Forty years ago, I was allowed to sit in on an adult Sunday school class taught by my then pastor, Dr. Richard Tow. I was fifteen years old at the time, and the teaching sparked an interest in me, as a teenager, for a verse-by-verse study in the book of the Revelation. Now, having been a pastor myself for over thirty years, I was extremely honored to be invited to both read and offer any critiques on Dr. Tow's examination of this very important subject. His honest and thorough look into the three common positions concerning the church and the Tribulation answered several questions that I have had over the years and affirmed some of the things that I have considered as a pastor and Bible teacher. I would encourage anyone interested in a work that is not designed to simply proof text the author's own presuppositions to read this book.

Pastor Troy D. Bohn
Director—Raven Ministries International and Board
of Directors of Legacy Ministry College

My friend and fellow minister for many years, Richard Tow has written a must-read book if you are interested in eschatology. His comprehensive, scholarly, non-dogmatic research of Scripture, and the positions held on the Tribulation and the Rapture of the church, leave it up to the individual reader to decide for him or herself which view to espouse. *Rapture or Tribulation* is the kindest, most thorough book I have read on the topic.

Dr. Loren Houltberg
Professor, Author, and Regional Pastor for the Foursquare Church

Rapture or Tribulation by Richard Tow is a timely book, for recently there has been increased interest in the timing of the Second Coming of Jesus as it relates to the Tribulation and the predicted catching up of the Church. We are told by the Apostle Paul that we are not to be ignorant of these things and that this day should not surprise us. It's critical, therefore, that we pursue a clearer understanding of this vital topic so as to be alert and ready. *Rapture and Tribulation* is just the book needed, by pastors and laymen, to help navigate this sometimes-confusing topic. Dr. Tow has done an extraordinary job in illuminating the issues and guiding the reader towards a more comprehensive understanding of what the scriptures reveal. Questions are answered; new questions are discovered. Whatever the readers preferred viewpoint, *Rapture and Tribulation* will be a treasured resource.

Pastor and Missionary John Leon Rusk
Director of Desert Dove Prophetic Intercessors
and Frontlines Development Group

We find ourselves in an hour that requires great spiritual preparation for the unique dynamics that are still ahead for the church, Israel, and the world as it is and will be. I am thankful for any and every resource that gives courage to godly men and women to see where the world is going and embrace the unique role that the church serves this generation. Therefore, I am thankful for Richard Tow and his timely service to the body of Christ in laboring to produce this important book. A generation of believers, young and old, are searching for biblical truth with depth on the subject of the return of Jesus because of the recent escalation of trouble and darkness. I highly recommend that Richard's book be a priority for any searching for a clearer sense of the "why behind the what" of the timing of the tribulation that precedes the Lord's return.

David Sliker
President, International House of Prayer University

RAPTURE

or

TRIBULATION

Will Christians Go Through the Coming Tribulation?

Richard W. Tow

WESTBOW
PRESS®
A DIVISION OF THOMAS NELSON
& ZONDERVAN

WestBow Press books may be ordered through booksellers or by contacting:

WestBow Press
A Division of Thomas Nelson & Zondervan
1663 Liberty Drive
Bloomington, IN 47403
www.westbowpress.com
844-714-3454

ISBN: 978-1-6642-6098-6 (sc)
ISBN: 978-1-6642-6099-3 (hc)
ISBN: 978-1-6642-6097-9 (e)

Library of Congress Control Number: 2022904977

Print information available on the last page.

WestBow Press rev. date: 04/04/2022

This book is dedicated to

Dr. Joe Dan Vendelin and Rev. Denny Stevens, my friends and ministry partners who invested precious time improving the text. Appreciation is also extended to my congregation, Life Church, which supported me throughout the publication process.

Watch therefore, for you do not know what hour your Lord is coming.
— Matt. 24:42 NKJV

For the Lord Himself will descend from heaven with a shout, with the voice of an archangel, and with the trumpet of God. And the dead in Christ will rise first. Then we who are alive and remain shall be caught up together with them in the clouds to meet the Lord in the air. And thus we shall always be with the Lord.
— 1 Thess. 4:16–17 NKJV

Behold, I tell you a mystery: We shall not all sleep, but we shall all be changed — in a moment, in the twinkling of an eye, at the last trumpet. For the trumpet will sound, and the dead will be raised incorruptible, and we shall be changed.
— 1 Cor 15:51–52 NKJV

CONTENTS

PREFACE

This book seeks a biblical answer to the question: Will Christians go through the Tribulation period? That question has occupied the minds of believers for many years. However, rapid changes in today's world events have alerted many to the urgency of the question. The signs pointing to Christ's return are more evident than ever.

In Daniel 12:4 God gave two signs that would mark "the time of the end." One sign is the increase in travel: "many shall run to and fro." That sign is being fulfilled through the invention of the automobile and airplane. Prior to 1900, travel was primary on foot or by horseback. Today people fly all over the world with relative ease. The traffic on our highways is ongoing testimony that people are running to and fro. The second sign given to Daniel is that "knowledge shall increase." While we may not be getting wiser, knowledge has increased exponentially. Scientific breakthroughs are common, and with today's internet, an abundance of information is available to much of the world's population. Those two signs alone alert us to the importance of end-time revelation. The angel told Daniel to "shut up the words and seal the book until the time of the end; many shall run to and fro, and knowledge shall increase" (Dan. 12:4).

Additionally, the birth of the nation of Israel in 1948 and the Israeli reoccupation of Jerusalem in 1967 are evidence the prophetic clock is moving quickly toward the end of the age. In 2017 the United States officially recognized Jerusalem as the capital of Israel. Secular developments toward globalization and interfaith ecumenical movements set the stage for end-time events. The coronavirus pandemic has disrupted societies, opening the door for more governmental control worldwide. Table 1 provides additional indicators that the end is near. The invasion of Ukraine by Russia has heightened tension with increased threat of world war and severe economic consequences. We are living in momentous times full of challenges, but also full of opportunities. *Rapture or Tribulation* equips believers to navigate those challenges and capitalize on the opportunities.

Ten Indicators of End Times		
Bible Ref.	*Subject*	*Comments*
1. Dan. 12:4	Travel	Radical increase with invention of automobile and airplane
2. Dan. 12:4	Knowledge	Available globally through internet
3. Amos 9:14-15	Israel	Restoration of nation of Israel in 1948 opening possibility for end-time fulfillment
4. Rev. 11:1–12	Satellite technology	Global capacity to collectively watch an event in Jerusalem
5. Matt. 24:14	Global evangelism	Made possible through travel and internet
6. Rev. 13:16-17	Digital tracking	Global tracking with increased central control
7. Rev. 17:1–6	Ecumenical movement	Peace movement toward one compromised religion
8. Matt. 24:21–22	Nuclear capacity	Potential for global destruction
9. 1 Tim. 4:1	Deception	Increased availability of error through internet and moral decline
10. 2 Pet. 3:3–4	Scoffers	Unable to discern the times and mocking biblical warning

Table 1. Ten Indicators of End Times[1]

Assumptions

The author is a conservative premillennialist and assumes certain theological beliefs. This book is written from that perspective, with a futuristic view of eschatology, including a literal seven-year Tribulation period at the end of the age. Of course, these views must have scriptural foundation and are legitimate areas of debate. However, they are not the focus of this study.

The divine inspiration and inerrancy of Scripture are taken for granted, and the Bible serves as the final referee on truth. The challenge we all face is to rightly divide and interpret that revelation. That is particularly challenging for the subject at hand because of the vast number of biblical texts on end-time prophecy and the symbolism that is often employed.

Approach

This topic must be approached with humility and grace.[2] We must first acknowledge that there are many pieces of the puzzle that we simply do not have (1 Cor. 13:9). Although Deuteronomy 29:29 was given under a previous covenant, the principle still applies. "The secret things belong to the Lord our God; but the things that are revealed belong to us and to our children forever, that we may do all the words of this law" (RSV). There are secret things that God has not revealed to us, and we must be very cautious when we fill in the blanks with our limited understanding. We must also remember that the revelation God has given us is not intended for mere academic purposes. The things that are revealed are designed to guide us into obedience to the will of God. If our investigation of Scripture does not move us toward loving God and loving our neighbor (Matt. 22:37–40), we have missed the point somewhere. Therefore, in this study we will seek to apply God's word in our lives toward those ends.

There are three theories proposed as the best answer to the question at hand. The pretribulationist position is that the Rapture will occur before the Tribulation period. Midtribulationists place that event somewhere near the middle of that seven-year period. And the posttribulation position is that the Rapture occurs at the end of the Tribulation period in conjunction with Christ's Second Coming back to earth. All three camps agree on the reality of the Rapture as described in 1 Thessalonians 4:13–18 and the

Second Coming of Christ described in Revelation 19:11–21.[3] This agreement provides a strong foundation of unity that should be preserved (Eph. 4:1–3).

Since the timing of the Rapture could profoundly affect Christians' experience in the days ahead, this matter warrants diligent investigation and debate. However, we should never break our fellowship in Christ over the *timing* of the Rapture. Instead, we should extend grace toward one another as fellow learners under Christ's training and instruction.

This study does not advocate one of the three positions. Instead, it evaluates the strengths and weaknesses of each in the light of Scripture. The Greek word translated disciple in the New Testament is *mathētēs*. It indicates a learner or pupil.[4] That is how we are proceeding: as a learner. I have studied this subject for many years, but in this book, I return to the topic with a fresh openness to be taught by the Spirit from the Word of God. We all come to Scripture with presuppositions based on previous experience and understanding. That is inevitable. But we can come with a teachable spirit. This is what we are trying to do in this book. May the Lord lead us as we explore his word together.

The hermeneutical spiral below illustrates how we come to Scripture with the knowledge we have but allow the Bible to enhance our understanding in each cycle of study.[5]

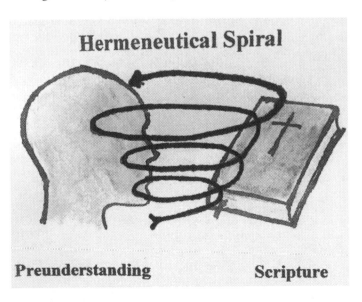

Figure 1. Hermeneutical Spiral

Ultimately, our answers must come from the Bible. While wise, informed Bible teachers can help us understand Scripture, the ultimate referee on truth is found in the Word of God. Therefore, I quote Scripture often. That is our authority for believing what we believe. Each chapter begins with a biblical quote relevant to the content of the chapter.

Structure

This study is structured under three sections.

Section I establishes two foundational concepts and evaluates a variant of the pretribulation position known as the partial Rapture theory. The two concepts that are addressed are first, the interpretation method used for understanding Scripture and second, the biblical purpose of the Tribulation period.

Section II evaluates the strengths and weaknesses of each theory.

In *Section III* the Olivet Discourse is analyzed for further understanding of how the Rapture fits into Jesus's prophecies. This discourse is examined carefully because it is foundational to our understanding of the subject. All the apostles based their eschatology on Jesus's teaching. The position we adopt on the timing of the Rapture must reflect the predictions Jesus makes in the parallel passages of Matthew 24–25, Mark 13, and Luke 21.

Most of the technical issues are addressed in the chapter endnotes so that the main narrative is easier to follow. In addition to providing citation credit, the endnotes contain supplementary analysis and scriptural support for stated conclusions. For the sake of readers who may not be familiar with the Greek language, the transliterated form for these words is used. A Scripture index and a subject index are provided in this book.

Appendices A and B are designed to supply added clarity concerning the book of Revelation and the critical issue of *imminence*. Appendix C provides discussion questions to facilitate interaction for those using the book as a class or group study.

The following abbreviations are to reference translations of Scripture:

NIV: New International Version

KJV: King James Version

NKJV: New King James Version
NLT: New Living Translation
RSV: Revised Standard Version

All Scripture quotations are from the New King James Version unless indicated otherwise.

May God bless our study of his word.

Endnotes: Introduction

1   The list in Table 1 is not exhaustive and only provides one Bible reference for each indicator. There have been signs throughout history, but the global nature of the signs and the convergence of *all* the signs (Matt. 24:33) is what adds certainty that the end is drawing near. Some scholars believe Daniel 12:4 is referring to people running to and fro in pursuit of Daniel's prophecy, and knowledge of Daniel's prophecy will increase. While that interpretation is possible, the text does not demand it. There is no reason that God could not make a general prediction about travel and knowledge in Daniel 12:4. If those scholars are correct, history has taught us that the fulfillment happens in the context of the general increase in travel, communication, and knowledge.

    The indicators on this table have implied assumptions about how prophecy will be fulfilled that are not being critically analyzed because the sole purpose of the table is to simply illustrate the fact that today's social and technological environment sets the stage for the fulfillment of end-time prophesy much more than in previous generations.

2   Extreme dogmatism on this subject is usually an indication of one's lack of knowledge, rather than perfect knowledge.

3   In this book I typically refer to the event when living Christians are caught up to be with the Lord as the Rapture, and I refer to the event when Christ returns to the earth to set up his kingdom as the Second Coming. Although the English word Rapture is not in English Bibles, the Greek word *harpazō* is in the original text (1 Thess. 4:17) and carries the idea, usually translated "caught up." The Vulgate translated *harpazō* with the Latin words *rapiemur* which accounts for the popular use of the term Rapture.

4   James Strong, *New Exhaustive Strong's Numbers and Concordance with Expanded Greek-Hebrew Dictionary* (Originally published: *The Exhaustive Concordance of the Bible*, Cincinnati: Jennings & Graham, 1890). Accessed in electronic data base: Biblesoft, Inc., 2010), s.v. "NT: 3101."

5   G. R. Osborne, *The Hermeneutical Spiral* (Downers Grove: InterVarsity, 1991) 10, 324 as quoted by William Klein, Craig Blomberg, and Robert Hubbard, Jr., *Introduction to Biblical Interpretation* (Grand Rapids: Thomas Nelson, 1993), 114. Hermeneutics is simply the principles employed in interpreting literature. Osborne's hermeneutical spiral is based on the concept of the hermeneutic circle conceived by German philosopher Martin Heidegger in 1927. Martin Heidegger, *Being and Time*, John Macquarrie and Edward Robinson, trans. (Oxford, UK: Blackwell, 1962) as quoted by Anne-Laure Le Cunff, "The hermeneutic circle: a key to critical reading," *Nesslabs*. Accessed at: The hermeneutic circle: a key to critical reading - Ness Labs. "St. Augustine of Hippo was the first philosopher and theologian to have introduced the hermeneutic cycle of faith and reason. . . ."

"Hermeneutical Circle," *Wikipedia*. Accessed at https://en.wikipedia.org/wiki/ Hermeneutic_circle#cite_note-1. I am using the term hermeneutical cycle to refer to one fresh engagement or attempt to understand the subject as revealed in Scripture. With a complex subject like the timing of the rapture, it is essential that we repeat these cycles with humility and openness to better understanding.

SECTION I

PRELIMINARIES

CHAPTER 1

Interpretation Method for Understanding End-Time Prophecy

These were more fair-minded than those in Thessalonica, in that they received the word with all readiness, and searched the Scriptures daily to find out whether these things were so.

Acts 17:11 NKJV

Rapid changes in world events have caused many people to think more about the end times. The invasion of Ukraine, the coronavirus pandemic, and economic upheaval have set the world on edge and occasioned dramatic shifts in social structures. If that many changes can occur in such a short time, how quickly will we move toward the final days of this age? One lesson we have learned is that a single incident can trigger a swift chain of events that reshape the world as we know it. It makes one wonder what changes are coming in the days ahead. Will the pace of change continue? Will it slow down? Will it accelerate and race toward the end of the age?

I am optimistic about our future as Christians. God always takes care of his people! But alarming trends are also evident: moral decline in society, increased governmental control, pressures toward globalization, and compromise made by the ecumenical movement toward one-world religion.[1] These developments point toward the end of the age prophesied in Scripture. They awaken in us questions that need to be answered from a reliable source. For us that source is the Word of God!

Focus of the Study

In this study, we are exploring one question: Will Christians go through the Tribulation period? Or we might put it this way: Will the church go through the Tribulation period prophesied in the book of Revelation? If so, will it go through the whole seven years or just the first three and a half years? Will *all* the church go through the Tribulation or only those Christians who were not ready for the Rapture? These are difficult questions to answer. There are many complications involved in attempting to answer our central question. The three dominate theories among conservative Christians that offer an answer are: the pretribulation position, which says the church will be raptured before the seven-year Tribulation period begins the posttribulation position, which believes the church will be caught up at the end of that period and the midtribulation Rapture theory, which predicts the church will be raptured halfway through the Tribulation period.

There are good, knowledgeable people in each of these camps. I respect the scholarship and sincerity of all those leaders. I do not approach this subject as someone with all the answers. Instead, I come as a student of the Bible with a desire for more understanding. Eschatology, the branch of theology that studies last things, constitutes a large portion of Scripture. Any answer about the Rapture's timing in relation to the Tribulation period must be consistent with *all* biblical revelation on the subject. For that reason, we must not rely on quick proof texts to support a position. We must examine Scripture in a more comprehensive way.

Before assessing these positions and attempting an answer, we need to establish some foundational concepts. Within the scope of this study, we cannot do that in an in-depth manner. But three vital issues must be considered if we are to proceed effectively. We will address the first one in this chapter and the other two in the next chapter. The three foundational concepts are:

1. the method to use for interpreting Bible prophecy,
2. God's purpose for the Tribulation period, and
3. the mystery of the church age.

Importance of Hermeneutical Method

The primary reason there are so many different opinions on this subject is that people are using different methods of interpreting Scripture. Hermeneutics is "the discipline that deals with principles of interpretation."[2] A valid hermeneutical method must be consistently applied if we are to makes sense of what the Bible says about the last days. Hermeneutics is a huge subject, and we cannot deal with it in depth. Bible colleges and seminaries require at least one course in the subject, and serious Bible students should become knowledgeable of the subject.

If we get the method of interpretation wrong, we will probably interpret biblical passages incorrectly and arrive at misguided answers. It is like building a house on a crooked, defective foundation. Without a solid foundation it is impossible to construct a stable, efficient home. Likewise, we must begin with a reliable hermeneutical method.

Two Prevalent Methods of Interpreting Biblical Prophecy

The two prevalent methods used in interpreting prophecy are the allegorical and the literal methods. The literal method is often called the grammatical-historical method.

The allegorical method minimizes the literal meaning of a passage and looks for a hidden, spiritual meaning. It is influenced by platonic thought. "Plato taught that true reality actually lay behind what appeared to the human eye."[3] In this approach, what the text actually says is not nearly as important as the allegorical, spiritual meaning assigned to it by the reader. The Jewish scholar, Philo used this method in his interpretation of the Old Testament. Later, the church father, Origin popularized it in Alexandria.[4]

The problem with the allegorical method is that the interpretation is open to the subjective whim or imagination of the interpreter. It abandons the common sense of the words and fails to uphold the basic authority of Scripture itself. Using the allegorical method, the interpreter can inject his or her own ideas, justifying them as a higher, more spiritual meaning. There is no objective way to test the allegorized interpretation.[5] This approach is not a reliable way to interpret the Bible. Therefore, we reject it in favor of the literal method.

In contrast to the allegorical method, the literal (grammatical-historical) method interprets Scripture according to the normal meaning of the words and grammar. Before making an application of the passage, the interpreter seeks to understand what the historical writer was saying to the historical audience in that context. In this school of thought there can be many applications of the principles being communicated, but there is only one interpretation. And that interpretation is based on what the author communicated to the listener in his day.

Ramm explains this method in the following way: "*The customary, socially-acknowledged designation of a word is the literal meaning of that word. The 'literal' meaning of a word is the basic, customary, social designation of that word. The spiritual, or mystical meaning of a word or expression is one that arises after the literal designation and is dependent upon it for its existence. To interpret literally means nothing more or less than to interpret in terms of normal, usual, designation*" (emphasis Ramm's).[6]

Even though the emphasis is on the words, grammar, and context of the biblical author and audience, the interpreter must depend on the Holy Spirit to understand the message of a passage. Paul explained this in 1 Corinthians 2. In verse 14, he wrote, "But the natural man does not receive the things of the Spirit of God, for they are foolishness to him; nor can he know them, because they are spiritually discerned." To understand Scripture the interpreter must be born of the Spirit (John 3:3) and yield to the Holy Spirit (Gal. 5:25). Failure to recognize this has produced a plethora of theological errors.[7] We need the objective grounding of the literal words inspired in the text by the Spirit, but we also depend on the Holy Spirit to enlighten us as to his message in the passage. This illumination is very different from attaching fanciful interpretations using the allegorical method.[8]

The literal method grounds the interpretation in objective, testable data: the historical context, grammar, and the normal meaning of words.[9] It leaves the authority of meaning with the Bible itself, rather than the subjective imaginations of the interpreter. Therefore, we embrace this method in interpreting Bible prophecy.

Specific Considerations When Using the Literal Method

I stated these two methods in simplistic terms to highlight the basic difference between them. In all fairness, the differences are complicated by several factors. While the interpreter should use the literal method rather than the allegorical, there are specific considerations that cannot be ignored. I will mention a few of these.

The New Testament does use typology.[10] For example, types and shadows are prevalent in the book of Hebrews. In Hebrews 9 the author talks about the Levitical priesthood and the tabernacle. Then in verse 9, he says, "It was symbolic for the present time." So, we cannot throw out all symbolism and typology. However, just as in this example, we are often told in the biblical text that it is symbolic.[11] We see that happening in the interpretation of dreams by Joseph and by Daniel. Dreams and visions usually employ symbolism to communicate the message.

Revelation 12:3 portrays a "fiery red dragon having seven heads and ten horns, and seven diadems on his heads." But, in verse 9, we are told that dragon is "that old serpent, called the Devil and Satan." So, we do not understand the fiery red dragon to be a literal dragon. But why do we not interpret it literally? It is because the Scripture specifically tells us not to. If we are not to interpret something literally, the Bible itself will give us clues as to the symbolism being used.[12]

There are various genres of literature in the Bible. There are historical narratives, letters, poetry, and parables to name a few. The type of literature being used to convey the message has to be taken into consideration. This adds another layer of complexity to the interpretation process. For example, poetry often uses figures of speech to convey its message. In Psalm 57:4 the author writes, "I am in the midst of lions; I lie among ravenous beasts—men whose teeth are spears and arrows, whose tongues are sharp swords" (NIV). A literal object (spears and arrows) is used to highlight a figurative meaning (perhaps verbal slander). The psalmist is not saying his enemies literally have spears and arrows for teeth. In this poetic genre we first understand what literal spears and arrows are. But from that imagery, just as we do in our common speech today, we are to understand the figurative meaning along with the emotion associated with that meaning.[13] So we must be cognizant of the literary genre.

The Bible often alerts us to symbolism in the text itself. When introducing a parable, the gospels often say something like, "Another parable He put forth to them, saying: 'The kingdom of heaven is like. . . .'"[14] That lets us know the media being used and the metaphorical nature of the message. The words "as" and "like" are often clues that something is being presented to represent something else.

Here is a good general rule for understanding Scripture: If a literal interpretation makes sense and is consistent with the rest of Scripture, then interpret it literally.[15] Do not try to attach some allegorical meaning to something that can be logically interpreted literally. The allegorical method of interpretation leaves the interpretation open to all kinds of fanciful conclusions generated in the imagination of the reader. We want to simply understand what the historical author wanted to communicate to the historical hearer. Then we can make applications to current situations. The New Testament writers used the literal method of interpreting the Old Testament even though they dealt with types and shadows and figurative language.[16]

Sometimes, New Testament writers apply the underlying principle in an Old Testament text to a current situation. In doing that, they are not abandoning the literal interpretation. The original text stands, but an application of the principle is being made. For example, in 1 Corinthians 9:9, Paul quotes Deuteronomy 25:4: "You shall not muzzle an ox while it treads out *the grain.*" Then he applies the principle to financial provision for ministers. The Old Testament passage tells the Israelite to not muzzle the ox. The ox must be allowed to eat from the grain it was threshing.[17] The underlying principle is explained in 1 Corinthians 9:10: "he who plows should plow in hope, and he who threshes in hope should be partaker of his hope." The NIV says, "they ought to do so in the hope of sharing in the harvest." 1 Timothy 5:18 makes the same application of the Deuteronomy passage. There the principle is stated in verse 18: "The laborer is worthy of his wages." We always begin with a literal interpretation of what is said *before* we make an application of the principle. So, another rule of thumb is this: Make sure you understand what the historical author was saying to the historical audience before you make an application of the underlying principle. If we get sloppy about that, we can misinterpret biblical prophecy.

Interpreting prophecy is complicated further by what is known as "the law of double reference." "The same prophecies frequently have a double meaning, and refer to different events, the one near, the other remote. . . ."[18] There is often a partial fulfillment as a kind of earnest guarantee of the complete fulfillment in the future. For example, the promise made to David in 2 Samuel 7:12–16 was partially fulfilled in Solomon, but ultimately fulfilled in Christ (Heb. 1:5).

When interpreting Scripture, we should also be aware of another principle called progressive revelation. This principle recognizes the way revelation is built upon previous revelation in the Bible. A truth will first be given in seed form. Then it will bud into more detail. Finally, it blossoms into a full flower of truth. The fuller revelation builds upon previous revelation and never contradicts it.[19]

Take for example, the all-important revelation in Genesis 3:15 spoken by God to Satan after Adam's fall. "I will put enmity between you and the woman, and between your seed and her seed [Messiah]; he shall bruise your head, and you shall bruise his heel [at the cross]" (RSV). That is the first prophecy of Christ and the cross. Not much detail is given, but the truth is provided in seed form. In the Old Testament the revelation is expanded to reveal that Christ (Messiah) would come through the tribe of Judah (Gen. 49:10), and later it was revealed that Messiah would be a descendant of David (2 Sam. 7:16). Of course, the gospels' account of the death and resurrection of Jesus provides much more insight on exactly what Genesis 3:15 meant. Then the epistles explain its significance more fully. Understanding this principle is very helpful for interpreting biblical prophecy.

What are the implications of this for interpreting the Bible? The more current revelation in Scripture never contradicts the previous, less-complete revelation. It builds upon what has already been revealed and opens the truth more fully. Additionally, the increased detail and clarity of a truth in the New Testament, can help the reader understand the earlier revelation better.[20] For example, we understand Daniel 9:24–27, a passage we will look in the next chapter, with more clarity because Jesus explained it more fully in Matthew 24, and the book of Revelation deals with those truths in even more detail.

Using the literal method can be challenging. But knowing some of the principles we have just discussed will make it easier. When we use the grammatical-historical method skillfully, we can have a reasonably high level of assurance that we understand what the Bible is telling us. Then we can make appropriate applications to our own lives. The allegorical method does not lead to this level of confidence.

Impact of Allegorical Method

Those who use an allegorical method tend to be amillennialists. "Millennial" is another way of saying one thousand years. The prefix "a" negates the primary term. Therefore, amillennialists *do not* believe in a literal thousand-year reign as stated in Revelation 20:4. Instead, they spiritualize that as merely symbolic of a long period of time. Augustine systemized Origin's non-literal view of the Millennium "into what is known as amillennialism."[21] Augustine's book, *The City of God*, was instrumental in that process. Augustine "taught that the church is the kingdom of God and there would be no literal fulfillment of the promises made to Israel."[22] That thinking has a profound impact on misinterpreting Bible prophecy. For example, Catholic Church commentators often interpret the book of Revelation as a description of the church age. Using the allegorical method, they place the Millennium in the past "and therefore something no longer to be anticipated in the future."[23]

Millennialists believe there will be a literal thousand-year reign of Christ on the earth immediately following the Tribulation period and the Second Coming.[24] We take the statements in Revelation 20 about Christ's reign at face value and accept it for what it says. We interpret the one thousand years, stated in Revelation. 20:1–7, to literally mean one thousand years.

So here is a major divide between the results of the allegorical method versus the literal method. Those using the allegorical method usually attribute Old Testament promises made to Israel as fulfilled in the church. They spiritualize promises made to that nation and rob them of any literal fulfillment. Those using the literal method recognize that many promises are made to the nation of Israel and will be fulfilled exactly as stated.

Lessons from Fulfillment of Prophecy at the First Advent

We can learn something about how to interpret unfulfilled prophecy by examining how prophecy was fulfilled at Christ's First Advent. For example, the prophecy in Micah 5:2 that Messiah would come forth out of Bethlehem was literally fulfilled at the birth of Jesus. The events at the cross, described in Psalm 22, were literally fulfilled. The prediction in verse 18, "They divide My garments among them, And for My clothing they cast lots," literally happened. The way previous prophecy was fulfilled teaches us how to interpret unfulfilled prophecy. That is why we embrace the literal method of interpretation.

Necessity of Systematized Eschatology

One final difficulty needs to be mentioned: the volume of prophetic material. It takes a vast knowledge of Scripture to deal with this subject holistically. It is common for people to pull out a few proof texts to defend a position. But when they do that, there are often numerous passages not being considered.[25] And the text being quoted is often not understood in its literary context. Proof-texting is "quoting biblical passages to prove a doctrine or standard for Christian living without regard for the literary context."[26] We must avoid that approach to our subject.

About 27 percent of the Bible is prophecy, according to *The Encyclopedia of Bible Prophecy.*[27] For an answer to our question, we need a sound understanding of that corpus as a whole. That is no small task, especially when many of those passages are difficult to interpret. In 2 Peter 1:20 we are told, "no prophecy of Scripture is of any private interpretation." That means each verse must be interpreted in the context of other passages comparing scripture with scripture.[28] If the interpretation is contrary to the meaning of those other passages, the interpretation is flawed. But to make that comparison, we must know and understand what those other passages say. That requires diligent study by disciplined followers of Christ.

Necessity of Grace and Humility

No one has all the i's dotted and all the t's crossed on this subject. Even if a theologian thoroughly understood all the passages in Scripture, his or her knowledge of the future is still limited. We currently see through a glass darkly. We all know in part according to 1 Corinthians 13:9. There were things God showed John the Revelator that John was forbidden to share. For example, after hearing a divine revelation in Revelation 10:4, John was about to write down what he heard. But he was then told to seal it up and not write it. No one alive knows that prophetic revelation.

All the theories about the timing of the Rapture have unanswered questions. It is a subject that must be approached with humility. The difficulties mentioned above should not cause us to shy away from the subject. On the contrary, it should inspire diligence, dependence on the Holy Spirit, and grace toward those who disagree with us.

My approach to this subject is not dogmatic for two reasons. First, the timing of the Rapture is not a foundational test of orthodoxy. In contrast, the physical resurrection of Jesus and his visible, literal return in his glorified body (not just a "spiritual coming") is an essential of the faith.[29] That is a test of orthodoxy. But we should never break fellowship with other Christians over the timing of the Rapture.

Second, God has sovereignly hidden some information on the subject. For that reason, we have to make some educated inferences when developing a systemized eschatology. Anytime we do that, we could be wrong!

In Mark 13:32 Jesus said, "But of that day or that hour no one knows, not even the angels in heaven, nor the Son, but only the Father" (RSV). From that statement, we know that the absence of more information about this in Scripture is not accidental; it is intentional on God's part. He could have given us more specifics about the timing of the Rapture. But in his wisdom, he has left us with a degree of uncertainty that is surely for our protection and benefit. On the one hand, we rest in the degree of uncertainty intended by God. On the other hand, we diligently search the scriptures to understand that which he has revealed. Deuteronomy 29:29 makes this distinction between the revealed and the hidden: "The secret things belong to the Lord our God; but the things that are revealed belong to us and to our children for ever, that we may do all the words of this law" (RSV). We do our best to put our eschatological puzzle together, but there are always some missing pieces when we are done. The proper response to that reality is humility and grace toward those who may differ from us on this subject.

Conclusion

We have briefly examined the two main methods of interpretation. We have rejected the allegorical method of interpretation because of its lack of grounding in what the Bible literally says. The allegorical method relies too heavily on the whim and imagination of the interpreter. Instead, we have chosen the literal method of interpretation which relies on the customary, basic meaning of words in the context of the author and audience.

Some challenges of applying the literal method have been explored, and ways to deal with those challenges have also been discussed. The way prophecy was fulfilled at the First Advent provides helpful guidance in understanding how prophecy will be fulfilled at the Second Advent. Nevertheless, there are some things left unsaid in Scripture. This requires interpreters to make some inferences when shaping a systemized eschatology. Having done that, we must deal with the matter in humility and with grace toward others.

Endnotes: Chapter 1

1   The signing of "Human Fraternity for World Peace and Living Together" by Pope Francis and Islamic Grand Imam Leader of Egypt Al-Azhar on February 4, 2019 is an example. See "Apostolic Journey of His Holiness Pope Francis to the United Arab Emirates (3–5 FEBRUARY 2019)," Vatican. http://www.vatican.va/content/francesco/en/travels/2019/outside/documents/papa-francesco_20190204_documento-fratellanza-umana.html.

2   Walter Kaiser, Jr. and Moises Silva, *An Introduction to Biblical Hermeneutics: The Search for Meaning* (Grand Rapids: Zondervan, 1994), 15.

3   E. R. Goodenough, *An Introduction to Philo Judaeus*, rev. ed., (New York: Barnes and Noble, 1963) as quoted by Klein, Blomberg, Hubbard, Jr., *Introduction to Biblical Interpretation*, 26. Cf. Kaiser and Silva, *An Introduction to Biblical Hermeneutics*, 220.

4   Klein, Blomberg, Hubbard, Jr., *Introduction to Biblical Interpretation*, 26. However, the Reformers as a rule rejected the allegorical method. "Martin Luther (1483–1546), the great Reformer, started his career as a biblical interpreter by employing the allegorical method but later abandoned it." "New Testament Interpretation: A Historical Survey" by D. S. Dockery in David A. Black and David S. Dockery, eds., *New Testament Criticism and Interpretation* (Grand Rapids: Zondervan, 1991), 47.

5   Cf. J. Dwight Pentecost, *Things to Come: A Study in Biblical Eschatology*, 1958 (Grand Rapids: Zondervan, 1973) 4–6.

6   Bernard Ramm, *Protestant Biblical Interpretation*, (Boston, MA: W. A. Wilde Company, 1950), 64 as quoted by Pentecost *Things to Come*, 9.

7   "A strict naturalist allows for nothing supernatural in the Bible or anywhere else." Robert McQuilkin, *Understanding and Applying the Bible* (1983; rev. ed, Chicago: Moody Press, 1992), 27. For an analysis of the three most influential forms of naturalistic interpretation see this text, pages 27–36. These three naturalistic approaches are: rationalism, literary criticism, and cultural relativism. "For the naturalist," McQuilkin writes, "when a clear teaching in Scripture is found to be in conflict with some human way of thinking, revelation must give way" (p. 35).

8   "The aim of good interpretation is simple: to get at the 'plain meaning of the text.' And the most important ingredient one brings to that task is enlightened common sense." Gordon D. Fee and Douglas Stuart, *How to Read the Bible for All Its Worth: A Guide to Understanding the Bible* (Grand Rapids: Zondervan, 1982), 16. This book is an excellent resource for understanding how to interpret the different genres in Scripture.

9   Pentecost, *Things to Come*, 11.

10   In Gal. 4:21–31 Paul is explaining an allegory, not using the allegorical method. For an explanation of the difference see Pentecost, *Things to Come*, 7–8.

11   Cf. John F. Walvoord, *Bibliotheca Sacra*, 150, no. 600 (Oct – Dec 1993): 387–396.

12   Rev. 1:20 is another example.

13   Klein, Blomberg, Hubbard, Jr., *Introduction to Biblical Interpretation*, 26. Also see Kaiser and Silva, *An Introduction to Biblical Hermeneutics*, 251.

14   Matt. 13:24.

15   Randolph O. Yeager, *Renaissance New Testament*, vol. 3 (Bowling Green, KY: Renaissance Press, 1978), 385.

16   Cf. Pentecost, *Things to Come*, 10.

17   "The text reflects the ancient agricultural practice of driving an ox drawing a threshing-sledge over the grain to release the kernels from the stalk. Out of mercy for the laboring animal the Israelites were forbidden to muzzle the ox, so that he might have some 'material benefit' from his labor." Gordon D. Fee, *The First Epistle to the Corinthians*, The New International Commentary of the New Testament, Stone, Bruce, and Fee, eds. (Grand Rapids: Eerdmans, 1987), 406–07.

18   Thomas Hartwell Horne, *Introduction to the Critical Study and Knowledge of the Holy Scriptures*, I, 390 as quoted by Dwight Pentecost, *Things to Come*, 46.

19   "The things that God revealed to humanity were not all given at once. His revelation was given in stages. This is known as progressive revelation." Don Stewart, "What is Progressive Revelation?" *Blue Letter Bible*. https://www.blueletterbible.org/faq/don_stewart/don_stewart_1203.cfm.

20   Augustine is credited with saying, "The New Testament lies concealed in the Old, the Old lies revealed in the New." Augustine, *Questions on the Heptateuch* 2.73.

21   Pentecost, *Things to Come*, 381. Walvoord writes, ". . . there are no acceptable exponents of amillennialism before Augustine . . . Prior to Augustine, amillennialism was associated with the heresies produced by the allegorizing and spiritualizing school of theology at Alexandria, which not only opposed premillennialism but subverted any literal exegesis of Scripture whatever. . . ." John F. Walvoord, "Premillennialism," *Bibliotheca Sacra*, no. 106 (October 1951) :420–421 as quoted by Pentecost, *Things to Come*, 381. Chafer details this history in Lewis Sperry Chafer, *Systematic Theology*, vol. 4, 1948 (Dallas, TX: Dallas Seminary Press, 1974), 270–284. Cf. Erich Sauer, *The Triumph of the Crucified* (Grand Rapids: Eerdmans, 1951). 144–53. Cf. John F. Walvoord, *The Blessed Hope and the Tribulation: A Historical and Biblical Study of Posttribulationism* (Grand Rapids: Zondervan, 1976) 11–13.

22   Pentecost, *Things to Come*, 382.

23 Chafer, *Systematic Theology*, vol. 4, 281. The reformers tended to see Revelation as "a prophecy of the history of the church," although they identified "the Beast and the False Prophet with the papacy in its political and religious aspects." George Eldon Ladd. *A Theology of the New Testament*, (1974; rev. ed., Grand Rapids: Eerdmans, 1993), 672.

24 At the conclusion of Christ's millennial reign and the final judgment of the wicked (Rev. 20:7–15), Christ will submit himself and the kingdom to the Father (1 Cor. 15:28) for the ushering in of the eternal kingdom.

25 Proof texting is "quoting biblical passages to prove a doctrine or standard for Christian living without regard for the literary context." Klein, Blomberg, Hubbard, Jr., *Introduction to Biblical Interpretation*, 160.

26 Klein, Blomberg, Hubbard, Jr., *Introduction to Biblical Interpretation*, 160.

27 J. Barton Payne, *The Encyclopedia of Bible Prophecy* as quoted by Jack Kelley, "How Much of the Bible is Prophecy?" *Ask the Bible Teacher*. https://gracethrufaith. com/ask-a-bible-teacher/much-bible-prophecy/.

28 Since Scripture is inspired and inerrant (2 Tim. 3:16; 2 Pet. 1:21), the passages must harmonize for there to be a correct interpretation. "Always insisting that Scripture interprets Scripture, Calvin rejected allegorical interpretation and emphasized the necessity of examining the historical and literary context while comparing Scriptures which treated common Subjects." "New Testament Interpretation: A Historical Survey" by D. S. Dockery in Black and Dockery, eds., *New Testament Criticism and Interpretation*, 48. The RSV says, "First of all you must understand this, that no prophecy of scripture is a matter of one's own interpretation" (2 Pet. 1:20).

29 Cf. 1 Cor. 15:12–18; 2 Tim. 2:16–18. For this reason, full preterism is heretical. We will examine some of the problems associated with partial preterism in chapter 9: "Matthew 24:15–31: The Great Tribulation." The Resurrection is not past. The Rapture is not past. And it is a serious error to say that it is. Often New Testament believers are reminded to keep it in mind and live with an expectancy of it. Additionally, the Rapture is not merely a spiritual event. The believer's physical body will be caught up into the air if he or she is still alive when Jesus returns for his bride. That is made abundantly clear in 1 Cor. 15 and 1 Thess. 4.

CHAPTER 2

Daniel's Seventieth Week:
The Tribulation Period

Seventy weeks are determined For your people and for your holy city. . . .
know therefore and understand, That from the going forth of the command
To restore and build Jerusalem Until Messiah the Prince, There shall be
seven weeks and sixty-two weeks. . . . And after the sixty-two weeks
Messiah shall be cut off, but not for Himself; And the people of the prince
who is to come Shall destroy the city and the sanctuary. . . . Then he shall
confirm a covenant with many for one week; But in the middle of the
week He shall bring an end to sacrifice and offering. And on the wing of
abominations shall be one who makes desolate.

Daniel 9:24–27 NKJV

<hr/>

We are pursuing an answer to the question: Will Christians go through
the Tribulation period? Finding an answer to that one question is not
easy. To intelligently answer it, we must consider a vast amount of biblical
revelation. Twenty-seven percent of the Bible is prophecy. It involves 150
chapters of scripture.[1] Quoting a few proof texts to defend a position is
simply inadequate. Instead, we need a comprehensive approach to our
inquiry.

So, we began by identifying three concepts foundational to our understanding of prophecy. We are exploring these three subjects before pushing toward an answer to the question. The three concepts are:

1. the method to use for interpreting Bible prophecy,
2. God's purpose for the Tribulation period, and
3. the mystery of the church age.

In the previous chapter we addressed the first issue: the method used for interpreting Scripture. Of the two prevalent methods of interpretation, we chose the literal method, also called the grammatical-historical method. We rejected the allegorical method because it fails to give adequate weight to what the Bible literally says, and it allows too much opportunity for the interpreter to inject his or her own ideas into the interpretation. Instead, we chose the literal method because it holds us more accountable to the *inspired* words of Scripture.

In this chapter, we explore God's purpose for the Tribulation period. Any answer to our question must coincide with this vital issue. The purpose of the Tribulation period in Scripture is two-fold: the outpouring of God's wrath on the unbelieving Gentile nations and the preparation of Israel to receive her Messiah. That is the reason there is a Tribulation period.[2] Incorporated in this discussion is an analysis of the mystery of the church age as it impacts our understanding of eschatology.

The Wrath of God Poured Out on the Ungodly Nations

During the Tribulation period, God will pour out his wrath on the Gentile nations. The theme of wrath is prominent in the book of Revelation. It is referenced at least a dozen times. For example, Revelation 6:15–17 says, "And the kings of the earth, the great men, the rich men, the commanders, the mighty men, every slave and every free man, hid themselves in the caves and in the rocks of the mountains, and said to the mountains and rocks, 'Fall on us and hide us from the face of Him who sits on the throne and from the wrath of the Lamb! For the great day of his wrath has come, and who is able to stand?'"

In Revelation 15:1 John declares, "Then I saw another sign in heaven, great and marvelous: seven angels having the seven last plagues, for in them the wrath of God is complete." In 15:7 he continues, "Then one of the four living creatures gave to the seven angels seven golden bowls full of the wrath of God who lives forever and ever." This wrath is not designed to correct God's children or purify his church. It is God venting his wrath on the wicked world and, in the process, offering opportunity to repent.[3]

In contrast, Paul tells the Christians at Thessalonica, "For God did not appoint us to wrath, but to obtain salvation through our Lord Jesus Christ" (1 Thess. 5:9). Jesus bore the wrath of God on the cross for believers so that we would never come under that condemnation. Christians receive correction and discipline (Heb. 12:3–11), but they are not subject to the wrath of God.

The message of the Rapture is a message of comfort for the believer. After declaring the coming Rapture/Resurrection of the Just, Paul concludes with these words in 1 Thessalonians 4:18, "Therefore comfort one another with these words." The message of the Rapture is not a warning of pending wrath for the believer. It is a message of comfort and assurance. This point is emphasized by the pretribulationists.[4]

The Preparation of Israel to Receive Messiah

The second purpose of the Tribulation period is to complete God's preparation for Israel to receive her Messiah. Jeremiah 30:7 refers to this as "the time of Jacob's trouble." It is never referred to as the time of the church's trouble.[5] The seven-year Tribulation period is primarily related to Israel rather than the church.

The key passage that prophesies this seven-year period is Daniel 9. In that chapter Gabriel is talking to Daniel about God's plan for Israel. In Daniel 9:24 Gabriel says, "Seventy weeks are determined For your people [Daniel's people is Israel] and for your holy city [Jerusalem], To finish the transgression, To make an end of sins, To make reconciliation for iniquity [to finish the appointed judgment for the nation's unfaithfulness], To bring in everlasting righteousness, To seal up vision and prophecy, And to anoint the Most Holy." At the conclusion of the seventy weeks, the righteous rule of Messiah will be established.

Seventy weeks refers to 490 years to prepare Israel for the Millennium. Each week represents seven years.[6] Seventy times seven years is 490 years. Daniel 9:25 continues, "Know therefore and understand, That from the going forth of the command To restore and build Jerusalem Until Messiah the Prince, There shall be seven weeks and sixty-two weeks; The street shall be built again, and the wall, Even in troublesome times." This period began in 445 BC with the commandment by Artaxerxes to restore Jerusalem (Neh. 2). The seven weeks (49 years) was from the time of that decree to the covenant renewal celebrated at Jerusalem in Nehemiah 9 (396 BC).[7] The 62 weeks (434 years) was from the dedication of the second temple to the crucifixion of Christ (Fig. 2). Daniel 9:26: "And after the sixty-two weeks Messiah shall be cut off, but not for Himself. [That's a reference to the cross.] And the people of the prince who is to come Shall destroy the city and the sanctuary. The end of it shall be with a flood, And till the end of the war desolations are determined." In 70 AD the city (Jerusalem) and the sanctuary (the temple) were destroyed just as Jesus prophesied in Matthew 23:37–24:2.

So, the 49 years plus the 434 years is 483 years. That leaves seven of the 490 unfulfilled. Since the first 483 years were literally fulfilled, it follows the last seven years will be literal years. That is the seven-year Tribulation period. It is the final week of God's preparation of Israel to receive Jesus as Messiah and enter the Millennium under the reign of Christ.[8]

Because Israel rejected the Messiah at his First Advent, God turned to the Gentiles with the gospel and ushered in the church age on the Day of Pentecost. The church age between Christ's crucifixion and the final week of God's dealings with Israel was a mystery not revealed in the Old Testament.[9] So there is a lengthy gap between Daniel 9:26 and Daniel 9:27 (when the final seven years are fulfilled).

The people who destroyed the city of Jerusalem and the sanctuary after Jesus's death on the cross was the Romans. The prince mentioned in 9:27 is the Antichrist. "Then he [the Antichrist] shall confirm a covenant with many [with Israel] for one week [seven years]; But in the middle of the week [3½ years] He shall bring an end to sacrifice and offering. And on the wing of abominations shall be one who makes desolate Even until the consummation, which is determined, Is poured out on the desolate."

Jesus spoke about the abomination that makes desolate in Matthew 24:15 as a *future* event. There He warned, "Therefore when you see the 'abomination of desolation,' spoken of by Daniel the prophet, standing in the holy place (whoever reads, let him understand), then let those who are in Judea flee to the mountains. Let him who is on the housetop not go down to take anything out of his house. And let him who is in the field not go back to get his clothes. But woe to those who are pregnant and to those who are nursing babies in those days! And pray that your flight may not be in winter or on the Sabbath. [Notice how Jewish this setting is] For then there will be great tribulation, such as has not been since the beginning of the world until this time, no, nor ever shall be" (Matt. 24:15–22). Those last three and a half years will be a time of horrific trouble worldwide with intense persecution and control by the Antichrist. The record in Revelation, especially chapters 12 and 13, details this out more fully.[10]

So that is the two-fold purpose of the Tribulation period. God will be completing his agenda for the nation of Israel, and he will be judging the Gentile nations. This chart may help the reader visualize what Daniel 9:24–27 is predicting. It is a key passage for understanding end-time prophecy.[11]

SEVENTY-WEEK PLAN FOR ISRAEL

Daniel 9:24–27

Ref.	"week" = 7 years not 7 days	Years	From	To
V. 24 Total	70 weeks (7 years)	70 x 7 = 490 years	445 BC	Beginning of Millennium
V. 25	7 weeks	7 x 7 = 49 years	Decree by Artaxerxes in 445 BC	Renewal of Covenant in 396 BC (Neh. 9)
V. 25	62 weeks	62 x 7 = 434 years	Dedication of 2nd Temple in 396 BC	Crucifixion of Messiah in 32 AD
Sub total	**69 weeks**	**69 x 7 = 483 years**	**445 B. C**	**32 AD**

V. 26		Destruction of Jerusalem by Titus in 70 AD		
Gap	Hidden Mystery	Church Age	Day of Pentecost (Acts 2)	Rapture
V. 27	**1 week**	**1 x 7 = 7 years**	**End of Church Age**	**End of Tribulation Period**
Total	70 weeks	483 + 7 = 490 years		

Table 2. Seventy-Week Plan for Israel

This revelation came in the context of Daniel seeking God about Israel's future.[12] In answer to his prayer, God sent Gabriel with the revelation.

In Daniel 9:25, why were the seven weeks distinguished from the 62 weeks? Why didn't verse 25 simply say there would be 69 weeks "from the going forth of the command To restore and build Jerusalem Until Messiah the Prince"? It is because there would be a partial fulfillment in the relatively near future in Nehemiah's day,[13] but the ultimate fulfillment would not come until the full 70 weeks were accomplished at the end of the Tribulation period.

Interpreting the Seven *Shabua* as Years

Two questions about our interpretation must be answered before we move on.

First, how do we know the weeks spoken of in this passage are seven years and not seven days. This question arises because of the English translation. For the typical English reader, a week means seven days. But for the Jew in Daniel's day, the Hebrew word *shabua* meant seven days or seven years depending on the context. Jews were socially cognizant of the seven-year *shabua* because key ordinances revolved around it. They were to till the land six years and let the land rest on the seventh year (Lev.25:3–4). A Hebrew servant was to serve six years, and on the seventh year he was to be set free (Deut. 15:12). The context of Israel's restoration included a return of the Jewish captives to the land, followed by the rebuilding of the city and the temple. It would not have been reasonable to include all those events in 490 *days*. So, Daniel immediately understood the week in our passage as referring to seven years.[14] In confirmation of this understanding, we can look back in history and affirm the prophecies were not fulfilled in 490 *days*. We can also look back at the first 69 weeks and see they were precisely fulfilled in 483 lunar *years*.[15]

Recognizing a Gap between the 69th and 70th Week

The bigger issue is how do we know there is a gap between the 69th and 70th week, between verses 26 and verse 27. The mystery is explained in the New Testament, and we will deal with those passages shortly. When the gap is recognized, then a lot of Scripture that would not otherwise make sense, falls into place.

The only alternative to the gap is that there is not a gap. The absence of a gap creates all kinds of interpretation problems. Those who do not recognize a prophetic gap between verses 26 and 27 either say the abomination of desolation spoken of in Daniel 9:27 was fulfilled in about 167 BC when Antiochus IV defiled that sanctuary, or they say it was fulfilled in 70 AD when the temple was destroyed. The theory that Antiochus IV fulfilled the abomination of desolation in Daniel 9:27 must be rejected for four reasons:

1. That event happened *before* Messiah was cut off (v. 26) while Daniel places this abomination (v. 27) *after* Christ's crucifixion.
2. The objectives of these 70 weeks (Dan. 9:24) were not accomplished within a few years of the Antiochus event.
3. In the first century AD, Romans 9–11 tells us that God is not finished with his program for Israel.
4. Most importantly, Jesus spoke of the abomination as a future event (Matt. 24:15).

As often happens in Old Testament prophecy, the Antiochus event *foreshadowed* the end–time event, but it was not its fulfillment.

The theory that Daniel 9:27 was fulfilled in 70 AD requires more analysis and will be explored more fully when the Olivet Discourse is discussed. Most conservative scholars agree that Daniel 9:26 refers to Christ's crucifixion followed by the destruction of Jerusalem in 70 AD. Then the question becomes: Was Daniel's abomination of desolation fulfilled during the 70 AD event or was Jesus pointing to a later end-time event? Preterists place the fulfillment in 70 AD and reject the gap between Daniel 9:26 and 9:27. Other scholars place the ultimate fulfillment after a gap (the church age) and the first three and a half years of the Tribulation during the end times. The latter position is the best when biblical revelation as a whole is considered.

The obvious weakness in the gap theory is that Daniel 9:26–27 does not specifically say it is there. However, an unstated time gap is commonly found in Old Testament prophecies.[16] That can be easily demonstrated by analyzing First Advent fulfillments. Secondly, the fact that the last week of the seventy weeks is set apart from the others implies the need to deal with it in a special way. Also, notice in verse 26, the unstated gap of about 40 years between the crucifixion and the destruction of Jerusalem (described in the last part of the verse).[17] That gap is undeniable; history records it. So, taking the position that there can be no time gaps in this prophecy is unsustainable. Look at verse 26: "And after the sixty-two weeks Messiah shall be cut off, but not for Himself [the crucifixion of Christ]; And the people of the prince who is to come Shall destroy the city [Jerusalem] and the sanctuary [the temple]. The end of it shall be with a flood, And till the end of the war desolations are determined." That destruction of Jerusalem happened in 70 AD.

What happens when we insist that no gap exists? Let us consider that question. It is easy to understand verse 26 refers to the time of Christ's crucifixion, followed by the destruction of Jerusalem in 70 AD. But if you allow no gap, then some amazing things must happen within a few years immediately following the destruction of the temple in 70 AD. [18]

1. The *worst* tribulation ever experienced in the world follows the abomination of desolation. As bad as the suffering was in 70 AD, there have been tribulations more severe and more universal than that, and the suffering described in the book of Revelation is without question worse. In conjunction with Daniel's abomination

of desolation, Jesus said, "For then there will be great tribulation, such as has not been since the beginning of the world until this time, no, nor ever shall be" (Matt. 24:21).

2. *Immediately* after that tribulation an unmistakable upheaval in nature will manifest. Jesus described those events in Matthew 24:29–30: "Immediately after the tribulation of those days the sun will be darkened, and the moon will not give its light; the stars will fall from heaven, and the powers of the heavens will be shaken. Then the sign of the Son of Man will appear in heaven, and then all the tribes of the earth will mourn, and they will see the Son of Man coming on the clouds of heaven with power and great glory."[19]

3. Most importantly, the Second Coming of Christ would occur.

None of that happened in the first century. There was no time of trouble "such as was not since the beginning of the world to this time, no, nor ever shall be" (Matt. 24:21). The trouble during World War II was far more devastating than anything that happened in the first century. The sun and moon did not stop shinning; the stars did not fall from heaven. Christ did not return "on the clouds of heaven with power and great glory" (Matt. 24:30). Instead of becoming the head of the nations at the end of the events in the first century and enjoying all the prominence and blessing promised by God through the prophets, Israel was scattered and was not even a nation until 1948. Taking the gap out results in an interpretation that history clearly proves to be false.[20] If the 70 weeks were fulfilled in the first century, then the Parousia would have occurred, and the glorious restoration of Israel as prophesied for the nation would have immediately followed. All the blessings listed in Daniel 9:24 would be fulfilled.

Therefore, acknowledging a time gap between Daniel 9:26 and verse 27 makes much more sense than not recognizing it.[21] That gap is what we typically refer to as the church age. We will now examine New Testament passages that tell us it was hidden in the Old Testament and is, in fact, currently happening. So, we move to our third foundational concept.

Mystery of the Church Age

Our explanation of the gap between verses 26 and 27 of Daniel 9 is the church age. How do we know that there is a gap of time there? The answer cannot be found in the Old Testament. The revelation of that gap did not come until after Israel rejected and crucified Messiah. The offer of full restoration to Israel at Christ's First Advent was a bonified offer. Had Israel received her Messiah, there would have been no gap. Of course, God who knows all things knew what would happen.[22] But the church age was hidden in the Old Testament so that Israel would be free to receive Jesus as the Messiah if she would do so.

Notice how the last (seventieth) week in Daniel 9:24–25 is set off from the others. Verse 24 says 70 weeks are determined. But, in verse 25, only 69 weeks are discussed as seven plus 62. That is a hint that there is something unique about the seventieth week. And the rest of Scripture affirms this.

Daniel 9:26 says, "And after the sixty-two weeks Messiah shall be cut off, but not for Himself; [That's the crucifixion.] And the people of the prince who is to come Shall destroy the city and the sanctuary. The end of it shall be with a flood, And till the end of the war desolations are determined." That is the destruction of Jerusalem in 70 AD. That rejection of Messiah marked the temporary end of God's dealings with Israel as a nation. It concluded the 69 weeks and marked the beginning of the church age, which was launched on the Day of Pentecost (Acts 2).

The church age is described in the New Testament as a mystery. A mystery [*mustērion*] in biblical terms is not something puzzling that you can figure out. It is a truth that can only be known if God reveals it.[23] God did not reveal it to Daniel or any of the other Old Testament saints. After Jesus was rejected, crucified, and ascended into heaven, God revealed to Paul and the apostles this mystery of the church age.[24]

In Ephesians 3:2–6 Paul wrote, "If indeed you have heard of the dispensation of the grace of God [that's the church age] which was given to me for you, how that by revelation He made known to me the mystery [*mustērion*] (as I have briefly written already, by which, when you read, you may understand my knowledge in the mystery of Christ), which in other ages was not made known to the sons of men, [it was hidden in the Old Testament] as it has now been revealed by the Spirit to His holy apostles and prophets: that the Gentiles should be fellow heirs, of the same body, [the church] and partakers of His promise in Christ through the gospel."[25]

During this church age, the wall of separation between Jew and Gentile is broken down (Eph. 2:13–22). A biological Jew gets saved the same way a Gentile gets saved. They are both saved into one body. Galatians 3:26–29 says, "For you are all sons of God through faith in Christ Jesus. For as many of you as were baptized into Christ have put on Christ. There is neither Jew nor Greek, there is neither slave nor free, there is neither male nor female; for you are all one in Christ Jesus."[26]

In contrast, during the old covenant, the distinction between Jew and Gentile was strictly observed. A Gentile could only be saved by becoming a Jewish proselyte and must worship at the temple in the court of the Gentiles. Similarly, during the Tribulation period, we see God sealing 144,000 Jews in Revelation 7. The woman being persecuted in Revelation 12 is probably Israel. The nation of Israel is in focus there. In this current church age, "There is neither Jew nor Greek [Gentile]" (Gal. 3:28 RSV).

Paul deals with this matter extensively in Romans 9–11. Without this interlude called the church age, it is impossible to make any sense of Romans 9–11. In Romans 11:25 Paul wrote, "For I do not desire, brethren, that you should be ignorant of this mystery, lest you should be wise in your own opinion, that blindness in part has happened to Israel until the fullness of the Gentiles has come in."[27] A judicial blindness came on the nation of Israel after they rejected Messiah. However, in the end times, that blindness will be lifted, and they will ultimately receive Jesus as their Messiah. But God's program from the Day of Pentecost until the initiation of Daniel's seventh week is the church—something not anticipated in the Old Testament.

There are two great mountains of Old Testament prophecy. One mountain is those predictions concerning the First Advent of Christ, and the other mountain is the predictions concerning his Second Advent. Between those mountains, hidden from the Old Testament saints, was a great valley of time, the church age.[28]

If God started his program with the church when he ended the sixty-ninth week of his dealings with Israel, it is logical that he would conclude the church age as he starts up the seventieth week for the Jewish nation. That conclusion of the church age may be the Rapture as an event, just as the Day of Pentecost was an event that began the church age. It is not impossible that God would continue the church age into the Tribulation period, allowing a seven-year overlap. But that would seem inconsistent with the more distinct timing on the Day of Pentecost. It seems more likely that he will conclude the church age with the Rapture, as he resumes his program (seventieth week) with Israel. That is not a conclusive argument for a pretribulation Rapture, but it should be considered.

Conclusion

We have now considered three foundational concepts:

1. the method to use for interpreting Bible prophecy,
2. God's purpose for the Tribulation period, and
3. the mystery of the church age.

That is preparation for attempting to answer the one question: Will Christians go through the Tribulation period?

We have spent significant time looking at Daniel 9:24–27 because it is a pivotal passage in biblical prophecy. God's program for Israel is revealed in those verses. It provides an outline of God's eschatological plan from the time of Daniel into the Tribulation period. When Israel rejected and crucified Messiah, God put his program for the nation of Israel on pause. He initiated the church age on the Day of Pentecost in Acts 2. At the beginning of the Tribulation period, he will restart his program to prepare Israel to receive Messiah. According to pretribulationists, the Rapture will occur at the beginning of that Tribulation period. Posttribulationists believe it will occur at the end of that seven-year period, and midtribulationists say it happens near the middle.

Before evaluating each of those positions, we will consider a variant of the pretribulation position. The partial Rapture theory places the Rapture at the beginning of the Tribulation period. However, only those waiting and watching for Christ's return will be raptured according to that model.

Endnotes: Chapter 2

1 "There are more than one hundred and fifty chapters in the Bible about the end of the age. The amount of information about this coming hour is staggering." David Sliker, *Biblical Foundations of Eschatology* (Kansas City, MO: Forerunner Books, 2006), 1.

2 Posttribulationists and midtribulationists add a third purpose: to prepare the bride of Christ for the Second Coming, including the great ingathering of souls into the church numbers. In those models, people are still being saved into the church and being refined through the persecution experienced. While insisting the church is not on earth during the Tribulation period, pretribulationists reject that idea. They do, however, believe a great number of Gentiles will turn to God for salvation during that time. Those Gentiles who are saved during the Tribulation, according to the pretribulation model, do not become a part of the church but have a unique place in God's program.

3 We know from passages like Rev. 7:7–14 and 14:6–7 that many will be saved during the Tribulation period. However, verses like Rev. 9:20–21 and 16:9–11 inform us that the vast majority of people living at that time will not repent. Nevertheless, God's work of grace affords them that opportunity, and they are without excuse. Out of his heart of love, God provides ample opportunity to repent. The following principle of judgment should be kept in mind: "God's end-time judgments will remove all that hinders love. He will use the least severe means to reach the greatest number at the deepest level of love without violating anyone's free will." Mike Bickle, *Studies in the Book of Revelation* (Kansas City, MO: Forerunner Books, 2014), 25.

4 The debate among posttribulationist, midtribulationists, and pretribulationists concerning wrath will be progressively analyzed in this study, especially in chapters 4, 6, and 7.

5 Ladd. *A Theology of the New Testament,* 673.

6 This understanding is confirmed by the way the first 69 weeks were fulfilled.

7 There were four edicts about the rebuilding of Jerusalem: (1) by Cyrus in 536 B.C. (Ezra 1) (2) by Darius (Ezra 6) (3) by Artaxerxes (Ezra &) (4) by Artaxerxes in 445 BC (Neh. 2). See W. A. Criswell, *Expository Sermons on the Book of Daniel,* vol. 4 (Grand Rapids: Zondervan, 1972), 116.

8 Jack W. Hayford, ed., *The New Spirit Filled Life Bible,* (Nashville, TN: Thomas Nelson, 2002), s.v. "Dan. 9:24–27" by Coleman Cox Phillips, 1135–36.

9 See Col. 1:26–27 and H. A. Ironside, *Lectures on the Epistle to the Colossians,* 1929 (Neptune, NJ: Loizeaux Brothers, 1979), 57–58.

10 For a rebuttal of opposing views on the interpretation of Dan. 9:24–27, see *The Moody Bible Commentary.* Any interpretation that does not lead to the fulfillment of the objectives stated in Daniel 9:24 cannot be the correct

interpretation. "The first three objectives deal with the issue of sin:" (1) "To finish the transgression" (end Israel's rebellion) (2) "To make an end of sins" (through righteous judgment) (3) "To make reconciliation for iniquity" (reconciliation with God through the cross). The last three objectives establish the kingdom of righteousness: (1) "To bring in everlasting righteousness" (surely this has not already happened) (2) "To seal up vision and prophecy" (3) "And to anoint the Most Holy." From the beginning of this passage, we are told the seventy weeks are designed to accomplish those ends. Michael Rydelnik and Michael Vanlaningham, eds., *The Moody Bible Commentary* (Chicago: Moody Publishers, 2014) 1305.

11 Three decrees had authorized the rebuilding of the temple: (1) by Cyrus (2 Chron. 36:22–23; Ezra 1) (2) by Darius confirming Cyrus's decree (Ezra 6) and (3) by Artaxerxes in his seventh year (Ezra 7). But all those *only* authorized the rebuilding of the temple. In his 20ᵗʰ year (445 B.C.) Artaxerxes's decree authorized the restoration of the *city* Jerusalem as well. That is when the prophetic clock for the seventy weeks (Dan. 9:24) began.

12 The first verse tells us when this revelation came to Daniel. It was the first year of Darius's reign, or about 538 BC. When Daniel found in Jer. 25 and 29 that the Babylonian captivity would be for 70 years, he began to intercede for his nation.

13 This fulfillment in 396 BC is marked by the renewal of the covenant in Nehemiah 9. Criswell provides an interesting observation about 396 BC. He observes, "The year 396 BC marks the end of the ministry of Malachi and the sealing and completion of the Old Testament canon." Criswell, *Expository Sermons on the Book of Daniel*, vol. 4, 117.

14 Cf. Alva J. McClain, *Daniel's Prophecy of the Seventy Weeks* (Grand Rapids: Zondervan, 1940), 12–15 quoted by Pentecost, *Things to Come*, 243. Daniel began his prayer when he saw in Jeremiah's prophecies that the Babylonian captivity would be for 70 years (10 x 7 years) (Dan. 2:2).

15 For a detailed analysis of the 483 years (483 x 12 mos. X 30 days = 173,880 days) adjusted from the biblical 30-day lunar months to the solar calendar used in the Western world see Robert Anderson, *The Coming Prince*, (London: Hodder & Stoughton, 1909), 121–123. One way we know Daniel's weeks are measured by the lunar calendar is John's description of the last three and a half years as 1,260 days (Rev. 11:3;12:6). During Noah's flood five months is reckoned as 150 days (Gen. 7:11 to 8:4) (Gen. 7:24; 8:3).

16 For example, there is a gap between "the acceptable year of the LORD" and "the day of vengeance of our God" in Isa. 61:2 and an unstated gap between Hosea 3:4 and Hosea 3:5. Cf. John F. Walvoord, "Is the Church the Israel of God," *Bibliotheca Sacra*, no. (October 1944): 403–416. The gap of time in prophetic passages is commonly referred to as telescoping. David Reagan

explains, "Another peculiar feature of prophetic literature is called "telescoping." This occurs when a prophet compresses the time interval between two prophetic events. This phenomenon is very common. The reason for it has to do with the perspective of the prophet. As he looks into the future and sees a series of prophetic events, they appear to him as if they are in immediate sequence. It is like looking down a mountain range and viewing three peaks, one behind the other, each sequentially higher than the one in front of it. The peaks look like they are right up against each other because the person viewing them cannot see the valleys that separate them." David R. Reagan, "The Interpretation of Prophecy: An exercise in imagination or the application of plain sense?" *Lamb & Lion Ministries*. https://christinprophecy.org/articles/the-interpretation-of-prophecy/.

17 "Given the forty-year spread between these two events [crucifixion of Messiah and destruction of Jerusalem], it is enough to indicate that the final seven in the seventy will not come in sequence with the other sixty-nine." Walter C. Kaiser, Jr., P. H. Davids, F. F. Bruce, M. T. Brauch, *Hard Sayings of the Bible* (Downers Grove: IL: InterVarsity Press, 1996), 319.

18 Some try to avoid this conclusion by saying the seven years "represent" an indefinite period of time rather than seven literal years. But the 483 years were literal years, and there is no reason to assume the last seven years are not literal years. Even Jeremiah's prophecy of the seventy-year Babylonian captivity were literal years.

19 Preterists try to avoid the fact that these events did not occur in the first century by allegorizing/spiritualizing the events recorded in Matt. 24:29–30. We will discuss the problems with their position more fully in chapter 9: "Matthew 24:15–31: The Great Tribulation." When the interpreter spiritualizes the upheavals in sun, moon, and stars, he often spiritualizes the Second Coming in order to maintain consistency in his interpretation. But Jesus will literally and physically return in his glorified body. The promise in Acts 1:11 is that Christ "will so come *in like manner* as you saw Him go into heaven" (emphasis added). It was physical, visible, and literal.

20 For a more detailed analysis of this, see Pentecost, *Things to Come*, 246–49.

21 Those who argue against the church-age gap are forced by history to recognize a forty-year gap in Dan. 9:26. If the forty-year gap is accepted, why must the church-age gap be rejected? Had Israel accepted her Messiah, there would have been no church-age gap. That is why God's revelation was given to Daniel the way it is recorded in Dan. 9:26–27. In this chapter, we identify some of the New Testament support for recognizing a church-age gap. For Brown and Keener's arguments against the church-age gap, see Michael L. Brown and Craig S. Keener, *Not Afraid of the Antichrist: Why We Don't Believe in a Pre-Tribulation Rapture* (Minneapolis, MN: Chosen, 2019), 68–78. For arguments supporting the church-age gap, see Pentecost, *Things to Come*, 246–50.

22 Acts 15:18.

23 In his definition, Zodhiates writes, "Some sacred thing hidden or secret which is naturally unknown to human reason and is only known by the revelation of God (Rom. 11:25; 1 Cor. 4:1; 14:2; 15:51; Col. 2:2; 1 Tim. 3:16; see 1 Cor. 2:2)." Spiros Zodhiates, *The Complete Word Study Dictionary: New Testament,* 1992 (Iowa Falls, IA: World Bible Publishers, 1994), 1,000. See also Douglas J. Moo, *The Epistle to the Romans,* The New International Commentary on the New Testament, N. Stonehouse, F. Bruce, and G. Fee, eds. (Grand Rapids. Eerdmans,1996), 714–718.

24 Rom. 16:25–26: "Now to Him who is able to establish you according to my gospel and the preaching of Jesus Christ, according to the revelation of the mystery kept secret since the world began, but now has been made manifest, and by the prophetic Scriptures has been made known to all nations, according to the commandment of the everlasting God, for obedience to the faith."

25 Criswell comments on this text, "The secret was this: that between the suffering of our Lord and the kingdom appearance a dispensation of mercy, and that in that period of time God was going to form another entity. It would be made up of Jews and Gentiles alike and they would be of the same body belonging to the same household of faith. That was the mystery. Even the angels did not know it. First Peter says, '. . . which things the angels desire to look into' (1:12) wondering what God was doing." W. A. Criswell, *Ephesians: An Exposition by W. A. Criswell* (Grand Rapids: Zondervan, 1974), 102–03.

26 Notably, 1 Cor. 10:32 divides humanity into three groups: Jews, Gentiles, and the church.

27 "These considerations suggest that the Gentiles' 'fullness' involves a numerical completion: God has determined to save a certain number of Gentiles, and only when that number has been reached will Israel's hardness be removed." Moo, *The Epistle to the Romans,* 719. In our Western culture we recon time by a date on the calendar. But here God's plan seems to be reckoned by the completion of an event. The "fulness" of the Gentiles is not the same thing as the "times" of the Gentiles mentioned in Luke 21:24. Luke 21:24 identities "the times of the Gentiles" with the city of Jerusalem being "trodden down by the Gentiles."

28 Criswell, *Ephesians,* 103.

CHAPTER 3

Partial Rapture Theory: A Variant of Pretribulationism

But take heed to yourselves, lest your hearts be weighed down with carousing, drunkenness, and cares of this life, and that Day come on you unexpectedly. For it will come as a snare on all those who dwell on the face of the whole earth. Watch therefore, and pray always that you may be counted worthy to escape all these things that will come to pass, and to stand before the Son of Man.

Luke 21:34–36 NKJV

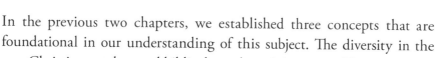

In the previous two chapters, we established three concepts that are foundational in our understanding of this subject. The diversity in the way Christians understand biblical prophecy is immense. This is partially due to the complexity of the subject and challenges in understanding the immense volume of material involved. But it is also due to the different methods of interpretation used in the process. We briefly discussed the two primary methods of interpretation: allegorical and literal. In chapter 1, we found the literal method to be more reliable and objective than the allegorical method.

In chapter 2, we analyzed Daniel 9:24–27 in detail. That is the key passage that tells us the Tribulation period will last for seven years. That seven-year period will begin with the Antichrist signing a peace treaty with Israel which he will break in the middle of the seven-year period. For thousands of years, such a treaty seemed impossible since there was no nation of Israel that could sign the agreement. But in 1948, Israel became a nation, and with that event, the possibility of a literal fulfillment of Daniel 9:27 became an evident reality!

Interpreting the Book of Revelation

Before proceeding, we need to address the book of Revelation briefly. John's revelation, in the last book of the Bible, expands our understanding of the seven-year period prophesied in Daniel 9:27. It is the most extensive document of biblical prophecy in the New Testament. The way we interpret that book significantly affects our eschatological understanding. For that reason, we want to quickly examine the four basic approaches to interpreting the book of Revelation.[1]

One is the preterist approach. This approach sees most of the prophecies in Revelation as already fulfilled during the first century.[2] In order to support this approach, one must reject the generally accepted timeframe in which John wrote Revelation. For good reason, most scholars date the writing of Revelation to be about 95 AD. Since preterists see in Revelation a prediction of the destruction of Jerusalem in 70 AD, they argue a date for this book to be before 70 AD. Without that earlier date, their approach breaks down. However, the evidence for the latter date is overwhelming.[3]

Historicists believe Revelation is "describing a long chain of events from Patmos to the end of history." They emphasize Revelation as a prediction of major events in church history to the present time. It takes a lot of allegorical interpretation to support this approach.

The idealists view the book "as symbolic pictures of timeless truths." They do not try to connect the message with any specific reference to time. Instead, they see it as depicting the "ongoing struggle between good and evil." This approach also relies heavily on the allegorical method of interpretation.

We are in the futurist camp. We interpret most of Revelation 4–22 as prophecy to be fulfilled in the future. Pretribulationists, midtribulationists, and posttribulationists generally embrace the futurist approach.

Of course, there are many variations within each of these camps.

Some even add a fifth school of thought: the eclectics who combine pieces from the four major approaches.[4] Whatever approach an interpreter takes to the book of Revelation is typically consistent with the way he or she is approaching biblical prophecy in general.[5]

With the internet and the increased availability of viewpoints on Bible prophecy, it is more important for believers to understand these different approaches to interpreting Revelation than it used to be. In the past, believers were almost exclusively taught doctrine by the church they attended. They did not access the other approaches. The negative side of that was that they did not get their thinking challenged by other theories. But the positive side was they did not encounter the possible confusion inherent in hearing a little from one school of thought, then a little from another, then trying to make sense of it all. Christians need to know at least the basic approaches potentially encountered when searching this subject out on the internet.

Back to our central question: Will Christians go through the Tribulation period? *Futurists* hold three different theories as to when the Rapture will occur in relationship to the Tribulation period: pretribulationism, midtribulationism, and posttribulationism.

Before critiquing each of those positions, we want to consider a variation that is perhaps exclusively associated with the pretribulation theory. It is called the partial Rapture theory, sometimes referred to as the split Rapture position. The stance in this camp is that some of the church will be raptured before the Tribulation period begins, and the rest will go through the Tribulation period. Those who are ready will be raptured and will not have to go through the Tribulation period. God will use the Tribulation period to refine those who were not ready. Among others, the godly Englishman, Austin Sparks held this view.

Strengths of the Partial Rapture Position

The many New Testament exhortations to be ready for the Lord's coming lend support to this theory. This is an important theme in the Bible, and some of the passages do imply a consequence of not being prepared. Here are a few passages where we find this.

In Luke 21, Jesus gave a lengthy prophetic teaching. Then, in verses

34–36, he said to his followers, "But take heed to yourselves, lest your hearts be weighed down with carousing, drunkenness, and cares of this life, and that Day come on you unexpectedly. For it will come as a snare on all those who dwell on the face of the whole earth. Watch therefore, and pray always that you may be counted worthy to escape all these things that will come to pass, and to stand before the Son of Man."[6] The gravity of this warning is obvious. Anytime Jesus says, "Take heed to yourselves" we should pay attention. It's a foolish thing to take lightly what he says following such an alert.

The warning is against preoccupation with other things, rather than seeking first the kingdom of God.[7] The warning is that something is coming that will be "a snare on all those who dwell on the face of the whole earth." Notice this warning is not just about Judea. This will affect "all those who dwell on the face of the whole earth."

So, what did Jesus say to do? Take heed to yourselves: pay attention to your spiritual condition. "Above all else, guard your heart" (Prov. 4:23 NIV). Paul warned the Corinthians, "Examine yourselves as to whether you are in the faith. Test yourselves" (2 Cor. 13:5). In his first epistle, the Apostle John gave specific tests to use in the self-examination.[8] This partial Rapture position alerts Christians to the importance of doing this.

Jesus also says in Luke 21:36, "Watch therefore, and pray always." That command calls for disciplined consistency. The implication of Jesus's words in that text is that if you do not watch and pray, you might not be counted worthy to escape "all these things." That thought tends to support to the partial Rapture theory.

The partial rapture position also finds support in the words spoken by Jesus to the church at Ephesus. There Jesus said to Christians, "Because you have kept My command to persevere, I also will keep you from the hour of trial which shall come upon the whole world, to test those who dwell on the earth" (Rev. 3:10). Jesus did not say that he would keep them from the hour of trial because they said the sinner's prayer and were born again. Keeping Christ's command to persevere was required. It is an argument from silence, but the implication is that if they did not persevere, then Christ would not keep them from the hour of trial. We know "the hour of trial" is not just a personal trial because Jesus defines it using the Greek article "the" (*tēs*) hour of trial. He further identifies it as *tēs* hour of trial "which shall come upon the whole world." That description fits the Tribulation period.[9]

The New Testament also seems to tie the promise of the Rapture to those who love Christ's appearing—those who eagerly wait for him. Hebrews 9:28 is an example: "So Christ was offered once to bear the sins of many. To those who eagerly wait for Him He will appear a second time, apart from sin, for salvation." The phrase "To those who eagerly wait for Him" might indicate a qualification. Second Timothy 4:8 makes a similar statement. Paul says, "Finally, there is laid up for me the crown of righteousness, which the Lord, the righteous Judge, will give to me on that Day, and not to me only but also to all who have loved His appearing." In Philippians 3:20, Paul also writes, "For our citizenship is in heaven, from which we also eagerly wait for the Savior, the Lord Jesus Christ." Are all those today who profess Christ "eagerly" waiting for the Savior?

The Apostle John talked about our blessed hope in 1 John 3:2 "Beloved, now we are children of God; and it has not yet been revealed what we shall be, but we know that when He is revealed, we shall be like Him, for we shall see Him as He is." That refers to the transformation we will experience at the Rapture/Resurrection of the Just. Then John adds this statement: "And everyone who has this hope in Him purifies himself, just as He is pure" (1 John 3:3). Is John saying, "everyone who has this hope in Him" *should* purify himself? Or is he saying something more significant. Is he saying, "everyone who has this hope in Him" *does* purify himself? The indicative present tense of the verb "purifies" (*hagnizō*) indicates something that does happen, not just should happen. Commenting on this verse, Martyn Loyd-Jones wrote, "He [John] does not say, he *ought* to purify himself, he says that he *does*, and therefore it becomes a very thorough test of what we truly are" (emphasis Loyd-Jones's).[10] So, the partial Rapture approach does recognize the biblical call to watch and be prepared for Christ's coming.

Another strength of this position is that it recognizes the quality of the bride of Christ. Will Christ be coming back for a bride that loves this world, has little interest in her bridegroom, and is preoccupied with other things? Or will he come for a bride living for him and longing to be with him? When we look at the church today, we are forced to ask questions like that. This position sees the bride as being prepared to meet her bridegroom.

Ephesians 5:27 tells us Christ will have a bride who is glorious "not having spot or wrinkle or any such thing, but that she should be holy and without blemish." It is hard to see lukewarm, half-hearted, compromising Christians in that light. We get another view of the bride in Revelation 19 that confirms this description. Verse 7 says, "The marriage of the Lamb has come, and His wife has made herself ready." The phrase "has made herself ready" implies some responsibility on her part. Verse 8 goes on to say, "And to her it was granted to be arrayed in fine linen, clean and bright, for the fine linen is the righteous acts of the saints." She is beautifully arrayed "in fine linen, clean and bright." That attire is defined as "the righteous *acts* of the saints" (emphasis added). This is not referring to the imputed righteousness of Christ that Christians receive in their initial experience when justified by faith. It is referring to the outworking of that. It is referring to righteous works that have been done by the bride of Christ.

Paul exhorted the church at Philippi to "work out your own salvation with fear and trembling; for it is God who works in you both to will and to do for His good pleasure" (Phil. 2:12–13). The sanctification in that passage is not possible unless God is working in a person "to will and to do for His good pleasure." However, there is a responsibility for the believer to work that inner grace out into godly behavior—righteous *acts*.

Titus 2:12–13 says the grace of God teaches us to deny ungodliness and worldly lusts and to "live soberly, righteously, and godly in the present age, looking for the blessed hope and glorious appearing of our great God and Savior Jesus Christ." The description of the bride in Ephesians 5:27 and Revelation 19:8 seems to indicate a bride who is obedient to that command. Titus 2:14 says Christ's purpose in his First Advent was not just to save us from hell, but to "redeem us from every lawless deed and purify for Himself His own special people, zealous for good works."[11] The bride revealed in the New Testament is clothed in those good works. This partial Rapture position does recognize the importance of those good works.

Personal Experience with the Partial Rapture Theory

Years ago, I attended a church that not only believed in a split Rapture but took great pride in the revelation. Since most Evangelical churches in the area held to a traditional pretribulation stance, we felt like this revelation positioned us a notch above others. Of course, we were sure that we would go up, as the bride, in the Rapture while many other Christians would not make it. Our problem was not so much the doctrine itself. I cannot tell you with certainty that this position is wrong. The problem was not with the teaching itself. The problem was the spirit in which it was held and defended. Behind our assertion of this partial Rapture interpretation was spiritual pride. Anytime an individual, a church, or a movement becomes prideful of its "superior" knowledge, that person, church, or movement is in trouble. Even if right doctrinally, they are in trouble.

After 40 plus years of ministry, I have come to this conclusion: Nothing is more destructive that spiritual pride! Deception accompanies spiritual pride. And when people are full of pride and deceived by the Devil, it gets very difficult to help them. They cannot hear correction. They cannot hear reason. They are too busy trying to straighten everybody else out. Because of pride, Lucifer fell. Because of spiritual pride, the scribes and Pharisees rejected Christ and orchestrated his crucifixion. They knew a lot of Scripture, but they did not maintain a biblical humility before God and other people.

It would be nice if I could teach the reader unequivocally which position on the timing of the Rapture is correct and back it up with the Bible. But far more beneficial is teaching people to maintain a humble spirit. "He has showed you, O man, what is good; and what does the Lord require of you but to do justice, and to love kindness, and to walk humbly with your God?" (Mic. 6:8 RSV). That is a weightier issue than exactly when and how the Rapture occurs.[12] Whatever your position on when the Rapture occurs, are you walking humbly with your God and with your fellow believers? Are you esteeming others better than yourself (Phil. 2:3)?

God let Paul go through all kinds of suffering with the goal of protecting him from spiritual pride. When Paul asked God to remove his awful thorn in the flesh, God's answer was "My grace is sufficient for you, for My strength is made perfect in weakness" (2 Cor. 12:9). He was telling Paul that instead of removing it, he would give him grace/strength to bear it. Why? Because God was using it as a means of protecting him from pride. We know Paul understood that revelation because in 2 Corinthians 12:7 he wrote, "And lest I should be exalted above measure by the abundance of the revelations, a thorn in the flesh was given to me, a messenger of Satan to buffet me, lest I be exalted above measure."

Knowledge and revelation tend to puff us up.[13] That is why a purely academic study of the word without applying its exhortations to our lives is a spiritually dangerous endeavor. This mistake is one reason brilliant theologians get deceived while studying the Bible. We must continually humble ourselves under the mighty hand of God. It is a humbling thing to live the message out because we often come short of the perfection we are pursuing (Rom. 3:23). God allows trials and tribulation to come into our lives, just as He did in Paul's life, to remind us of our dependence on him.

Whenever you see a group with a "pet doctrine"—a doctrine that is central to their identity and in their own eyes sets them above the other Christians, watch out![14] In the past some of my fellow Pentecostals developed an attitude of superiority based on their experience in the baptism in the Holy Spirit. They were right about the doctrine but wrong in their attitude toward other believers. They were condescending in the way they communicated the truth they had received. As a result, many people who would have benefited from it were put off by the prideful way it was communicated and never entered into the baptism of the Holy Spirit. That was a net loss for the kingdom of God. We want to be right about our doctrine, but we must maintain a right spirit in our pursuit of knowledge. The Devil has all kinds of tricks up his sleeve, and his most lethal weapon is spiritual pride.

The pastor of that church was a gifted Bible teacher. He taught the partial Rapture theory because that was what he was taught in Bible school. However, over the years, he diligently searched the scriptures on this subject. Out of those studies, he concluded that the Rapture included the whole church, not just part of the church. To his credit, he had the courage to follow his convictions and teach the church some of the problems in this split Rapture position. Regardless of which theory is correct, he led the congregation out of that prideful attitude of heart, and the church grew as a result. Whatever position is embraced concerning the Rapture, we must maintain a humble, teachable spirit.

Weaknesses of the Partial Rapture Position

First, this position fails to recognize the fundamental qualification of believers through faith in Christ's death and resurrection. We are not accepted based on our good works. We are "accepted in the Beloved [in Christ]" (Eph. 1:6). Our justification rests on what Christ did on our behalf. Romans 8:30 says, "Moreover whom He predestined, these He also called; whom He called, these He also justified; and whom He justified, these He also glorified." First Corinthians 15 and 1 Thessalonians 4 tie the Rapture with the Resurrection of the Just. That is when our glorification happens. Paul concluded Romans 8:30 with this statement: "whom He justified, these He also glorified." Being justified by faith is the qualification for glorification. Our resurrection is guaranteed by his resurrection. It is problematic to make the timing of the resurrection dependent on good works, and it is problematic to do that with the Rapture since they occur together.

Second, with a partial Rapture, one is left with questions about the resurrection of dead believers. Logically, only the "good" ones would be resurrected as well. But Paul specifically says in 1 Thessalonians 4:14, "God will bring with Jesus those who have fallen asleep in him" (NIV). There are no works given as a qualification except that they "have fallen asleep in him." Additionally, 1 Corinthians 15:51 says, "Behold, I tell you a mystery: We shall not all sleep, but we shall all be changed." Paul's language there would include *all* believers.

Third, the partial Rapture divides the Body of Christ.[15] That seems to violate the unity of the body taught in Ephesians 4:1–13 and 1 Corinthians 12:12–13. Ephesians 4:4 says, "There is one body and one Spirit, just as you were called in one hope of your calling." I have the same blessed hope as all my brothers and sisters in Christ have. There is one body . . . one hope. In conjunction with that statement, God tells us to endeavor "to keep the unity of the Spirit in the bond of peace." It seems strange that he would break that unity which he has told us to diligently guard. It is even more problematic that he would divide the body at the most glorious, climactic moment. On the day of the Rapture, we will rejoice that *all* of us are there with him. On that day Christ will rejoice that *all* of us are there with him.

Fourth, the split Rapture position leaves God's program with the church only partially fulfilled as He renews his program with Israel. It is not impossible that God would do that, but it is less likely. It raises difficult questions. For example, during the overlap, is there still neither Jew nor Gentile (Gal. 3:28)? How do we reconcile the trigger event of "the fullness of the Gentiles" (Rom. 11:25) with the partial Rapture position? In the Tribulation period God will have restarted the seventy-week prophetic clock for Israel. The partial Rapture theory contends that he almost finished the church age. Will this age end in that way? Possibly, but it will more likely be a complete work instead.

Fifth, the partial Rapture theory seems to confuse the rewards Christians receive at the Judgment Seat of Christ with the privilege of the Rapture/Resurrection. Paul says in 2 Corinthians 5:9–10, "Therefore we make it our aim, whether present or absent, to be well pleasing to Him. For we must all appear before the judgment seat of Christ, that each one may receive the things done in the body, according to what he has done, whether good or bad." The word "all" in verse 10 implies a unity of the whole church. Therefore, rather than making the Rapture, and by extension the Resurrection, a reward, it is more reasonable to see the Judgment Seat of Christ as the occasion when rewards are given.

While there are some strengths in the partial Rapture position, the weight of the evidence is against it. It is much more likely the whole church will be raptured at the same time.

Analysis of the Distinction between Those Raptured and Those Left Behind

Before concluding, we need to further analyze this theory's distinction between those raptured and those left behind.

To its credit, the partial Rapture theory recognizes a problem with people living ungodly lives and being caught up in the Rapture as part of the bride of Christ. It offers a rationale to explain how Christ's bride will be pure, honorable, and holy. If we do not accept that explanation, then we need to account for how that problem is to be resolved.

The problem begins here: In our culture anyone who makes a profession of Christ is recognized as a Christian. Yet, Jesus said, "Not everyone who says to Me, 'Lord, Lord,' shall enter the kingdom of heaven, but he who does the will of My Father in heaven" (Matt. 7:21). Many people today say to Christ, "Lord, Lord," but they do not do the will of the Father. They are professors of the faith but not possessors of the faith. James insisted that true faith would be demonstrated by one's lifestyle—by the way the person lives (James 2:19–20). The Apostle John wrote, "Little children, let no one deceive you. He who practices righteousness is righteous, just as He is righteous" (1 John 3:7). A Christian is not verified by having his name on the church membership role or performing a religious ritual. We know he is really a Christian because he "practices righteousness." Practicing righteousness does not make him a Christian. It demonstrates that he is one. John also said, "If we say that we have fellowship with Him, and walk in darkness, we lie and do not practice the truth" (1 John 1:6). In that verse, walking is used as a metaphor for the way a person lives. There are many people in the visible church who "say" they have fellowship with Christ, but they "walk in darkness." Those people will not go up in the Rapture.

In 1 Corinthians 6:9–10 Paul wrote, "Do you not know that the unrighteous will not inherit the kingdom of God? Do not be deceived. Neither fornicators, nor idolaters, nor adulterers, nor homosexuals, nor sodomites, nor thieves, nor covetous, nor drunkards, nor revilers, nor extortioners will inherit the kingdom of God." People who live like that won't just miss the Rapture. They will miss heaven altogether unless they repent. They will not have delayed rewards; they will have their part in the lake of fire.

We have made the narrow gate broad; then we called those living ungodly lives "carnal" Christians. We have replaced the difficult path of self-denial with a pursuit of the American dream; then we adapted our theology to the change. When we view people living ungodly lives as Christians, then it is difficult to see the whole group as the bride of Christ.

But in the parable of the wheat and tares, Jesus made a distinction between two groups of people in the visible church. He said the two groups would grow up together until the end. In that parable the tares are burned in the fire. That is imagery generally associated with unsaved people. The tares are characterized as "those who practice lawlessness." And the warning is "There will be wailing and gnashing of teeth" (Matt. 13:41-42). All that sounds more severe than a delay of heavenly rewards for the immature, carnal Christian. The parable tells us that tares (people who are not regenerated) will be in the visible church along with true believers until the end of the age (Matt. 13:36–43). When we look at the visible church today, we are seeing wheat and tares. We are seeing people living in darkness and people living in the light. Only part of those people will be raptured. Only the genuine followers of Christ will be caught up to be with the Lord.[16]

The perseverance and eagerness for the coming of the Lord that we quoted earlier in support of the partial Rapture theory may be descriptions of true believers in contrast to mere professors of the faith. The whole "visible" church will not be raptured. Only true believers will be raptured. All true believers may fit the description given in those passages. They may be those who love his appearing and are eagerly awaiting his return. They are exhorted to maintain that attitude in preparation for Christ's coming.

The partial Rapture position is often supported with the parable of the ten virgins. However, we know the foolish virgins are not Christians by the answer the Lord gives them when they ask him to open the door to them. "But he answered and said, 'Assuredly, I say to you, I do not know you'" (Matt. 25:12). The Lord knows those who are truly his. In John 10:14, he said, "I am the good shepherd; and I know My sheep, and am known by My own." Second Timothy 2:19 says, "Nevertheless the solid foundation of God stands, having this seal: 'The Lord knows those who are His.'" These foolish virgins are not carnal Christians.[17] They are people who do not really *know* the Lord.

I wonder how many people we think are carnal Christians are in fact not Christians at all. That's a difficult thought to consider, but we can't ignore the possibility. We need to help those people make their calling and election sure (2 Pet. 1:10). We need to preach the word in such a way that if they are not saved, they will get saved. One of the greatest harvest fields on earth today is the visible church in America. The people I have led to the Lord this year have been church people who had never been born again. One had been in church for decades. May God help us to reach that great harvest.

Conclusion

If you do not have an assurance in your heart that Christ is your Lord and Savior, seek him until you get that assurance. Get people of faith to pray with you. God's Spirit will bear witness with your spirit when you have been born of the Spirit (Rom. 8:16). Consider praying this prayer:

"Dear God, I ask you for an inner assurance that I am saved and belong to you. Reveal to me my true condition in your eyes. Forgive me for my sins. Change me where I need to be changed. Above all else, I want to be right with you. I know that is only possible through Jesus's sacrifice on the cross. Based on what Jesus has done for me, I ask you for mercy. I open my heart to you and ask you to take over my life entirely. I surrender my life to you and receive your transforming love and grace. By your word, and by your Spirit, confirm my salvation in Jesus's name. Amen."

Endnotes: Chapter 3

1   For additional information on interpreting the book of Revelation see Appendix A: "The Book of Revelation."

2   For a summary of problems in the preterist interpretation of the Olivet Discourse see Douglas J. Moo, "A Case for Posttribulation Rapture, *Three Views on The Rapture: Pretribulation, Prewrath, or Posttribulation,* by Craig Blaising, Alan Hultberg (gen. ed.), and Douglas J. Moo, (1984; rev. ed., Grand Rapids: Zondervan, 2010) 215–216.

3   Donald Guthrie, *New Testament Introduction,* (1961; rev. ed., Downers Grove, IL: InterVarsity Press, 1990), 948–962.

4   Cf. Barker, Kenneth L., ed., *The NIV Study Bible,* 1985 (Grand Rapids: Zondervan, 1995) s.v. "Introduction Revelations" by Robert Mounce and David O'Brian. See also Leon Morris, *The Revelation of St. John,* The Tyndale New Testament Commentaries, R. Tasker, gen. ed. (Grand Rapids: Eerdmans, 1981) 16–19; "5 approaches to interpreting Revelation," *Zondervan Academic.* https://zondervanacademic.com/blog/how-read-revelation; Ladd, *A Theology of the New Testament,* 671–675.

5   While we do not question the sincerity of those who hold the other views, we believe the weight of biblical evidence supports the futurist approach. Evaluating the strengths and weaknesses of each approach is beyond the scope of this study.

6   This emphasis on watchfulness is also recorded in Matt. 24:36–44 and Mark 13:32–37.

7   Cf. Prov. 6:33.

8   Cf. Richard W. Tow, *Authentic Christianity: Studies in 1 John* (Bloomington, IN: WestBow Press, 2019).

9   For a pretribulation interpretation of Revelation 3:10 see Chafer, *Systematic Theology,* Vol. 4, 369–371. For a posttribulation rebuttal see Robert H. Gundry, *The Church and the Tribulation* (Grand Rapids: Zondervan, 1973), 53–61.

10   Martyn Loyd-Jones, *Life in Christ: Studies in 1 John* (Wheaton, IL: Crossway, 2002), 297.

11   The prediction in Matt. 1:21 was "you shall call His name Jesus, for He will save His people from their sins."

12   Cf. Matt. 23:23.

13   Paul says in 1 Cor. 8:1 that knowledge puffs up. Then in the next verse, he makes this comment about people who are in that prideful state: "And if anyone thinks that he knows anything, he knows nothing yet as he ought to know." After exhorting toward a submissive humility in 1 Tim. 6:1–2, Paul characterizes those who would teach otherwise with these words: "he is proud, knowing nothing, but is obsessed with disputes and arguments over words." (v. 6).

14 The central message of the New Testament is Christ and Him crucified (1 Cor. 2:2). There are many important truths peripheral to that center that need to be taught. But we must not let any of them take that central place.

15 Govett's partial Rapture theory is built mainly on interpreting parables and symbolic language. His projection of three Raptures seems highly unlikely. He writes, "There may be a Rapture—the Rapture of *especial reward*, promised to Philadelphia—which takes place *before the main one destined for the watchful church*—and lastly, a third for those who have to pass through the great tribulation" (emphasis Govett's). R. Govett, *The Saints' Rapture to the Presence of the Lord Jesus*, originally published in London during the mid-1800s (Miami Springs, FL: Conley & Schoettle Publishing, 1984), 295.

16 Worldwide changes are occurring rapidly. For example, the pandemic in 2020 became the catalyst for dramatic changes in church life and in societies all over the world. If the falling away that we are seeing in those turning from "the faith" to "Progressive Christianity" continues, the distinction between wheat and tares may become more evident. Additionally, if persecution of the church intensifies, the American church may look very different in the future—perhaps more like the church in China. A refined, persecuted church tends to look more like the bride of Christ that we see in Scripture than an affluent, self-indulgent church. The partial rapture theory offers an explanation for Christ coming for a praying people eagerly awaiting his return. But we do not know when the Rapture will occur, and we do not know what the visible church will look like when He returns.

17 My stance here may be somewhat overstated since parables are stories designed to make one point, and the details may not be solid ground for building doctrine. Nevertheless, the harshness of the answer and the seriousness of Christ's point in this parable seems to support my position. The point of this parable is stated in Matt. 25:13: "Watch therefore, for you know neither the day nor the hour in which the Son of Man is coming."

SECTION II

EVALUATION OF POSITIONS

CHAPTER 4

Pretribulation Position: Strengths

For God did not appoint us to wrath, but to obtain salvation through our Lord Jesus Christ.

1 Thessalonians 5:9 NKJV

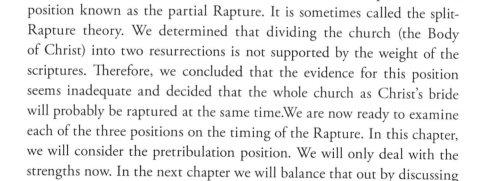

In the previous chapter, we examined a variant of the pretribulation position known as the partial Rapture. It is sometimes called the split-Rapture theory. We determined that dividing the church (the Body of Christ) into two resurrections is not supported by the weight of the scriptures. Therefore, we concluded that the evidence for this position seems inadequate and decided that the whole church as Christ's bride will probably be raptured at the same time.We are now ready to examine each of the three positions on the timing of the Rapture. In this chapter, we will consider the pretribulation position. We will only deal with the strengths now. In the next chapter we will balance that out by discussing its weaknesses. Analyzing the other two positions will go faster because we will deal with many of the major issues while evaluating the pretribulation position.

Typically, when people teach on this subject, they simply present their preferred position. When doing that, they usually emphasize the strengths of that position with minimal discussion of the weaknesses. In some settings that is appropriate. However, in this study we want to present both strengths and weaknesses of each position as objectively as possible.

No one does that perfectly, but we are trying to look at it from more than one perspective. That requires more thought on the part of the reader, but it empowers that person to personally evaluate the matter and arrive at his or her own conclusion.

There are many issues of eschatology that I am absolutely convinced of as scripturally correct. I believe Jesus is literally, visibly, and physically returning to the earth in his glorified body to rule and reign as King of Kings and Lord of Lords. I believe Christians will be literally and physically resurrected with a glorified body like the one Christ has. I could go on and on with doctrines that are so clear in Scripture that there is no debate about them as far as I am concerned.

But the timing of the Lord's return is something no one fully knows. Even the angels do not know the day and hour of Christ's return. We are looking at this subject through a glass darkly with a teachable spirit. We are searching the scriptures like the Bereans did to learn what we can. The final answer that we arrive at is important, but so is what we will learn in the process. Simply being told an answer to accept is not nearly as beneficial. So, I hope you will persevere as we seek to understand what we can and trust God with the secret things he has not revealed.

What are the strengths of the pretribulation position? This model has a lot of strong points to recommend it. That is why so many conservative, Bible-believing scholars embrace it. Like the other two positions, it is built on a literal interpretation of Scripture. But in what ways might this approach be preferable over the other two positions.

It Recognizes the Biblical Purpose of the Tribulation Period.

In chapter 2, we identified two primary purposes for the seven-year Tribulation. Do you remember what they are? They are the outpouring of wrath on the ungodly Gentile nations and the final preparations for Israel to receive the true Messiah. This model places the church in heaven during the Tribulation with those two objectives as the focus of God's dealings on earth during that time.

It is easy to read Scripture with ourselves at the center of the interpretation. Replacement theology does that, in my opinion. Instead of recognizing Israel's rightful place in God's plan, everything said to them is about *me* as a Christian. At a lesser degree, it is possible to put the church at the center of the Tribulation period when Israel is really the focus. I am speaking on behalf of this pretribulation position when I say that. Those in the other two camps argue the Tribulation period also serves to prepare the bride of Christ for her groom.

The book of Revelation provides the most detail about the Tribulation period. Its content and symbolism are very Jewish. The revelation was given to a Jew knowledgeable of Old Testament Scripture. That should be kept in mind by anyone trying to understand the book. Some estimate nearly 70 percent of the verses contain Old Testament references.[1] In his exposition of Revelation, W. A. Criswell points out some of the Jewish symbolism and writes, "Though he never quotes from the Old Testament directly, John reflects the prophetic language and visions of the books of the Old Testament. When we see the symbols and the signs and the pictures in the Revelation, we can go back to the Old Testament and find their meaning."[2] Pretribulationists point to the Jewishness of this book as an indication that John is primarily describing the last week of God's dealings with the nation of Israel. John sees the church in heaven in chapters 4, 5, 11, and 19. But we do not see any explicit references to the church being on earth in chapters 4–18.

Some expositors point to the mention of "saints" as proof that the church is present on earth. But the Greek word simply means "set apart to or by God, consecrated; holy, morally pure, upright."[3] For example, Revelation 13:7 says, "It was granted to him [Antichrist] to make war with the saints [*hagios*] and to overcome them." "Saints" is a valid translation, but it does not necessarily refer to those who are a part of the church. In fact, the context follows the comments about the woman in chapter 12, which is probably a reference to Jews.[4] Criswell, a pretribulationist, makes an interesting observation about the exhortation that follows in Revelation 13:9: "If anyone has an ear, let him hear." Criswell writes, "Here again is an example of the fact that if we interpret this book correctly, every little piece and detail will fall into place. 'If a man have an ear, let him hear what the spirit saith to the churches' [Rev. 13:9 KJV]—this is the word of the Lord seven times in chapters 2 [verses 7, 11, 17, and 29] and 3 [verses 6, 13, and 22]. But we do not have that last phrase here— '. . . what the spirit saith to the church,' for they are gone. God has taken them out of this awful trial and tribulation."⁵ The pretribulation theory gives prominence to God's purpose for Israel during that seven-year period.⁶

Additionally, it supports the biblical statement that God has not appointed Christians to wrath. We demonstrated in a previous teaching that God's wrath is poured out during the Tribulation period. In fact, that is the other clear reason for the Tribulation period. The classic verse quoted by pretribulationists is 1 Thessalonians 5:9: "For God did not appoint us to wrath, but to obtain salvation through our Lord Jesus Christ."

Posttribulationists answer this issue by claiming "wrath in that verse refers to eternal wrath alone." But the argument is weak. If God did not appoint Christians to wrath, he does not subject them to his wrath in any context. In fact, the promise in 1 Thessalonians 5:9 is in the context of the Tribulation period. This issue will be explored more fully in later chapters.

That is the first strength of the pretribulation position; it recognizes God's purpose for the Tribulation period.

It Organizes the Whole Biblical Revelation on Eschatology in a Logical, Unified System.

The pieces fit together well.⁷ Perhaps too well, but at least it makes sense.⁸

It avoids the challenges found in overlapping the church age with the last week for Israel. With the overlap, questions arise. For example, is the declaration in Galatian 3:28 that says, "There is neither Jew nor Greek" still in effect? If the church age is still operational during the Tribulation, do not those who turn to God simply become Christian? If so, why does the book of Revelation give such prominence to Jews during that time?

The church age began with a specific event on the Day of Pentecost that coincided with the closing of God's work with Israel when the nation rejected Messiah. It seems reasonable that it would end with a specific event called the Rapture and coincide with the resumption of God's work with Israel at the beginning of the seventieth week. The argument that God let the temple stand forty more years is not persuasive because the New Testament makes it clear that anyone turning to God during those forty years was saved into the church.⁹

A reasonableness argument like that is not as strong as a chapter and verse with a clear statement of revelation. Nevertheless, having the church going through the Tribulation period does raise questions about which program is in effect during that time and how events transpire when the church is raptured. We will deal with some of those issues when we talk about the weaknesses in the posttribulation model.

Midtribulationism and posttribulationism have organized systems that address the whole biblical revelation on the subject. However, the pretribulation position seems to be the most logically organized of the three. That does not prove it is right. But the more "loose-ends" that we have in our interpretation the less confident we become.

The Pretribulation Position Seems to Follow the Sequence in the Book of Revelation.

In Revelation 4:1, John is caught up and sees a vision of heaven.[10] The transition in that verse begins with the words, "After these things" (*meta tauta*).[11] John is marking a significant shift in his narrative. Prior to this, he is addressing the seven churches on earth. Now he sees into heaven, and one of the things he sees is 24 elders around the throne of God. There are good reasons to see these 24 elders as representative of the church in heaven.[12] In Revelation 4:4, John writes, "Around the throne were 24 thrones, and on the thrones I saw 24 elders sitting, clothed in white robes; and they had crowns of gold on their heads." The fact that they are seated (Eph. 2:6; Rev. 3:21), clothed in white robes (Rev. 3:5), and have crowns on their heads all point to the church. The crowns are *stephanos* which were the wreaths given to the winners in the Olympic games. It is indicative of overcoming.[13] Perhaps the greatest evidence that they represent the overcoming church is found in their expression of worship in Revelation 5:9–10. There they sing, "You are worthy to take the scroll, And to open its seals; For You were slain, And have redeemed us to God by Your blood Out of every tribe and tongue and people and nation, And have made us kings and priests to our God; And we shall reign on the earth." If they are the church, we are seeing them in heaven, not on the earth at this point. They continue to be seen in chapters 7, 11, 14, and 19. Throughout Revelation 4–19, there is no specific reference to the church on earth.[14] That is an indication that the church is in heaven during the Tribulation.

As important as the church is in New Testament theology, it would be strange that she is not specifically seen on earth during the Tribulation period if she is there.

In Revelation 19, John sees the bride of Christ in heaven. Ephesians 5:25–27 lets us know the church is the bride of Christ. She is seen in heaven before the Second Coming. Revelation 19:6–8 says, "And I [John] heard, as it were, the voice of a great multitude, as the sound of many waters and as the sound of mighty thunderings, saying, 'Alleluia! For the Lord God Omnipotent reigns! Let us be glad and rejoice and give Him glory, for the marriage of the Lamb has come, and His wife has made herself ready.' And to her it was granted to be arrayed in fine linen, clean and bright, for the fine linen is the righteous acts of the saints."

Her attire described in that last phrase which says, "for the fine linen is the righteous acts of the saints" suggests an event that is not explicitly stated in this passage but is taught elsewhere in the New Testament. The "righteous acts of the saints" is not a reference to imputed righteousness but to the righteous *acts* that flowed out of the new nature. The church is seen here clothed with her righteous acts. That terminology suggests that her works have already been tested and approved at the Judgment Seat of Christ.[15] Addressing fellow Christians, Paul wrote in 2 Corinthians 5:10, "For we must all appear before the judgment seat of Christ, that each one may receive the things done in the body, according to what he has done, whether good or bad." There is no indication in Revelation 19 that the bride is on her way to be judged. Yet, the posttribulation position would seem to require that.

In addition to the Judgment Seat of Christ event, there is also "the marriage of the Lamb" mentioned in Revelation 19:7. When do those two events happen? In the pretribulation position, they happen in heaven during the Tribulation period. John sees all of this before the Second Coming described in Revelation 19:11–16. But the posttribulation position requires that both these major events happen instantaneously as Jesus returns to earth.[16] That is simply not logical.

Describing Jesus's return to the earth at his Second Coming, Revelation 19:14 says, "And the armies in heaven, clothed in fine linen, white and clean, followed Him on white horses." They are coming to earth with him. They are not being caught up; they are coming down with him. We know these armies include the church because of the promise in Colossians 3:4: "When Christ who is our life appears, then you also will appear with Him in glory." And Jude 1:14 quotes Enoch's prophecy saying, "Behold, the Lord comes with ten thousands of His saints."

The posttribulation position has the church coming up to meet the Lord in the air as Christ is coming down to judge the wicked. In defense of the posttribulation position, advocates point to the custom in ancient times of "emissaries from a city going out to meet the dignitary and escort him on his way to their city." Keener says the word translated meeting (*apantēsis*) in 1 Thessalonians 4:17 when paired with a royal coming "normally" referred to this.[17] However, Greek scholar, Clinton Arnold, rejects this argument. He says Paul often relied on the Septuagint in the language he used in his letters, and this Greek word "is regularly used in the Septuagint just in the simple sense of meeting without any technical sense of going out and escorting a dignitary back to the city." Arnold insists this idea of emissaries going out from a city to meet dignitaries "is certainly not inherent in this Greek word."[18] If the posttribulation position is right, this offers a beautiful picture to describe it. But it offers no real argument for the position.

The Pretribulation Theory Offers a Meaningful Explanation of the Purpose for the Rapture.

In his debate on this subject, Clinton Arnold asked the thought-provoking question: "Why is there a Rapture in the first place?" He criticized the posttribulation position for substantially removing the need for a Rapture. In that scheme, the church goes up and comes right back down.[19] In the pretribulation position, the Rapture removes the church from the wrath being poured out on the earth; it concludes the church age as the seventieth week for Israel begins; it places the church in heaven during the Tribulation period where the Judgment Seat of Christ and the Marriage Supper take place. In the pretribulation position, there is a clear purpose for the Rapture.

The Pretribulation Model Effectively Supports the Biblical Issue of Imminence.

The dictionary definition of imminent is "ready to take place; *esp* : hanging threateningly over one's head."[20] Pretribulationists equate imminence with "at any moment" coming. Henry Thiessen writes, ". . . they [the early church fathers] held not only the premillennial view of Christ's coming, but also regarded that coming as imminent. The Lord had taught them to expect His return at any moment, and so they looked for him to come in their day. Not only so, but they also taught His personal return as being immediately. Only the Alexandrians opposed this truth; but these Fathers also rejected other fundamental doctrines. We may say, therefore, that the early church lived in the constant expectation of their Lord, and hence was not interested in the possibility of a Tribulation period in the future."[21]

In his discourse on the Mount of Olives, Jesus warned his followers to be ready for his return and said in Matthew 24:44, "for the Son of Man is coming at an hour you do not expect." He followed that up with parables emphasizing the importance of continual readiness. The pretribulation position places emphasis on eagerly watching and staying prepared for his return. In Revelation 16:15, Jesus warned, "Behold, I am coming as a thief. Blessed is he who watches, and keeps his garments, lest he walk naked and they see his shame."[22]

In the upper room before his trial, Jesus taught his disciples to live in anticipation of his return. In John 14:1–3, he said to them: "Let not your heart be troubled; you believe in God, believe also in Me. In My Father's house are many mansions; if it were not so, I would have told you. I go to prepare a place for you. And if I go and prepare a place for you, I will come again and receive you to Myself; that where I am, there you may be also." The assurance that this promise could be fulfilled at any moment would bring much comfort. The idea that one would face seven years of the worst tribulation ever experienced would not be as comforting.

We find the promise of Christ's return confirmed at his ascension. Acts 1:4–8 says, "And being assembled together with them, He commanded them not to depart from Jerusalem, but to wait for the Promise of the Father, 'which,' He said, 'you have heard from Me; for John truly baptized with water, but you shall be baptized with the Holy Spirit not many days from now.' Therefore, when they had come together, they asked Him, saying, 'Lord, will You at this time restore the kingdom to Israel?' And He said to them, 'It is not for you to know times or seasons which the Father has put in His own authority. But you shall receive power when the Holy Spirit has come upon you; and you shall be witnesses to Me in Jerusalem, and in all Judea and Samaria, and to the end of the earth.'"

The disciples wanted to know about God's plan for the end times, in particular whether Christ would restore the kingdom to Israel "at this time." It is easy to understand why they would ask that question because the church age had not yet been revealed. But Jesus's answer communicates the priorities every Christian must keep in mind.

In verse 7, Jesus says, "It is not for you to know times or seasons which the Father has put in His own authority." God has not chosen to reveal a full answer to the question that was asked. It is a legitimate question, but it should not be the center of attention. Instead, there are two things that Christians should focus on. Those are stated in verse 8: empowerment by the Spirit and evangelism. "But you shall receive power when the Holy Spirit has come upon you; and you shall be witnesses to Me in Jerusalem, and in all Judea and Samaria, and to the end of the earth." Even though we are currently studying "the times and seasons" of God's plan to restore the kingdom to Israel, the details are not central to our gospel message.[23] In this church age, the central concern is the empowerment of the Spirit for being a witness of Christ to the whole world. Knowing that helps us keep this current study in perspective.

We should not fret because we cannot perfectly put all the pieces together in our eschatology. Some of the pieces are not revealed. Deuteronomy 29:29 tells us, "The secret things belong to the Lord our God; but the things that are revealed belong to us and to our children forever, that we may do all the words of this law" (RSV). We do not waste a lot of time theorizing on the secret things God has not revealed in his word. Instead, we seek to understand by his grace that which He has revealed. And we don't do that as a mere academic exercise. We do it so that we can live pleasing to him: "that we may do all the words of this law." We do it so that we can live obediently within the behavioral boundaries he has established for us as our God and heavenly Father.

In this book, we are studying end-time prophecy. But we do that in the context of our mission to evangelize the world. We keep our eschatology in the context of our mission and gospel message. Twenty-seven percent of Scripture is prophecy. Those passages are not to be ignored. But we also want to deal with the other 73 percent. That way, we maintain balance in our walk forward.

Continuing in Acts 1:9–11, we are told what happened next when Jesus ascended into heaven. "Now when He had spoken these things, while they watched, He was taken up, and a cloud received Him out of their sight. And while they looked steadfastly toward heaven as He went up, behold, two men stood by them in white apparel, who also said, 'Men of Galilee, why do you stand gazing up into heaven? This same Jesus, who was taken up from you into heaven, will so come in like manner as you saw Him go into heaven.'" The assurance of Christ's return is affirmed. That verse does not necessarily prove the pretribulation position.[24] But it does reinforce an anticipation of his coming. The exclamation mark of that moment is that he is coming back!

This passionate anticipation of the Lord's return runs throughout the New Testament. For example, Titus 2:11–13 says, "For the grace of God that brings salvation has appeared to all men, teaching us that, denying ungodliness and worldly lusts, we should live soberly, righteously, and godly in the present age, *looking for* the blessed hope and glorious appearing of our great God and Savior Jesus Christ" (emphasis added). Just reading that passage for what it says, one would not be looking for a Great Tribulation and then the glorious appearing of the Lord. Instead, the tone is that we would live in anticipation of his imminent return.

And there should be an eagerness in that waiting. In Philippians 3:20, we read, "For our citizenship is in heaven, from which we also eagerly wait for the Savior, the Lord Jesus Christ." Notice Paul includes himself and the Philippian Christians in that anticipation of the Lord's return. He communicates the possibility of the return in his generation.

The New Testament authors write with an anticipation of the imminent return of Christ. James says in 5:8 of his epistle, "You also be patient. Establish your hearts, for the coming of the Lord is at hand." The NIV says, "You too, be patient and stand firm, because the Lord's coming is near."

Notice how Paul includes himself in 1 Corinthians 15:51–53. "Behold,

I tell you a mystery: We shall not all sleep, but we shall all be changed — in a moment, in the twinkling of an eye, at the last trumpet. For the trumpet will sound, and the dead will be raised incorruptible, and we shall be changed." Paul expresses the possibility and even the anticipation of being raptured: "*We* shall not all sleep, but *we* shall all be changed — in a moment, in the twinkling of an eye" (emphasis added). What I am pointing out is Paul's mindset of imminence.

The Apostle John, with all the revelation he received, had that mindset as well. He begins the book of Revelation this way: "The Revelation of Jesus Christ, which God gave Him to show His servants — things which must shortly take place" (Rev. 1:1). The New Living Translation says, "This is a revelation from Jesus Christ, which God gave him concerning the events that will happen soon." Then John closes that book in chapter 22 with a reminder of imminence. In verses 6–7, we read, "Then he said to me, 'These words are faithful and true.' And the Lord God of the holy prophets sent His angel to show His servants the things which must shortly take place. 'Behold, I am coming quickly! Blessed is he who keeps the words of the prophecy of this book.'" And verse 20 makes this final appeal from the Lord: "He who testifies to these things says, 'Surely I am coming quickly.' Amen. Even so, come, Lord Jesus!"[25]

Those are some of the passages alerting us to stay prepared for the coming of the Lord. None of those verses promise a seven-year refinement time that prepares us for his coming. The general idea is that we do not know the time when the Lord will return, so we are to stay prepared to meet him. Scholars of the other two positions answer the imminence issue by saying we do not know the "day and hour," but we can know the "season." There is some validity in that argument; we will discuss that when we examine the posttribulation position in chapter 7.[26]

Before we leave the subject of imminence, we should mention an application error that can easily happen with the other two positions. This is not an error in the doctrine held by mid or post tribulation camps. It is simply a tendency some in those camps can fall into. While those who hold the pretribulation position can easily fall into a mindset of escapism, those in the other two camps can easily get too focused on the signs and the coming Tribulation, rather than looking for Christ himself. Both errors should be avoided.

A strength of the pretribulation position is that it tends to focus our expectancy on Christ himself rather than the signs of his coming or the tribulation we are going to experience. The New Testament calls us to live in expectancy of the Lord's coming. Our mind is to be focused on him! We are not to focus on the coming tribulation or the Antichrist. With passionate love, we are to be eagerly waiting for our bridegroom. We are to look beyond the trouble and see the King! We must eagerly long for his appearing. Nothing should distract us from that.

When the biblical call to look for Christ's coming is understood as an "at any moment" possibility, the pretribulation position is particularly strong. It allows for no events in the eschaton to occur before the sudden Rapture of the church. I have viewed this issue of imminence as an extremely important concept regarding the Rapture. However, we will progress in our understanding of this issue as we proceed in this study.

Conclusion

We have discussed five strengths of the pretribulation position:

1. It properly recognizes the biblical purpose of the Tribulation period.
2. It organizes the whole biblical revelation on eschatology in a logical, unified system.
3. It seems to follow the sequence in the book of Revelation better.
4. It offers a meaningful explanation for the purpose of the Rapture.
5. It supports the biblical issue of imminence effectively.

Those are significant strengths. But there are also some serious weaknesses that we will consider in the next chapter.

I hope this study is stirring in you a longing for Christ's return. I hope you are holding the things of this world a bit more loosely as we turn our face toward the promise of his coming.[27] In the conclusion of his first letter to the Corinthians, Paul wrote with passion, "Maranatha" (1 Cor. 16:22 KJV) which means, "O Lord, come!"[28] In my early twenties, full of zeal, I found a bumper sticker that simply had the word "Maranatha." I got some interesting responses when I stuck it on my bumper. Most people didn't know what it meant and would ask. That was the open door I was looking for, and I gave them an ear full. It is the longing of our hearts, "O Lord, come!" It is our blessed hope: "Maranatha." It is our response to his promise to come quickly. "Even so, come Lord Jesus!"[29]

Endnotes: Chapter 4

1   "7 Tips for Understanding Revelation," Sept. 29, 2017, *Zondervan Academic.*
    https://zondervanacademic.com/blog/how-read-revelation.

2   W. A. Criswell, *Expository Sermons on Revelation: Five Volume Complete and
    Unabridged in One*, Vol. 1, 1962 (Grand Rapids: Zondervan, 1978), 20.

3   Barclay Newman, Jr., "A Concise Greek-English Dictionary of the New
    Testament" in *The Greek New Testament*, Barbara Aland, Kurt Aland, Johannes
    Karavidopoulos, Carlo Martini, and Bruce Metzger, eds., 4th ed. (United Bible
    Society, 1983), s.v. *"Hagios,"* 2.

4   There are verses in Revelation that could be referring to Christians on earth
    during the Tribulation period. The "offspring" in Rev. 12:17 is an example. The
    term is not specifically defined as Christians in the text, but the offspring of
    the woman (Israel) could very well be a reference to Gentile believers. Cf. Mike
    Bickle, *Book of Revelation Study Guide* (Kansas City, MO: Forerunner Books,
    2009), 54.

5   Criswell, *Expository Sermons on Revelation,* vol. 4, 110. Criswell is quoting
    the KJV.

6   However, Revelation is addressed to the churches in 1:4. It seems strange that
    the vast majority of the book would relate to Israel and not the church.

7   Stating the advantages of pretribulationism, Walvoord says, "pretribulationism
    moves logically from its premises and principles of interpretation to
    conclusion. . . . In contrast with posttribulational treatment . . . pretribulationists
    follow a consistent pattern of literal or normal interpretation." Walvoord, *The
    Blessed Hope and the Tribulation*, 166–67. Cf. Richard R. Reiter, "A History
    of the Development of the Rapture Positions," in *Three Views on the Rapture:
    Pre-, Mid-, or Post-Tribulational?* by Gleason L. Archer, Jr. (gen. ed.), Paul
    D. Feinberg, Douglas Moo, and Richard R. Reiter, 1984 (Grand Rapids:
    Zondervan, 1996), 41.

8   The lack of clarity in Scripture on some issues related to this subject poses
    challenges in developing a system of eschatology. We must make inferences from
    Scripture in order to develop a coherent, complete system. It is necessary to inject
    human logic in the process, which may not be correct. It is wise to distinguish
    inferences from clear scriptural statements.

9   Dwight Pentecost writes, "The church is manifestly an interruption of God's
    program for Israel, which was not brought into being until Israel's rejection of
    the offer of the kingdom. It must logically follow that this mystery program
    must itself be brought to a conclusion before God can resume His dealing with
    the nation of Israel, as has been shown previously He will do. The mystery
    program, which was so distinct in its inception, will certainly be separate at its

conclusion." Pentecost, *Things to Come*, 201. The posttribulation answer to this issue is discussed in chapter 7.

10   I will discuss later the fallacy of interpreting John's experience in 4:1 as the Rapture. The Rapture could happen at this point in Revelation, but 4:1 does not prove that. What we can see in that verse is a transition in the book of Revelation.

11   *Tauta* is in the accusative. *Meta* with the accusative means "after." John's use of the words *meta tauta* in this book is a strong indicator of sequence.

12   However, many scholars understand the twenty-four elders as representing both Israel and the church. For example, Kistemaker writes, "The traditional interpretation of the twenty-four elders is that this number is the total of twelve times two, namely, twelve Old Testament patriarchs and twelve New Testament apostles, the representative of those redeemed by Christ." Simon J. Kistemaker, *Exposition of the Book of Revelation*, New Testament Commentary (Grand Rapids: Baker Books, 2001), 187. Cf. J. Barton Payne, *The Imminent Appearing of Christ* (Grand Rapids: Eerdmans, 1962), 79–80; Douglas Moo, "Posttribulation Rapture Position" in *The Rapture: Pre-, Mid-, or Post-Tribulation?* by Gleason L. Archer, Jr. (gen. ed), Paul D. Feinberg, Douglas Moo, and Richard R. Reiter (Grand Rapids: Zondervan, 1984), 202; Alexander Reese, *The Approaching Advent of Christ* (London: Marshall, Morgan, Scott, 1937. Repr., Grand Rapids: Grand Rapids International, 1975), 19; George Eldon Ladd, *The Blessed Hope* (Grand Rapids: Eerdmans, 1956), 87–94. For a defense of the pretribulation position see Allen Beechick, *The Pretribulation Rapture* (Denver, CO: Accent Books, 1980), 174–177. For the prewrath position see Marvin Rosenthal, *The Pre-Wrath Rapture of the Church* (Nashville, TN: Thomas Nelson, 1990), 250–55.

13   Partial Rapture advocates identify these 24 elders as overcoming Christians in contrast to Christians who were not overcoming and had to go through the Tribulation period. There are various interpretations of who the 24 elders are. The meaning depends on one's interpretation of something symbolic. Therefore, reliance on this by pretribulationists must be tentative and inconclusive. However, it does tend to argue for the church being in heaven.

14   References to saints in verses like Rev. 13:7 do not prove the church is on the earth during the Tribulation because of the general meaning of the Greek word. The Greek word *hagios* simply means "set apart to or by God, consecrated; holy, morally pure, upright." Newman, "A Concise Greek-English Dictionary," s.v. "*hagios*," 2. This reference to God's people could refer to Christians. It is used in the Septuagint to refer to Old Testament followers of God (Exod. 19:6), and in Revelation it could refer to Tribulation saints who are God's people but not a part of the church. The point is that those references offer no proof that the church is present on earth during the Tribulation period.

15 1 Cor. 3:13 says, "each one's work will become clear; for the Day will declare it, because it will be revealed by fire; and the fire will test each one's work, of what sort it is." The tone in Rev. 19 suggests this has already happened, for the bride is ready for her bridegroom.

16 Posttribulationists have other explanations, but none are entirely convincing. None fit the systematic timing as well as the pretribulation model.

17 Craig S. Keener, *The IVP Bible Background Commentary: New Testament* (Downers Grove, IL: InterVarsity Press, 1993) 593. The imagery in the parable of the ten virgins (Matt. 25:6) is a better defense of the posttribulation position. Cf. Ladd, *The Blessed Hope*, 91.

18 Clinton Arnold, "Academic Forum, Segment I: Initial Remarks," *The Glorious Return of Our King*, Center for Biblical End-Time Studies, International House of Prayer. https://www.cbetskc.org/products/cbets-symposium-the-glorious-return-of-our-king/categories/1897596/posts/6355726. For an in-depth analysis of this issue, see Rydelnik and Vanlaningham, eds., *Moody Bible Commentary*, 1887–88.

19 Clinton Arnold, "Academic Forum, Segment I: Initial Remarks," *The Glorious Return of Our King*.

20 *Merriam Webster's Collegiate Dictionary*, 10th ed., s.v. "imminent" (Springfield, MA: Merriam-Webster, Incorporated, 1993), 580.

21 Henry Clarence Thiessen, "The Place of Israel in the Scheme of Redemption as Set Forth in Romans 9–11," *Bibliotheca Sacra*, no. 98 (April): 215. For a more extensive examination of imminence among the early church fathers, see Payne, *The Imminent Appearing of Christ*, 12–19.

22 Cf. Matt. 24:43; Luke 12:39; 1 Thess. 5:2, 3; 2 Pet. 3:10; Rev. 3:3. "That His coming is not secret is patently true. The fallacy of dispensationalism, which confuses the sense of Christ's coming 'as a thief,' which means its unexpectedness in time, with an assumed secrecy in manner, should be clear from the simple reading of any of a number of texts." Barton Payne, *The Imminent Appearing of Christ*, 102. We should keep in mind the statements in 1 Thess. 4:16 describe something very different from a secret, sneaky coming: "For the Lord Himself will descend from heaven with a *shout*, with the *voice* of an archangel, and with the *trumpet* of God" (emphasis added).

23 The Second Coming with the bodily resurrection of the dead is essential, but we must not get overly focused on end-time details to the neglect of the Great Commission.

24 In fact, the close connection in verse 11 made between the ascension and the return tends to support the posttribulation position.

25 Barton Payne comments, ". . . the Greek adverb *tachu* means, not 'soon,' but 'swiftly, all at once,' that is before one can be aware and make preparations." Payne, *The Imminent Appearing of Christ*, 86.

26 During this study I progressed in my understanding of imminence. A fuller analysis of the subject will be shared in the chapters that follow.

27 Cf. Luke 21:34–36; 1 John 2:15–17; Tow, *Authentic Christianity*, 95–110.

28 The Greek would also allow for it to be translated, "Our Lord has come." But given the overall message of the New Testament, it is more likely it expresses a longing for Christ's return, i.e., "O Lord, come!"

29 Rev. 22:20.

CHAPTER 5

Pretribulation Position: Weaknesses

Since it is a righteous thing with God to repay with tribulation those who trouble you, and to give you who are troubled rest with us when the Lord Jesus is revealed from heaven with His mighty angels, in flaming fire taking vengeance on those who do not know God, and on those who do not obey the gospel of our Lord Jesus Christ.

2 Thessalonians 1:6–8 NKJV

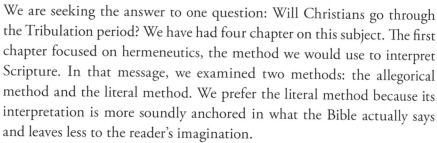

We are seeking the answer to one question: Will Christians go through the Tribulation period? We have had four chapter on this subject. The first chapter focused on hermeneutics, the method we would use to interpret Scripture. In that message, we examined two methods: the allegorical method and the literal method. We prefer the literal method because its interpretation is more soundly anchored in what the Bible actually says and leaves less to the reader's imagination.

In the second chapter, we considered the biblical purpose of the seven-year Tribulation period as an important foundation for our study. Those two reasons are: the outpouring of wrath on the ungodly Gentile nations and the final corrections of Israel to prepare that nation to receive Messiah Jesus. In that study, we analyzed Daniel 9:24–27 closely. Posttribulationists and midtribulationist often add an additional objective of refining and maturing the church. But all three camps agree on the two purposes we studied in chapter 2.

In the third chapter, we weighed the pros and cons of a variant of the pretribulation Rapture position known as partial or split Rapture. That study led to a conclusion that the Rapture will probably include all members of the church living at that time. However, many in the visible church may be tares rather than wheat.[1] Those who have not been genuinely transformed by the grace of God will not be raptured. Those three chapters prepared us to consider the strengths and weaknesses of the three main theories held by futurists on the timing of the Rapture: the pretribulation, the midtribulation, and the posttribulation positions.

In chapter 4 we identified major strengths in the pretribulation theory. We discussed the following five strengths of that model:

1. It recognizes the two-fold biblical purpose of the Tribulation period.
2. It organizes the whole biblical revelation on eschatology in a logical, unified system.
3. It seems to follow the sequence in the book of Revelation.
4. It offers a meaningful explanation of the purpose for the Rapture.
5. It effectively supports the biblical issue of imminence.

In this chapter, we will consider the weaknesses of that position. We will discuss the following five weaknesses in pretribulationism.

1. Second Thessalonians 1:3–10 seems to place the Rapture with the Second Coming of Christ.
2. The pretribulation interpretation of 2 Thessalonians 2:1–12 is unconvincing.
3. The relatively recent articulation of the pretribulation position may be a weakness.
4. Additional complaints against common applications of this position will also be discussed. These concerns are not so much against the theory itself as the way it is often applied.
5. The way the New Testament uses three Greek words when referring to the coming of the Lord points toward a posttribulation position.

Second Thessalonians 1:3–10 Seems to Place the Rapture with the Second Coming of Christ.

As we read this passage allow it to speak to you concerning the *timing* of the Rapture.

> We are bound to thank God always for you, brethren, as it is fitting, because your faith grows exceedingly, and the love of every one of you all abounds toward each other, so that we ourselves boast of you among the churches of God for your patience and faith in all your persecutions and tribulations that you endure, which is manifest evidence of the righteous judgment of God, that you may be counted worthy of the kingdom of God, for which you also suffer; since it is a righteous thing with God to repay with tribulation those who trouble you, and to give you who are troubled rest with us when the Lord Jesus is revealed from heaven with His mighty angels, in flaming fire taking vengeance on those who do not know God, and on those who do not obey the gospel of our Lord Jesus Christ. These shall be punished with everlasting destruction from the presence of the Lord and from the glory of His power, when He comes, in that Day, to be glorified in his saints and to be admired among all those who believe, because our testimony among you was believed (2 Thess.1:3–10).

Notice the word *when* in this passage as an indicator of timing. First, we see it in the middle of verse 7: "*when* the Lord Jesus is revealed from heaven with His mighty angels, in flaming fire taking vengeance on those who do not know God . . ." (emphasis added). That is clearly a description of the Second Coming to earth described in Revelation 19.[2] Now look at the second *when* in verse 10: "*when* He comes, in that Day, to be glorified in His saints and to be admired among all those who believe" (emphasis added). This *when* is linked with the previous *when* by the phrase "in that Day." At the same time, the Lord comes "in flaming fire taking vengeance on those who do not know God," he also comes, "in that Day, to be glorified in His saints and to be admired among all those who believe."[3] We cannot say that refers to Tribulation saints because Paul specifically includes the Thessalonian readers in the last part of verse 10: "because our testimony among *you* was believed" (emphasis added).

Pretribulationists might argue that the Lord will be glorified in his saints when they come back with him, having been in heaven for seven years. The argument is that this passage is not specifically dealing with the timing of the Rapture but only with the return of the Lord with his saints (Jude 1:14; Rev. 19:14).[4] While that explanation is possible, the natural reading of the text would suggest a posttribulation Rapture happening in conjunction with the Second Coming.

The promised reward translated *rest* in verse seven "commonly denotes relief from some type of affliction" in the New Testament. Gene Green writes, "The promise given to these believers who have suffered so much at the hands of their persecutors (see v. 4) is that God will reward them with *relief* at the time of the revelation of the Lord Jesus (v. 7b) (emphasis Green's).[5] The reward seems to come in conjunction with the destruction of their persecutors. Thus, 2 Thessalonians 1:3–10 seems to support a posttribulation position.

The Pretribulation Interpretation of Second Thessalonians 2:1–12 Is Unconvincing.

The passage poses a difficulty for the pretribulation position. A natural reading of this text expresses two events that must occur before "our gathering together to Him."

> Now, brethren, concerning the coming [*parousia*] of our Lord Jesus Christ and our gathering together to Him, [topic is about our gathering to him which is probably a reference to the Rapture], we ask you, not to be soon shaken in mind or troubled, either by spirit or by word or by letter, as if from us, as though the day of Christ had come. Let no one deceive you by any means; for that Day will not come unless the falling away comes first, and

the man of sin is revealed, the son of perdition, [That's a straightforward statement] who opposes and exalts himself above all that is called God or that is worshiped, so that he sits as God in the temple of God, showing himself that he is God. Do you not remember that when I was still with you I told you these things? And now you know what is restraining, that he may be revealed in his own time. For the mystery of lawlessness is already at work; only He who now restrains will do so until He is taken out of the way. And then the lawless one will be revealed, whom the Lord will consume with the breath of His mouth and destroy with the brightness of His coming. [the language in that verse indicates Christ's Second Coming back to earth in which he destroys His enemies]. The coming of the lawless one is according to the working of Satan, with all power, signs, and lying wonders, and with all unrighteous deception among those who perish, because they did not receive the love of the truth, that they might be saved. And for this reason God will send them strong delusion, that they should believe the lie, that they all may be condemned who did not believe the truth but had pleasure in unrighteousness (2 Thess. 2–12).

Consider these observations:

In verse 1, Paul introduces the subject as "the coming [*parousia*] of our Lord Jesus Christ and our being gathered to him."[6] That seems to point to the Rapture and Paul's teaching in 1 Thessalonians 4:13–18.[7] It is helpful that Paul states his subject explicitly.

In verse 2, the concern being addressed is the misinformation that "the day of Christ had come." The NIV correctly translates it: "the day of the Lord has *already* come" (emphasis added). This is difficult to interpret because we do not have the details of the error that caused the disturbance that Paul is addressing.[8] The Thessalonians had that information, so Paul did not need to explain the phrase more fully.

In the light of what Paul taught in his previous letter, one interpretation is that the false teaching was that the Rapture has already occurred, and they missed it. That would certainly be an upsetting thought.[9] It is easy to understand their receptivity to a message like that considering the heavy persecution they were experiencing (2 Thess. 1:4–5). It must have felt like something was wrong for their lives to be so difficult. With the limited information we have, we proceed cautiously with the assumption that they had been misled to believe the Rapture had already happened and they were not counted "worthy" to be a part of that glorious event.[10]

Paul's instruction in verse 3 is the key point of our current discussion. There he says, "Let no one deceive you by any means; for that Day[11] *will not come unless the falling away comes first,* and the man of sin is revealed, the son of perdition" (emphasis added). Of course, "the man of sin" is the Antichrist who will rise to power during the Tribulation period.

Here is a sign—something that must occur before the coming of the Lord. Paul then describes a falling away and the emergence of the Antichrist that will occur during the Tribulation period. Then, in verse 8, he follows that with a description of Christ's coming in power destroying his enemies. This verse weakens the insistence that imminence means there are no signs to be fulfilled before the Rapture.[12] And that weakens the pretribulation position. A natural reading of this passage would point to a posttribulation position.

Pretribulationist Schuyler English, and more recently Andy Woods, have tried to counter this by saying the word translated falling away [*apostasia*] in verse 3 "should be translated as 'departure' [and taken to mean 'physical departure,'] thus signifying the same event as the 'Rapture' in 1 Thessalonians 4:17, but there is no [or very little] linguistic basis for such a view."[13] In fact, pretribulationist John Walvoord admits, "the word probably refers to doctrinal defection of the special character that will be revealed in the day of the Lord." He acknowledges that English's interpretation of *apostasia* as a reference to the Rapture "has not met with general acceptance by either pretribulationists or posttribulationists."[14] Andy Woods bases part of his argument on the fact that several older translations (Latin Vulgate, Wycliffe Bible, Tyndale, Geneva Bible) simply translated *apostasia* with the phrase "departure" or "departing." But his conclusion that it was "communicating physical departure" is flawed.[15] That could be taken either as a physical departure or a spiritual departure.[16]

If Paul had intended to say Rapture, he could have been very clear by using the same Greek word he used in 1 Thessalonians 4:17: *harpazō*.

Other pretribulationist scholars accept *apostasia* as a falling away or rebellion,[17] yet use other arguments to explain the midtrib/posttrib interpretation away. Charles Giblin argues that Paul "is stressing the conditions on which God's judgment and salvation are to be manifested" (p. 135). He shifts the emphasis from the temporal-calendar chain of events to a reminder of this two-fold nature of "the day of Christ" which should bring comfort to these Christians (1 Thess. 4:18). His position is that "Paul does not seem to have regarded the events mentioned in vv. 3–4 as signs in the sense of 'things (temporally) to be watched for" (p. 137).[18]

Green argues against Giblin's position. Concerning the elliptical in the first part of verse 2, Green says, "He [Giblin] would understand the implied idea as something like, 'the judgment of God will not have been executed against the power of deception, removing them once and for all [described particularly in verse 8]' *until* etc. The other suggestion he makes to supply the missing apodosis is, 'The Lord will not have come in judgment to end definitively the deception that is the work of Satan' *until* etc." (emphasis Green's). Green contends for the simpler and more natural reading in keeping with Paul's emphasis on "the order of events throughout this section (vv. 3, 6–8)." He continues, "At the head they declare that 'first' (*proton*, rendered loosely in the *NIV* as *until*); that is, before the day of the Lord, two events will occur: *the rebellion occurs and the man of lawlessness is revealed*" (emphasis Green's).[19]

Pretribulationists also bolster their position by saying the restrainer mentioned in verses 6–7 is the Holy Spirit operating in the church. Therefore, when the church is raptured that restraining influence is removed and the Antichrist emerges. While this is an excellent guess as who the restrainer is in this passage, we are not explicitly told in Scripture who the restrainer is. Every identification of the restrainer is only an educated guess since the identity is not stated in the Bible. It must be someone very powerful since it restrains Satan and his program. For that reason, it is most likely a reference to God the Holy Spirit since he is currently the person of the Trinity at work in the earth. I personally think it is a reference to the Holy Spirit, but it is further speculation to define the lifting of the restraint as the Rapture.[20] Maybe so, and maybe not. We simply do not know.

Whether pretribulationist, midtribulationist, or posttribulationist, building one's eschatology on this passage has its limitations because there is so much here that we do not know. We do not know the details of what had these Thessalonians so disturbed. We do not know for certain exactly what Paul meant by the phrase "the day of the Christ" in 2 Thessalonians 2:2. We do not know who or what the restrainer is in verses 6–7. Paul is relying on knowledge the Thessalonians already had from his previous teachings. Because of all that, we are forced to fill in the blanks with a lot of guesses.[21] The more guessing we do, the less we can rely on our conclusions for establishing doctrine. For those reasons, this passage does not establish a decisive posttribulation position. On the other hand, it does point in that direction.

The Relatively Recent Articulation of the Pretribulation Position May be a Weakness.

Opponents of this position are quick to say John Darby invented it in about 1830 and C. I. Scofield popularized it with the Scofield Bible beginning in 1909.[22] Therefore, it could not be true. But there is a difference between inventing a doctrine and articulating it more clearly. The doctrine of the Trinity was not well articulated until the Council of Nicaea in 325 AD. It was in the New Testament, but it was put into a doctrinal statement 200 years later. That does not mean the Council of Nicaea invented it. They articulated it in a doctrinal statement form. That in no way diminished the biblical truth of the Trinity revealed in Scripture.

It is not surprising that biblical truth would be lost for hundreds of years by an apostate Catholic Church. In the early 1500s Luther articulated justification by faith. Paul had clearly taught that truth in Romans and Galatians, but a corrupt Catholic Church lost that truth and replaced it with a legalistic, ritualistic system. Do we reject justification by faith because for hundreds of years the Catholic Church did not teach it?

The Pentecostal/Charismatic truths taught by Paul in 1 Corinthians 12 and exemplified in Acts came alive at the beginning of the twentieth century.[23] Those truths were not invented in the twentieth century, but they had not been preached by very many for hundreds of years. Nevertheless, they are biblical. Millions throughout the world have experienced these supernatural realities.

Most early premillennialist church fathers held a posttribulation position. Reece, Ladd, and Gundry convincingly establish this probability.[24] However, Walvoord responds to the posttribulationist argument by pointing out how recent their version of posttribulationism was developed. He writes, "It may be conceded that the advanced and detailed theology of pretribulationism of today is not found in the church fathers, and there are some grounds for tracing this to Darby, who seems to have been the first to make this sharp distinction. What posttribulationists do not seem to realize is that the detailed arguments for posttribulationism as they are now advanced are even more recent than Darby; and if recency is an argument against pretribulationism, it is also an argument against posttribulationism."[25]

By the fifth century Augustine, influenced by Origen, had turned the established church to amillennialism and the voice of premillennialism was largely silenced. The Reformation leaders "such as Luther and Calvin continued this view" but with the inconsistency of accusing the Pope of being the Antichrist.[26] So through most of the centuries during the church age, amillennialism has been taught.

The oldest documents we have for building our eschatology are in the Bible. If a doctrine can be established from the inspired Word of God, I don't care if Origen or other church fathers held a different view. Much of the truth held by the early church was lost during the apostasy of the Catholic Church and had to be recovered. If a position can be supported by Scripture, it should not be dismissed because of writings by scholars during the church age. The argument that Darby *invented* the pretribulation theory cannot be proved. He did articulate the model held by most pretribulationists today. However, the fact that Darby and Scofield popularized it in recent history does not negate its validity. The final referee on doctrine is the inspired Scripture. The pretribulation position must stand or fall, based on what the Bible says.

It is conceded that the absence of pretribulationism in the teaching of the early church fathers might be an indication that it was not taught by the apostles. That is a just consideration. Verification of that can only be made by examining the New Testament itself.

Some Perceived Weaknesses in Pretribulationism Are in the Way It Is Applied Rather Than the Position Itself.

One accusation against pretribulationism is that it denies the many passages that say Christians will suffer tribulation. Some groups do use the pretribulation position to argue that way. But no scholarly pretribulationist would take the stance that God does not want Christians to go through trials.[27] In John 16:33, Jesus told His followers, "In the world you will have tribulation." That is unavoidable, and we just as well brace ourselves for it. Paul said in 2 Timothy 3:12, "all who desire to live a godly life in Christ Jesus will be persecuted" (RSV). He taught the early Christians "that we must through much tribulation enter into the kingdom of God" (Acts 14:22 KJV). Many other passages confirm this.

But the Tribulation period is a distinct time in God's program. To say Christians will not go through the Tribulation period is not to say they will not go through tribulation. On the contrary, we are appointed, and Paul even says privileged, to suffer for the name of Christ (Phil. 1:29).

Another complaint against the pretribulation position is that it is simply escapism: "I can't take the hardship of life anymore, so 'beam me up Scotty.'"[28] Some have erroneously applied the pretribulation position with an escapist mentality. However, that is not necessarily inherent in the position. One can be fully prepared to deal with the difficulties of life with joy, and at the same time be fully submitted to God's plan if it involves a Rapture before the Tribulation period. A Christian's desire should be to do the will of the Father whether it involves ascending into heaven or living through the Tribulation period. A pretribulation theological position and an escapist mentality are two different things. When weighing the validity of these three theories, we must distinguish flawed theory from flawed application.

The Way the New Testament Uses Language When Referring to the Coming of Christ Points toward the Posttribulation Position.

This is the greatest weakness in pretribulationism. The three Greek words used in the New Testament in reference to Christ's coming are *parousia, apokalupsis,* and *epiphaneia.* Each word emphasizes a particular aspect of the Lord's coming.

Parousia is the word most used. Its basic meaning is "coming, arrival; presence."[29] In 1 Thessalonians 4:15, it is used in a passage typically attributed to the Rapture.[30] "For this we say to you by the word of the Lord, that we who are alive *and* remain until the coming [*parousia*] of the Lord will by no means precede those who are asleep." But it is also used in passages referring to Christ's Second Coming to the earth.[31] For example, 2 Thessalonians 2:8 says, "And then the lawless one will be revealed, whom the Lord will consume with the breath of His mouth and destroy with the brightness of His coming [*parousia*]." So, the same term, *parousia,* is used in a text referring to the Rapture and a text referring to the Second Coming.

Apokalupsis comes from the root word *kaluptō* meaning to cover or hide and the prefix *apo* meaning from or away from.[32] Thus *apokalupsis* is a revelation or appearance.[33] First Peter 1:13 uses the term: "Therefore gird up the loins of your mind, be sober, and rest *your* hope fully upon the grace that is to be brought to you at the revelation [*apokalupsis*] of Jesus Christ." There *apokalupsis* is referring to the meeting of Christ with his church.[34] But 2 Thessalonians 1:7–8 is a clear reference to his coming in glory at his Second Coming.[35] "And to *give* you who are troubled rest with us when the Lord Jesus is revealed [*apokalupsis*] from heaven with His mighty angels, in flaming fire taking vengeance on those who do not know God, and on those who do not obey the gospel of our Lord Jesus Christ." Again, the same term is used to refer to the Rapture and the Second Coming.

The other Greek word used in reference to the Lord's coming is *epiphaneia.* We get our English word epiphany from this Greek term. It is a manifestation or appearance.[36] Second Timothy 4:8 uses the term in reference to the coming of the Lord for his church.[37] "Finally, there is laid up for me the crown of righteousness, which the Lord, the righteous Judge, will give to me on that Day, and not to me only but also to all who have loved His appearing [*epiphaneia*]." On the other hand, the term is used earlier in 2 Timothy 4:1 in regard to his Second Coming.[38] "I charge *you* therefore before God and the Lord Jesus Christ, who will judge the living and the dead at His appearing [*epiphaneia*] and His kingdom." Once again, the same term is used to refer to the Rapture and to refer to the Second Coming.

That seems to indicate the same event. The pretribulation theory makes a crucial distinction between the timing of the Rapture and the Second Coming. But if that distinction is that important, why didn't the New Testament writers distinguish them in the language they used? Granted, these terms were probably being used in a general sense and were not intended to be technical terms for the coming of the Lord. But if Paul held the pretribulation position, we would expect him to make a clearer distinction between the two events. This is a strong argument for posttribulationism and against pretribulationism and midtribulationism.[39] In his criticism of the pretribulation separation of Rapture and Second Coming, J. Barton Payne writes, "The Biblical terminology should bear out such a basic distinction as is proposed. That is, if *parousia* is used indiscriminately by the New Testament writers for either of the proposed phases of Christ's coming, one cannot but wonder whether the apostolic writers really intended to distinguish them in the first place. The burden of proof rests upon those who would demonstrate the two phases, for a single Greek name seems to require a single event, unless strong proof is offered to the contrary."[40]

The pretribulation position has much to recommend it. It should be taken seriously. However, there are weaknesses in the theory that should motivate us to dig deeper. Paul commended the Bereans because they did not just take what the preacher said and go with it. Instead, they searched the Scriptures themselves to make sure they were getting the truth.[41] Many Christians are biblically illiterate because they just want to be quickly told the right answer so they can move on to things that interest them more. Unfortunately, those things are often relatively unimportant. We are not all called to be theologians, but we are all called to study our Bibles. Hopefully, this teaching will inspire readers to search the scriptures for more truth on this subject.

Endnotes: Chapter 5

1 Cf. Matt. 13:30.

2 Notice the similar language in Rev. 19: 9. "These shall be punished with everlasting destruction from the presence of the Lord and from the glory of His power."

3 Holmes writes, "All that Paul has been talking about 'will happen when the Lord Jesus is revealed from heaven' (1:7b), that is, 'when he comes . . . on that day' (1:10, NRSV). This is the same event that Paul in his first letter referred to as Jesus' 'coming' (*parousia*, 1 Thess. 5:15) or 'the day of the Lord' (5:2). Michael W. Holmes, *1 and 2 Thessalonians,* The NIV Application Commentary, Terry Muck, gen. ed. (Grand Rapids: Zondervan, 1998), 215. Cf. Payne, *The Imminent Appearing of Christ*, 59.

4 For example, the explanation Wiersbe gives is essentially a statement of the differences between the Rapture and the Second Coming based on the pretribulation theory. Warren W. Wiersbe, *Be Ready* (Wheaton, IL: Victor Books, 1979, 131.

5 Gene L. Green, *The Letters to the Thessalonians*, The Pillar New Testament Commentary, D. A. Carson, ed. (Grand Rapids: Eerdmans, 2002), 287–88.

6 Interestingly, both phrases are modified by one article. Morris writes, "The subject of his request is twofold, but the coming of the Lord and the gathering of the saints are regarded as closely connected, as the use of the single article shows. These are two parts of one great event." Leon Morris, *The First and Second Epistles to the Thessalonians*, 1959, The New International Commentary on the New Testament, F. F. Bruce, gen. ed. (Grand Rapids: Eerdmans, 1979) 214.

7 Gordon Fee sees verse 1 as a condensed version of 1 Thess. 4:16–17. Gordon D. Fee, *The First and Second Letters to the Thessalonians*, The New International Commentary on the New Testament, gen. eds. Stonehouse, Bruce, Fee, and Green (Grand Rapids: Eerdmans, 2009), 272.

8 Even Paul does not seem to be certain whether this misinformation came "either by spirit or by word or by letter" (2 Thess. 2:2). What Paul is correcting is difficult to know in detail because we do not have the information on it that the Thessalonians had. Since they already had that information, Paul does not go into further detail. Forged letters were common in that day. It seems "fake news" was around long before the internet.

9 Some stop short of this and simply say they were misled to think they were in the Tribulation period. However, that may not adequately explain why they were so shaken and disturbed. Gundry does not think their emotional response to the false teaching was negative distress. He writes, "Thus, it was not sorrow over a missed Rapture which agitated the Thessalonians, but wild anticipations of an immediate return of Christ." He thinks this is an erroneous conclusion "that

Christ's coming lay in the immediate future, with resultant cession of work, fanatical excitement, and disorder." Gundry, *The Church and the Tribulation*, 121. Leon Morris says one weakness Paul wants these Thessalonians to avoid is, "'that ye be not quickly shaken from your mind,'" Then he concludes the statement "directs attention to the possibility of being caught up by a sudden excitement." Morris, *The First and Second Epistles to the Thessalonians*, 214.

Nevertheless, most scholars interpret *throeō* in this context as a negative disturbance. That understanding is reflected in most modern translations, e. g., NKJV ("shaken in mind or troubled") and NIV ("unsettled or alarmed"). Green understands it as anxiety. He writes, "The false teaching that had moved the Thessalonians away from their apostolic foundation and that caused them great anxiety was that *the day of the Lord has already come*" (emphasis Greene's). Green, *The Letters to the Thessalonians*, 305. For the Prewrath position on this see Alan Hultberg, "A Case for the Prewrath Rapture," in *Three Views on the Rapture* by Blaising, et al. (2010), 121–22.

10   Leon Morris writes, "We must bear in mind the gaps in our knowledge, and not be too confident in our interpretations of this notoriously difficult passage." Morris, *The First and Second Epistles to the Thessalonians*, 213. Fee agrees with A. M. G. Stephenson that the *enestēken* means "already come" and not just at hand or near. The translators of the NKJV and NIV seem to agree. However, Fee also states the following caution: "What this may have meant to its proponents, or how the Thessalonian believers would have understood it, lies ultimately in the realm of speculation." Fee, *The First and Second Letters to the Thessalonians*, 273. Regarding the disturbance in our text, Kaiser writes, "Such a claim was unsettling and alarming for it implied that they had been excluded from the event of Christ's return and 'shut out from the presence of the Lord and from the majesty of his power' (2 Thess 1:9)." Kaiser, et. al., *Hard Sayings of the Bible*, 662.

In opposition to Gundry, Walvoord takes the position that Paul had taught the Thessalonians a pretribulation Rapture, and they were disturbed because they thought the Tribulation period had already begun and they had been left behind. Cf. John F. Walvoord, *The Rapture Question*, (1957; rev. ed., Grand Rapids: Zondervan, 1979) 240–241. *The Moody Commentary* on this verse says, "The false teaching apparently affirmed that the Rapture had occurred and the day of the Lord had begun." Rydelnik and Vanlaningham, eds., *Moody Bible Commentary*, 1892.

These varying opinions reinforce the fact that we do not know exactly what thoughts caused the Thessalonians to be disturbed. We know in general that it was that "the day of Christ had come." But additional specifics are not available to us.

11   After asserting that Paul refers to the Parousia/Rapture as the Day of the Lord in 2 Thess. 5:1–2, prewrath-rapture advocate Alan Hultberg notes, "All

pretribulationists, as far as I know, agree with this. Most would understand that Paul uses the expression 'the day of the Lord' in its broadest sense here, that is for the entire complex of eschatological events from the Rapture to the millennium." Hultberg, "A Case for the Prewrath Rapture," in *Three Views on the Rapture* by Blaising, et al. (2010), 118.

12   We are left with a tension in the New Testament between the urgency of staying prepared for the imminent return of Christ and predictions of events that will transpire before that return. For example, Peter is told that he will grow old in John 21:18. Paul is shown what great things he must suffer in Acts 9:16. Jesus said, "And this gospel of the kingdom will be preached in all the world as a witness to all the nations, and then the end will come" (Matt. 24:1). In 1 Tim. 3 Paul described perilous times in the last days as a warning to the church. And here in 2 Thess. 2:3 we are told "that Day will not come unless the falling away comes first, and the man of sin is revealed, the son of perdition." Yet, we cannot and must not dismiss or ignore the New Testament passages that tell us to stay prepared for Christ's return, for it could happen at any time. No one knows the day and hour of Christ's return (Matt. 24:36).

Some posttribulationists reject imminence outright. Gundry, *The Church and the Tribulation*, 29–43. However, Douglas Moo's approach seems more in line with biblical revelation. He rejects the "any moment" definition of imminent in favor of the *Oxford English Dictionary* definition: "impending threateningly, hanging over one's head; ready to befall or overtake one, close at hand at its incidence; coming on shortly." *Oxford English Dictionary*, 3rd ed., Angus Stevenson, ed. (New York: Oxford University Press, 2010). See Moo, "A Case for the Posttribulation Rapture," in *Three Views on the Rapture* by Blaising, et al. (2010), 235–36. Hultberg points out, ". . . Jesus also mixed 'imminence' with signs, not least the abomination of desolation, in the Olivet Discourse (Matt. 24:32–33, 42–44, and parallels). Thus, both Paul and Jesus enjoin their audiences to watch for the Parousia." Hultberg, "A Case for the Prewrath Rapture," in *Three Views on the Rapture* by Blaising, et al. (2010), 128.

13   Michael W. Holmes, *1 & 2 Thessalonians*, 230. For English's position, see E. Schuyler English, *Re–Thinking the Rapture* (Travelers Rest, S. C.: Southern Bible, 1954), 65.

14   Walvoord, *The Rapture Question*, 240.

15   Pointing out the mistake of appealing to old translations, Gundry writes, "But the appeal to Early English translations unwittingly reveals weakness, because in the era of those versions lexical studies in NT Greek were almost nonexistent and continued to be so for many years." Gundry, *The Church and the Tribulation*, 116. For a scholarly and convincing rebuttal to English's suggestion that *apostasia* is indicating the Rapture, see Gundry, *The Church and the Tribulation*, 114–118. Cf. Payne, *The Imminent Appearing of Christ*, 76–77.

16 Andy Woods, *The Falling Away: Spiritual Departure or Physical Departure* (Taos, NM: Dispensational Publishing, 2018), 4, 38–40. Pentecost says *apostasia* "may be interpreted either as a departure from the faith or a departure of the saints to be with the Lord." He does not give much attention to this passage, considering the challenge it offers to his pretribulation position. Pentecost, *Things to Come*, 204–05, 332.

17 There is debate as to whether *apostasia* is referring to a falling away from the faith or a rebellion against God. But the two conditions mutually reinforce one another, rather than being mutually exclusive. Jewish tradition (Just. Apol., I, 50, 12) "speaks of a complete apostasy from God and His Torah shortly before the appearance of Messiah." G. Kittel and G. Friedrich, eds., *Theological Dictionary of the New Testament*, vol. 1 (Grand Rapids: Eerdmans, 1964), s.v. "*apostasia*" by Heinrich Schlier, 513.

18 Charles H. Giblin, *The Threat of Faith: An Exegetical and Theological Re–examination of 2 Thessalonians 2* (Rome: Pontifical Biblical Institute, 1967), 135–37.

19 Green, *The Letters to the Thessalonians*, 306–07. For debate on this issue, see Blaising, et al., *Three Views on The Rapture* (2010), 54–58, 83–85, 99–102. Chafer states his pretribulation position concerning the Day of the Lord by simply writing, "Reference to the Day of the Lord, it will be remembered, is to that extended period of a thousand years long predicted." Chafer, *Systematic Theology*, Vol. 4, 350.

20 Posttribulationist Robert Gundry understands the restrainer to be the Holy Spirit but does not include the concept held by most pretribulationists that it is the Holy Spirit *in the church*. Gundry, *The Church and the Tribulation* as summarized by Walvoord, *The Rapture Question*, 242–243. Walvoord's defense of pretribulationism in 2 Thess. 2 depends heavily on the assumption that Paul's restrainer language refers to the removal of the Holy Spirit's influence via the Rapture. Walvoord, *The Rapture Question*, 241–243. Cf. Ladd, *The Blessed Hope*, 95. Rosenthal's contention that the restrainer is Michael, the archangel, is adequately refuted by Showers. Cf. Rosenthal, *The Pre-Wrath Rapture of the Church*, 256–261, 271; Robert Van Kampen, *The Sign* (Wheaton, IL: Crossway, 1992), 199–200, 435–436, 472–473; Renald E. Showers, *The Pre-wrath Rapture View: An Examination and Critique* (Grand Rapids: Kregel, 2001), 190–97.

21 Two things make this passage difficult to understand. (1) Paul's objective is to comfort these Christians by quickly addressing their concern. He is not setting forth a methodical teaching on end-time events. Therefore, we must make some assumptions as we interpret the passage. (2) Paul reminds them in verse 5 of things he has already taught them when he was with them. Since they already know these things, Paul does not repeat them. But that leaves us without that

information. Therefore, the passage is somewhat obscure because of the missing information.

22 Brown and Keener, *Not Afraid of the Antichrist*, 60–63. Some posttribulationists say Darby's separation of the Rapture from the Second Coming originated with a subjective vision received by Margaret MacDonald. But Craig Keener concedes that this is probably not correct. Brown and Keener, *Not Afraid of the Antichrist*, 60–61.

23 For a defense of this statement see Roger Stronstad, *The Charismatic Theology of St. Luke* (Peabody, MA: Hendrickson, 1984).

24 Cf. Reese, *The Approaching Advent of Christ*, 19; Ladd, *The Blessed Hope*, 18–33; Gundry, *The Church and the Tribulation*, 172–88. Pretribulationist David Petterson quotes Irenaeus of Lyon (120–202) (a disciple of Polycarp who was a disciple of the apostle John) as referring to "the Church's being 'caught up' before the tribulation." The quote says," And therefore, when in the end the Church shall be suddenly caught up from *this* [the Tribulation], it is said, 'There shall be tribulation such as has not been since the beginning, neither shall be' (Mat 24:21). For this is the last contest of the righteous, in which, when they overcome they are crowned with incorruption." Irenaeus, *Against Heresies*, Book 5. David Petterson, "The Rapture: A Pre–Darby Rapture," *Truth and Tidings Magazine*. https://truthandtidings.com/2020/07/the-rapture-a-pre-darby-rapture/. However, many more quotes of Irenaeus can be indicating a posttribulation mindset. Cf. Gundry, *The Church and the Tribulation*, 175; Ladd, *The Blessed Hope*, 25–27.

25 Walvoord, *The Rapture Question*, 50. In 1990 Rosenthal wrote, "Pretribulation rapturism appeared on the stage little more than 150 years ago. . . . Midtribulation rapturism is even more recent in origin. . . . Gundry's considerable modification of posttribulationism is less than twenty years old. What is clear from early church nonbiblical documents is that they were unclear as to the timing of the Rapture. . . . No Rapture view, then, can legitimately claim support for its position either from the early church or the church during the first seventeen centuries of its existence." Rosenthal, *The Pre-wrath Rapture of the Church*, 266.

26 Keener says, "In the fourth and fifth century, Augustine developed the idea that the Millennium symbolizes the entire present age, and most medieval thinkers followed him. Sixteenth-century reformers such as Luther and Calvin continued this view." Brown and Keener *Not Afraid of the Antichrist*, 58–59.

27 For example, pretribulationist Craig Blaising states, "I need to point out here that pretribulationists do not claim that God has promised carte blanch to protect or exclude the church from suffering . . . The entire message of 1 Peter is built around this point." Craig Blaising, "A Pretribulation Response [to Moo]" in *Three Views on The Rapture* by Blaising, et al. (2010), 244.

28 This was a common line in the old TV series Star Trek.

29 Barclay Newman, Jr., "A Concise Greek-English Dictionary of the New Testament" in *The Greek New Testament*, Barbara Aland, Kurt Aland, Johannes Karavidopoulos, Carlo Martini, and Bruce Metzger, eds., 4th ed. (United Bible Society, 1983), s.v. *"Parousia,"* 136.

30 See also 1 Cor. 15:23; 1 Thess. 2:19; 5:23; 2 Thess. 2:1; James 5:7–8; 1 John 2:29 and possibly 2 Pet. 3:4.

31 See also Matt. 24:3, 27, 37, 3:9; 1 Thess. 3:13; 2 Thess. 2:8; 2 Pet. 1:16.

32 Newman, "A Concise Greek-English Dictionary," s.v. *"Apo"* and *"Kalupto,"* 20, 91.

33 Newman, "A Concise Greek-English Dictionary," s.v. *"Apokalupsis,"* 21; H. G. Lindell and Robert Scott, *Lindell-Scott Greek-English Lexicon* (Oxford: Oxford University Press, 1843) s.v. *"Apokalupsis."* Accessed in electronic data base: Bibleworks, v. 6.0, 2003.

34 See also 1 Cor. 1:7; 1 Pet. 1:7.

35 See also Luke 17:30; 1 Pet. 4:13.

36 Newman, "A Concise Greek-English Dictionary," s.v. *"Epiphaneia,"* 71; *Lindell-Scott Lexicon.* Accessed in electronic data base: Bibleworks, version 6.0, 2003.

37 See also 1 Tim. 6:14.

38 See also Titus 2:13.

39 After coming to this conclusion in my own studies of Scripture, I later found Douglas Moo stating these observations in defense of the posttribulation position. He wrote, "And, while some texts obviously place the coming *after* the final tribulation, there are *none* that equally obviously place it before the final tribulation" (emphasis Moo's). Moo, "A Case for the Posttribulation Rapture" in *Three Views on The Rapture* by Blaising, et al. (2010), 194–96.

40 Payne, *The Imminent Appearing of Christ*, 47. Ladd analyzes the New Testament Greek vocabulary of the blessed hope and concludes, "The vocabulary used of our Lord's return lends no support for the idea of two coming of Christ or of two aspects of His coming." Ladd, *The Blessed Hope*, 70. Cf. Moo, "A Case for the Posttribulation Rapture," in *Three Views on The Rapture* by Blaising, et al. (2010), 194–96. Having already discovered this in my own studies, these scholars confirmed this position for me.

41 Acts 17:11: "These were more fair-minded than those in Thessalonica, in that they received the word with all readiness, and searched the Scriptures daily to find out whether these things were so."

CHAPTER 6

Midtribulation Position: Including Prewrath Interpretation

Now, brethren, concerning the coming of our Lord Jesus Christ and our gathering together to Him, we ask you, not to be soon shaken in mind or troubled, either by spirit or by word or by letter, as if from us, as though the day of Christ had come. Let no one deceive you by any means; for that Day will not come unless the falling away comes first, and the man of sin is revealed, the son of perdition, who opposes and exalts himself above all that is called God or that is worshiped, so that he sits as God in the temple of God, showing himself that he is God.

2 Thessalonians 2:1–4 NKJV

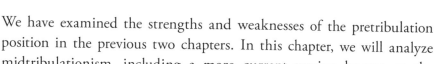

We have examined the strengths and weaknesses of the pretribulation position in the previous two chapters. In this chapter, we will analyze midtribulationism, including a more current version known as the prewrath position. Both midtribulationism and the prewrath theory place the Rapture after the midpoint of the Tribulation period.

A Brief Summary of the

Norman Harrison has been an important advocate of this model. He identifies the Rapture with the catching up of the two witnesses in

Revelation 11:12. "And they [the two witnesses] heard a loud voice from heaven saying to them, 'Come up here.' And they ascended to heaven in a cloud, and their enemies saw them." To take this position Harrison assumes "the two witnesses are symbolic of 'a larger company of witnesses.'" He sees these men as representing two classes of Christians: "Moses" represents dead Christians being resurrected, and "Elijah" represents living Christians being raptured.[1] However, there is nothing in the passage that identifies these two witnesses as groups of people. Sound exegesis would see them as two men anointed by God at that time.

Harrison attempts to bolster his position by identifying the seventh trumpet in Revelation 11:15 with the last trump of 1 Corinthians 15:52 and 1 Thessalonians 4:16.[2] However, he probably has the structure of the book of Revelation wrong. Posttribulationists place Revelation 11:15 at the end of the Tribulation period because of the declaration in that verse that says, "The kingdoms of this world have become the kingdoms of our Lord and of His Christ, and He shall reign forever and ever!"[3] If that is the case, Harrison has inadvertently supported the posttribulation position.[4]

Many scholars see no relationship between the trumpet series in Revelation and Paul's mention of the last trumpet. For example, pretribulationist Lewis Chafer writes, ". . . there is no connection whatsoever between the seventh and the last trump of Revelation and the last trump for the Church, as though God is restricted to one series of trumpets."[5] The continued debate about this subject demonstrates the uncertainty in Scripture associated with Harrison's identification of the seventh trumpet in Revelation 11:15 with the last trump in the Corinthian and Thessalonian texts.[6] Building doctrine on such symbolism produces a weak argument regardless of which of the Rapture positions one takes. Gordon Fee seems to have arrived at the most logical conclusion. He says the trumpet reference "is such common imagery for heralding of the End, it may carry no metaphorical freight whatever in this instance [1 Cor. 15:52]."[7] The bottom line is this: There is simply too much supposition in the interpretation of the trumpet references to establish a position on the timing of the Rapture.[8]

Midtribulationist Gleason Archer later rejects Harrison's position that the two men in Revelation 11 represent groups in the Rapture/Resurrection. Instead, he prefers identifying the Rapture with "events following the sounding of the seventh trumpet," especially in conjunction with the flight of Israel into the dessert in Revelation 12:13–17. However, Archer admits "there are too many obscurities and difficulties to make out a convincing case for this identification."[9] The lack of consensus on this pivotal matter says something about the weakness of the midtribulation theory.

A Brief Summary of the Prewrath Position

Marvin Rosenthal revised the midtribulation theory and renamed it "pre-wrath Rapture." Drawing on his analysis of Matthew 24, 1 Thessalonians 5:9, 2 Thessalonians 2:3, and Revelation 6, he places the Rapture sometime after the abomination of desolation but before the final outpouring of wrath.[10] He moves the position closer to the posttribulation position. However, his contention is that the church is raptured out of the earth before the outpouring of God's wrath during the second half of the seven-year period. In his theory the second half of the Tribulation period is divided into two parts: the Great Tribulation and the Day of the Lord.[11] The position is that wrath during what this system calls the Great Tribulation is the wrath of man and of Satan, but not of God. God's wrath is only poured out during the Day of the Lord at the end of the seven-year period. Rosenthal places the Rapture at the breaking of the seventh seal (Rev. 8:1), at which time the Day of the Lord begins.

Robert Van Kampen, the originator of the prewrath position, identifies the Rapture with Revelation 7:9: "After these things I looked, and behold, a great multitude which no one could number, of all nations, tribes, peoples, and tongues, standing before the throne and before the Lamb, clothed with white robes."[12] In his discussion of this group, Rosenthal writes, "This great multitude represents the true church which goes into the seventieth week of Daniel. They are raptured at the end of the Great Tribulation but before the Day of the Lord begins. They are raptured before God's wrath is poured out but are not exempt from the ultimate rebellion of unregenerate men. The symmetry, balance, and timing of Revelation 7 should not be missed. With chapter 8, the Day of the Lord will begin. Therefore, in chapter 7 the church is raptured."[13]

Seeing a parallel between Revelation 7–8 and Revelation 14–16, Alan Hultberg understands the heavenly group in Revelation 15:2 to be the same as the multitude in Revelation 7:9.[14] So these Christians are raptured before the outpouring of God's wrath is announced in Revelation 15:1 and its release in Revelation 16:1.

Challenges to viewing Revelation 7:9 as representing the Rapture include:

1. It is debatable whether the multitude being clothed with white robes represents having a glorified body.

2. There is no indication in the text that members of this multitude arrived in heaven suddenly and as a group—something which is necessary with the Rapture. It is just as likely, and perhaps more natural, to view them as people who died one-by-one and went into the presence of the Lord in heaven (2 Cor. 5:8).

3. John's ignorance of who the crowd is in Revelation 7:13–15 mitigates against this being the raptured church. Showers writes, "In response to the elder's question, 'What are these which are arrayed in white robes?' (Rev. 7:13), John expressed ignorance concerning the identification of the persons in the great multitude (v. 14). If, as the Pre-Wrath view teaches, the great multitude included all of the church saints, then it seems strange that John, as one of the church's apostles and part of its foundation (Eph. 2:20), did not recognize at least some of the persons in the multitude."[15]

4. The statement, "These are the ones who come out of the great tribulation," (Rev. 7:14) implies that they were people living during the Great Tribulation, not that they included those living prior to that time. The more natural reading would be that they represent Tribulation saints.

The point I'm making is that both the prewrath and midtribulation models depend too heavily on interpretation of symbolism for identifying the time of the Rapture. Moreover, these positions rest heavily on this timing. While their positioning of the Rapture after the abomination of desolation has direct support from 2 Thessalonians 2:1–3, basing the timing on pictures and symbols in Revelation lays a weak foundation for the models.[16]

The prewrath position is stronger than the traditional midtribulation theory. It offers the flexibility of a Rapture any time during the second half of the Tribulation period, whereas the midtribulation places it at the middle of that period with limited support for the assertion.[17] Most troubling is the substantial reliance on interpretation of symbolic language. The prewrath position depends on one's interpretation of the timing of the seven seals, especially the sixth and seventh seals (Rev. 6:12–17; 8:1). Both theories place the church on earth during the first three and a half years of the Tribulation period.

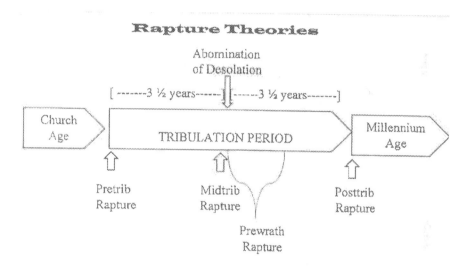

Figure 2: Rapture Theories

We will now evaluate some of the strengths of these theories. Then we will process some of the weaknesses and conclude with a summary of our observations. For simplicity, we will refer to both theories as the midtribulation position except when the distinction is crucial to the conversation.

Strengths of the Midtribulation and Prewrath Positions 2 Thessalonians 2

Like the posttribulation theory, the midtribulation position is more consistent with 2 Thessalonians 2 than the pretribulation theory. In that passage Paul writes, "Now, brethren, concerning the coming of our Lord Jesus Christ and our gathering together to Him, we ask you, not to be soon shaken in mind or troubled, either by spirit or by word or by letter, as if from us, as though the day of Christ had come. Let no one deceive you by any means; for that Day will not come unless the falling away comes first, and the man of sin is revealed, the son of perdition, who opposes and exalts himself above all that is called God or that is worshiped, so that he sits as God in the temple of God, showing himself that he is God" (2 Thess. 2:1–4).

In this chapter, we are limiting our discussion of this passage since we dealt with it in chapter 5. The misinformation that probably has these Thessalonians disturbed is that the Tribulation period has begun, with all the pending distress associated with it. Along with that, some postulate they may be concerned that they have missed the Rapture as taught in 1 Thessalonians 4:13–18. If that is correct, then Paul seems to be assuring them that two signs would precede the Rapture: a great apostasy or rebellion and the manifestation of the Antichrist in the abomination of desolation. Of course, that teaching would argue against the pretribulation position.

In the midtribulation position, Christians would see these two signs as indicators that the Rapture will follow. Midtribulation scholars parallel Paul's teaching here with Jesus's teaching in Matthew 24, where Christ points to deception and the abomination of desolation as signs to watch for (Matt. 24:15).

Wrath

The midtribulation position recognizes the protection from wrath promised to the church. Speaking to Christians, Paul writes, "For God did not appoint us to wrath, but to obtain salvation through our Lord Jesus Christ" (1 Thess. 5:9). Pretribulationists, midtribulationist, and prewrath advocates interpret that as an indication the church will be raptured before God pours his wrath out on the earth in the last days. Midtribulationists see that wrath beginning at the middle of the seventieth week. The prewrath position sees it happening sometime after the abomination of desolation but before the final outpouring of wrath designated as the *Day of the Lord*. In that theory the time in which the Day of the Lord begins is undetermined. Therefore, the midtribulation/prewrath position easily explains 1 Thessalonians 5:9 with a Rapture prior to the outpouring of God's wrath.

The posttribulation camp counters this in two ways: First, they say Paul is talking about eternal wrath that Christians are saved from through the cross. But this is not convincing because the context in 1 Thessalonians 5:9 is the coming of the Lord.[18] There were no chapter breaks in the original text, so chapter 5 flows immediately out of Paul's teaching about the Rapture in 1 Thessalonians 4:13–18. In chapter 5, he continues the thought. "But concerning the times and the seasons, brethren, you have no need that I should write to you. For you yourselves know perfectly that the day of the Lord so comes as a thief in the night. For when they say, 'Peace and safety!' then sudden destruction comes upon them, as labor pains upon a pregnant woman. And they shall not escape. But you, brethren, are not in darkness, so that this Day should overtake you as a thief" (1 Thess. 5:1–4). That is followed by exhortations to stay spiritually alert and to comfort one another, which is similar to the exhortation in 1 Thessalonians 4:18. Again, the context demands that we understand the promise in conjunction with the coming of the Lord and protection from eschatological wrath.

The other explanation given by posttribulationists is that the promise is to protect them while the wrath is being poured out around them during the Tribulation period. No doubt, God could do that.[19] But pretribulationists and midtribulationists argue that the Thessalonians would not have understood Paul's words in that way.[20] The midtribulation position can easily explain the promise in its context.

Midtribulation advocates make a good case for God's wrath being poured out in the last three and a half years, but not in the first half. The first three and a half years will be difficult because of the sorrows brought on by the Antichrist. However, this is the wrath of man, not the wrath of God. God does allow it. But the terminology describing the last half of the Tribulation period is different than what is said about the first half. The anticipation of God's wrath on the earth does not come in the book of Revelation until after the sixth seal is opened. Then we see the fear expressed that God's wrath is about to be released. Revelation 6:15–17: "And the kings of the earth, the great men, the rich men, the commanders, the mighty men, every slave and every free man, hid themselves in the caves and in the rocks of the mountains, [they got in their bunkers] and said to the mountains and rocks, 'Fall on us and hide us from the face of Him who sits on the throne and from the wrath of the Lamb! For the great day of His wrath has come, and who is able to stand?'"[21]

The language of "the wrath of God" is only used of the events after the abomination that makes desolate, which occurs at the midpoint of the Tribulation period. The seven bowls that are poured out on the earth in the last part of Revelation are full of the *wrath* of God. Revelation 16:1: "Then I heard a loud voice from the temple saying to the seven angels, 'Go and pour out the bowls of the wrath of God on the earth.'" This is not just man's inhumanity to man, as bad as that is. This is God's wrath being poured out on the whole earth. The midtribulation camp effectively explains their position on the issue of wrath. The pretribulation position is not weakened by the midtribulation arguments because pretribulationists exclude Christians from the outpouring of God's wrath as well.

Perseverance

A third strength of the midtribulation position is that it prepares Christians to persevere through tribulation. Of course, the posttribulation position does this as well. As mentioned in the previous chapter, the weakness of the pretribulation model in this regard is not inherent in the position itself. However, some people fail to understand that Christians should be braced for hardship and persecution, whether it happens during the Tribulation period or in earlier history. To its credit, the midtribulation position calls people to a readiness to persevere through any tribulation that may come.

Bride of Christ

The midtribulation position provides a preparation of the bride of Christ for her groom. Initially, this was the most attractive feature of this position for me. When I look at the condition of the church today, I find myself asking: How can this be a bride without spot or wrinkle? Yet, that is the description of Christ's bride in Ephesians 5:25–27: "Husbands, love your wives, just as Christ also loved the church and gave Himself for her, that He might sanctify and cleanse her with the washing of water by the word, that He might present her to Himself a glorious church, not having spot or wrinkle or any such thing, but that she should be holy and without blemish." This depiction of the bride is confirmed in Revelation 19:7–8: "'Let us be glad and rejoice and give Him glory, for the marriage of the Lamb has come, and His wife has made herself ready.' And to her it was granted to be arrayed in fine linen, clean and bright, for the fine linen is the righteous acts of the saints." The bride of Christ will reflect his purity and majesty.

So how does the bride of Christ get into that condition? The refining that comes through suffering must be part of the process. The Bible makes that clear in several places. For example, Peter acknowledges the tribulation first-century Christians were enduring, then writes, "But may the God of all grace, who called us to His eternal glory by Christ Jesus, after you have suffered a while, perfect, establish, strengthen, and settle you" (1 Pet. 5:10). The fact that this was happening in the first century tells us it does not have to happen during the Tribulation period. Even if the pretribulation position is correct, God may take the church through some tribulation to prepare her for the Rapture.

More notably, the argument against the pretribulation model based on the necessity of a pure bride is weakened by one fact: The last-days preparation of the church only addresses those living at the time. It does not address the preparation of all the previous generations.

Additionally, the primary preparation for the whole church is the glorification of the saints in the resurrection of the body. Flesh and blood cannot inherit the kingdom of God. "For this corruptible must put on incorruption, and this mortal must put on immortality" (1 Cor. 15:53). God uses all the work of the Spirit in this life, but the perfection of the bride happens at the Resurrection. John puts it this way: "Beloved, now we are children of God; and it has not yet been revealed what we shall be, but we know that when He is revealed, we shall be like Him, for we shall see Him as He is" (1 John 3:2–3).[22] The preparation of the bride for the groom will be complete and she will be without spot or wrinkle because of the transformation that will happen in the third phase of salvation (glorification).

Therefore, we should not put too much weight on the church's need of refinement in determining the timing of the Rapture. God could do some of that in the days before the Rapture, even in a pretribulation model. But, more importantly, the radical change will come because of the transformation brought about by the final stage of salvation, glorification/ resurrection.

Purpose of Rapture

The midtribulation position offers a meaningful explanation of the purpose of the Rapture. Why is there a Rapture to begin with? In both the pretribulation model and the midtribulation model, the Rapture exempts the church from the outpouring of wrath during the Tribulation period and positions the church in heaven for the Judgment Seat of Christ and the Marriage of the Lamb.[23] That seems to be missing in the posttribulation position.[24]

Weaknesses of the Midtribulation Position

Support for Timing

In this model the identification of when the Rapture occurs in Scripture is extremely weak. It is heavily dependent on symbolism and interpretation. Yet, everything in the model rests upon these interpretations.

The prewrath contention that the scene with the great multitude in heaven in Revelation 7:9 represents the timing of the Rapture is based on an allegorical method of interpretation and relies on one's interpretation of the imagery. We are not told enough in Scripture about how the multitude got in heaven (or who they are) to build a Rapture theory around it.

The pretribulationists use John's call to heaven in Revelation 4:1 to indicate timing for the Rapture. That position is vague and weak as well. God is simply calling John up, and it is a leap to say that represents the Rapture of the church.

There is no direct statement in Revelation about the timing of the Rapture. Because of the connection of the Rapture with the Resurrection of the Just, Revelation 20:4 is the closest thing we have to that. That verse would point toward a posttribulation position, not the midtribulation theory.[25]

Overlap of Church Age

The overlap of the church age with the seventieth week in God's program for Israel presents issues that must be addressed. We brought this matter up in chapter 4, so we only mention it here.

The church age is a work of God distinct in some ways from God's program for the nation of Israel. When Israel rejected and crucified Messiah, God launched the church age on the Day of Pentecost. His program for the nation of Israel was put on pause, and he began working through the church. The Day of Pentecost in Acts 2 was a distinct event on a specific day when the church age began. One would expect God to conclude the church age in a similar way, with a distinct event. Pretribulationists contend that event is the Rapture prior to a resumption of the seventy weeks prophesied in Daniel 9:24.

Granted, there were about forty years after Acts 2 before the temple was destroyed. But we know from the New Testament that Jews who turned to God during those forty years were saved into the church where there is "neither Jew nor Greek" (Gal. 3:28). Paul is an example of that. Therefore, the church age clearly began on the Day of Pentecost. After that day Jews were not saved by following the Old Covenant provisions, even though the temple was still standing for those forty years.

Looking at the precision in the way God began the church, we would expect it to end in a similar way, setting it apart from the unique program for Israel. The pretribulation model provides for this and eliminates some of the unanswered questions that were raised earlier in chapter 4. Pretribulationist Dwight Pentecost insists, "The mystery program [the church], which was so distinct in its inception, will certainly be separate at its conclusion."[26]

Could God end the church age with the overlap suggested by the midtribulation and posttribulation models? Of course, he could. For that reason, this issue is not decisive. However, in the pretribulation model the conclusion of the church age is more consistent with the way it began.

Imminence

Midtribulationism may not present as strong of a position on imminence as the pretribulation theory does. Pretribulationists argue that imminence is weakened by the signs placed before the Rapture.[27] We must examine this issue in the light of Scripture. What does the Bible say about our expectation of Christ's coming for his church?

Midtribulation advocates and posttribulationists say no one knows the day nor hour of the Rapture, but Christians can discern the nearness of the event by the signs given in Scripture. Even though end-time events will come as a thief in the night and take the world by surprise, alert Christians will discern the times and be prepared. First Thessalonians 5:1–11 says:

> But concerning the times and the seasons, brethren, you have no need that I should write to you. For you yourselves know perfectly that the day of the Lord so comes as a thief in the night. For when they say, 'Peace and safety!' then sudden destruction comes upon them, as labor pains upon a pregnant woman. And they shall not escape. But you, brethren, are not in darkness, so that this Day should overtake you as a thief. You are all sons of light and sons of the day. We are not of the night nor of darkness. Therefore let us not sleep, as others do, but let us watch and be sober. For those who sleep, sleep at night, and those who get drunk are drunk at night. But let us who are of the day be sober, putting on the breastplate of faith and love, and as a helmet the hope of salvation. For God did not appoint us to wrath, but to obtain salvation through our Lord Jesus Christ, who died for us, that whether we wake or sleep, we should live together with Him. Therefore comfort each other and edify one another, just as you also are doing.

Paul makes a clear distinction in verse 4 between how the coming of the Lord will take the world by surprise but should not catch Christians off guard. "But you, brethren, are not in darkness, so that this Day should overtake you as a thief" (1 Thess. 5:4). The warning that follows addresses the danger that Christians could be surprised by his coming *if* they do not stay alert and ready for his coming. In other words, there are signs that could alert believers to the nearness of his coming. However, Christians will only discern them if we are spiritually alert and ready.[28]

The readiness Paul prescribes is altogether *spiritual.* The error that is repeated again and again in history is trying to identify the time of Christ's coming and make *carnal* preparations. The focus usually becomes the troubles predicted for the end times and what we can do in the natural to protect ourselves. Therefore, people build bunkers, shift financial investments, and sometimes move off the grid. This is the carnal mind at work. But the preparation called for in 1 Thessalonians 5:8 is to "be sober [be spiritually alert], putting on the breastplate of faith and love, and as a helmet the hope of salvation." When our response to discerning the times moves us to take self-centered, carnal action, we are probably out of sync with Scripture. If our discernment of the times causes us to draw near to the Lord as our shepherd, commune with him more intimately, and live more obediently, then we are responding correctly. Gene Green points out the Thessalonian concern about when the Day of the Lord would arrive, then writes, "Paul answers this concern by teaching that living in faith, love, and hope is the proper way to be prepared so that the day of the Lord will not surprise them 'like a thief.'"[29]

The answer to the imminence debate by the midtribulationists and posttribulationists is somewhat convincing.[30] But the pretribulation model naturally lends itself to the call for readiness. An "at any moment' understanding of imminence is consistent with the pretribulation model. It is difficult to maintain in the other two models. However, midtribulationists and posttribulationists contend that they are faithful to the overall message on this subject in the New Testament. They argue it is possible to know the signs and seasons and still have a mindset that passionately longs for and prepares for the Rapture. Therefore, this is not a significant weakness in this model or the posttribulation model. We will continue to examine imminence as we proceed in this study.

Greek Terms

This midtribulation position fails to explain the lack of distinction made in the New Testament with the terms used in reference to the Rapture versus the Second Coming. We discussed this weakness in the previous chapter; we will only touch on it here.

The three Greek words used in the New Testament in reference to the coming of Christ are *parousia*, *apokalupsis,* and *epiphaneia*. All three words are used in reference to both the Rapture and the Second Coming. That tends to indicate events happening at the same time. The pretribulation and midtribulation theories make a crucial distinction between the timing of the Rapture and the Second Coming.[31] That distinction is weighty in those theories. But if that distinction is so important, why didn't the New Testament writers distinguish them in the language they used? If Paul held the pretribulation or midtribulation position, we would expect him to make a clearer distinction between the two events. If the two events occur at the same time, it is understandable that a more definite distinction is not made.

The pretribulationists answer given to this concern is to list the contrasting descriptions of these two events. Dwight Pentecost lists seventeen such contrasts, and the list is enlightening.[32] But it does not adequately explain the apparent merging of the events in some passages. These distinctions could simply explain the difference in the way groups are impacted by almost simultaneous events.

The prewrath position answers this by defining the Second Coming as a three-phase event of the Rapture, the Day of the Lord, and Christ's return to the earth. Posttribulationists generally agree that the Rapture of the godly, the judgment of the wicked, and Christ's return to the earth are involved in the Second Coming. However, the distance of at least five months (and probably more time for the outpouring of the seven bowls of wrath) between the Rapture and Christ's return naturally separates it from Christ's return to the earth. Thus, calling the three events the Second Coming seems more like a superficial play on words than a theory that answers the way New Testament writers used the terms *parousia, apokalupsis,* and *epiphaneia*.

While this complaint against the pretribulation and midtribulation positions is an argument from silence, it is an important consideration. The use of language is highly indicative of how an author is thinking.

2 Thessalonians 1:3–10

The midtribulation position offers an inadequate explanation as to why 2 Thessalonians 1:3–10 seems to portray Christians receiving rest in conjunction with the destruction of God's enemies at the Second Coming. This is closely associated with the fourth weakness we just discussed. In chapter 5, we examined this problem as a weakness for the pretribulation position as well.

Perhaps Paul is talking in general terms that would allow for the pretribulation and midtribulation models. But without question, the passage fits better with a posttribulation position.[33] In 2 Thessalonians 1:6–8, Paul says to the persecuted believers at Thessalonica: "since it is a righteous thing with God to repay with tribulation those who trouble you, and to give you who are troubled rest with us when [notice the time marker] the Lord Jesus is revealed from heaven with His mighty angels, in flaming fire taking vengeance on those who do not know God, and on those who do not obey the gospel of our Lord Jesus Christ."

Verses 9–10 seem to continue with this connection between the Lord being glorified in His saints along with the destruction of God's enemies at the Second Coming. "These shall be punished with everlasting destruction from the presence of the Lord and from the glory of His power, when [another time marker] He comes, in that Day, to be glorified in His saints and to be admired among all those who believe, because our testimony among you was believed."

Conclusion

We have examined the prewrath position along with its predecessor, the traditional midtribulation model. Overall, these models have fewer strengths and more weaknesses than the other two models. They do not fall outside the realm of possibility, but it is the most unlikely of the three positions. The prewrath model is stronger than the traditional midtribulation model. However, both depend heavily on identifying the time of the Rapture from the *symbolism* in the book of Revelation. Furthermore, the whole position depends on that timing. In the next chapter we will examine the posttribulation position.

Endnotes: Chapter 6

1   Norman B. Harrison, *The End: Re-Thinking the Revelation* (Minneapolis, MN: The Harrison Service, 1941), 116–117.

2   Harrison, *The End: Re-Thinking the Revelation*, 74–75. For a pretribulationist argument against Harrison's position on this see Pentecost, *Things to Come*, 188–92.

3   Brown and Keener, *Not Afraid of the Antichrist*, 109–110.

4   Moo thinks Revelation 11:11–12 may describe the Rapture, but he quickly adds, "If it does the Rapture would be posttribulational." Moo, "A Posttribulation Response [to Hultberg]" in *Three Views on the Rapture* by Blaising, et al. (2010), 174.

5   Chafer, *Systematic Theology*, vol. 4, 376. Feinberg also argues against equating the trump in Rev. 11:15 with the last trump of 1 Cor. 15:52 and 1 Thess. 4:16. Cf. Paul D. Feinberg, "Response [to Archer]," in *Three Views on the Rapture* by Archer, et al. (1996), 148–49. In his preference for prewrath over traditional midtribulationism, Hultberg agrees with Chafer and Feinberg on this point. Cf. Alan Hultberg, "A Case for the Prewrath Rapture," in *Three Views on the Rapture:* by Blaising, et al. (2010), 152.

6   For prewrath arguments on this subject, see Rosenthal, *The Pre-Wrath Rapture of the Church*, 187–94; Alan Hultberg, "A Case for the Prewrath Rapture," in *Three Views on the Rapture* by Blaising, et al. (2010), 152–53. For the posttribulation position, see Gundry, *The Church and the Tribulation*, 146–52; Brown and Keener, *Not Afraid of the Antichrist*, 30–31.

7   Fee, *The First Epistle to the Corinthians*, 801–02. Contra: Rosenthal, *The Pre-Wrath Rapture of the Church*, 189–94.

8   Considering all this, the weight of the argument tends to favor the posttribulation position.

9   Gleason L. Archer, Jr., "The Case for the Mid-Seventieth-Week Rapture Position," in *Three Views on the Rapture* by Archer, et al. (1996), 144.

10   Cf. Rosenthal, *The Pre-Wrath Rapture of the Church* (Nashville, 59. Showers credits Robert Van Kampen with originating the prewrath theory. He writes, "The view was publicized further in 1992 with the publication of Robert Van Kampen's book *The Sign* (Van Kampen was the originator and first advocate of the view)." Showers, *The Pre-wrath Rapture View*, 7. Also see Hultberg, "A Case for the Prewrath Rapture," in *Three Views on the Rapture* by Blaising, et al. (2010), 127. For a brief history of the development of the prewrath position and specific differences between prewrath and midtribulation theories, see Hultberg, "Introduction" in *Three Views on the Rapture* by Blaising, et al. (2010), 21–23.

11   Prewrath advocates recognize the last half of *the seventieth week* will not be cut short, but they believe Matt. 24:22 teaches *the Great Tribulation* will be cut

short to less than 3½ years, leaving the "Day of the Lord' to complete the 3½ years. Cf. Rosenthal, *The Pre-Wrath Rapture of the Church*, 107–13. This division marking out the "Day of the Lord" from the Great Tribulation is competently challenged by pretribulationist Renald Showers. Showers writes, "This argument of the Pre-Wrath Rapture view misses the fact that the biblical expression 'the Day of the Lord' has a double sense (a broad sense and a narrow sense) in relationship to the future. The broad sense refers to an extended period of time involving divine interventions related at least to the entire seventieth week of Daniel and the thousand-year Millennium. . . . The narrow sense refers to one specific day—the day on which Christ will return to the earth in His glorious Second Coming with His angels." Showers, *The Pre-wrath Rapture View*, 162.

While the day of Christ's coming is unique in its level of judgment and glory, the prewrath distinction is not convincing. Matt. 24:22 simply teaches that God has already shortened/limited the Great Tribulation to three and a half years, in his eternal decrees, for the elect's sake. "Actually," Barton Payne says, "'the day of the Lord' is whenever God acts." Payne, *The Imminent Appearing of Christ*, 60. The statement gives assurance to Christians reading Matthew's gospel that God sovereignly controls it all. Wilkins says it "is a proverbial way of indicating that God is in control even of these days of horror." Michael J. Wilkins, *Matthew*, The NIV Application Commentary, Terry Muck, ed. (Grand Rapids: Zondervan, 2004), 780.

12 For Van Kampen's defense of this interpretation see Robert Van Kampen, *The Rapture Question Answered: Plain and Simple*, 1997 (Grand Rapids: Fleming H. Revell, 2002), 155–65; Van Kampen, *The Sign*, 295–301.

13 Rosenthal, *The Pre-Wrath Rapture of the Church*, 185. For a pretribulationist critique of this position, see Showers, *The Pre–wrath Rapture View*, 139–51.

14 Cf. Hultberg, "A Case for the Prewrath Rapture" in *Three Views on the Rapture* by Blaising, et al. (2010), 135; H. L. Nigro, *Before God's Wrath: The Bible's Answer to the Timing of the Rapture*, rev. (Lancaster, PA: Strong Tower Publishing, 2002), 29–30.

15 Showers, *The Pre-Wrath Rapture View*, 150.

16 For a rebuttal of the prewrath position on Revelation 7:9, see Showers, *The Pre-Wrath Rapture View*, 140–51.

17 However, in the prewrath model the Rapture occurs long before Christ's return to the earth, an absolute minimum of five months (Rev. 9:1, 5) Cf. Rosenthal, *The Pre-Wrath Rapture of the Church*, 153.

18 Moo seems to concede the context as the coming of the Lord but argues the promise is not a rescue from the wrath poured out during the Tribulation but from wrath in general. His reasoning is that both living and dead Christians are exempted from wrath and only living Christians are raptured. Moo, "A Posttribulation Response [to Hultberg] in *Three Views on the Rapture* by Blaising,

et al. (2010), 170–172. However, if Christians are rescued from the wrath of God in whatever form it may come, then they are rescued from the wrath being poured out during the Tribulation period.

In response, Hultberg correctly reasserts the context of 1 Thess. 5:9 to be Parousia wrath, not just wrath in general. Hultberg understands "the day of the Lord" as referring to 'a complex of events' including the Rapture, the Tribulation period, and the Second Coming" (not just the final day of the Tribulation period). He points to the way Paul uses the phrase in 2 Thessalonians 2:2 as part of his argument. Hultberb, "A Prewrath Response [to Moo]" in *Three Views on the Rapture* by Blaising, et al. (2010), 267-69.

19 In fairness to the posttribulationists, there is significant precedence for this preservation in the midst of an outpouring of God's wrath. For example, Isaiah 26:20–21 says, "Come, my people, enter your chambers, And shut your doors behind you; Hide yourself, as it were, for a little moment, Until the indignation is past. For behold, the Lord comes out of His place To punish the inhabitants of the earth for their iniquity; The earth will also disclose her blood, And will no more cover her slain."

20 Brown and Keener, *Not Afraid of the Antichrist*, 123–126.

21 The prewrath position places this passage at some undetermined time in the second half of the Tribulation period. The sequence of events is Rapture, then the Day of the Lord in which God's wrath is poured out, then the glorious return of Christ. In this prewrath model these events are viewed as together constituting the Second Coming. Cf. Van Kampen, The Sign, 291, 423.

The combining of the Rapture with the Second Coming is consistent with New Testament terminology (*parousia, apokalupsis,* and *epiphaneia*) as discussed extensively in chapter 5: "Pretribulation Position: Weaknesses." However, the prewrath method of separating Rapture, the Great Tribulation, the Day of the Lord, and Christ's return is not sustainable. As stated earlier, in the prewrath model the Rapture occurs long before Christ's return to the earth, an absolute minimum of five months (Rev. 9:1,5) Cf. Rosenthal, *The Pre-Wrath Rapture of the Church*, 153.

22 See Tow, *Authentic Christianity*, 2019), 156–69.

23 Dwight Pentecost distinguishes between the marriage of the Lamb and the Marriage Supper. He says the marriage takes place in heaven, in contrast to the Marriage Supper which "becomes the parabolic picture of the entire millennial age. . . ." Pentecost, *Things to Come*, 227.

24 Payne offers alternatives to the pretribulation timing of the Judgment Seat of Christ, but they are not very convincing. Cf. Payne, *The Imminent Appearing of Christ*, 136.

25　Cf. Gundry, *The Church and the Tribulation*, 148; Moo, "A Posttribulation Response [to Hultberg]" *Three Views on the Rapture* by Blaising, et al. (2010), 172, 174–75.

26　Pentecost, *Things to Come*, 201.

27　Showers's comment is representative of the pretribulationist position: "Therefore, other things may happen before the imminent event, but nothing else must take place before it happens. The necessity of something taking place first destroys the concept of imminency." Showers, *The Pre-Wrath Rapture View*, 200–01.

28　Paul is probably basing his teaching here in 1 Thess. 5 on Christ's teaching in Matt. 24:32–25:46 which emphasized the warning to watch and stay spiritually prepared for his coming. This issue of being prepared is dealt with more extensively in chapter 11: "Matthew 24:45–25:30: Watching for the Return."

29　Green, *The Letters to the Thessalonians*, 230. Sliker writes toward the end of his book, "Yet here we are discussing biblical preparation for the hour in which we find ourselves. The centerpiece of our discussion must be our own prayer lives and the prayer lives of those we are discipling." David Sliker, *The Nations Rage: Prayer, Promise and Power in an Anti-Christian Age* (Minneapolis, MN: Chosen Books, 2020), 207.

30　For a pretribulation position on imminence, see Walvoord, *The Rapture Question*, 50–54, 73. For posttribulation position on imminence, see Brown and Keener, *Not Afraid of the Antichrist*, 126–130; Moo, "A Case for the Posttribulation Rapture" in *Three Views on the Rapture* by Blaising, et al. (2010), 235–239. See also Feinberg's response to the posttribulation position on imminence: Feinberg, "Response [to Archer]" in *Three Views on the Rapture* by Archer, et al. (1996), 150–58.

For a prewrath position on imminence, see H. L. Nigro, *Before God's Wrath*, 80–90. Nigro comments, "The distinction between imminence as an attitude of expectation and imminence as an 'any moment' return is important. . . . There is no question that imminence, in the sense of expectation, is found throughout the New Testament. . . . But does that mean the Lord could appear at any moment? There is not one verse in scripture that says so. In fact, this would be a direct contradiction with the many signs that Jesus gave to believers to help them discern when his Second Coming is approaching" (pp. 80–81). In his defense of the prewrath position, Rosenthal writes, ". . . Paul did not teach the Thessalonians that the *Rapture* was imminent. Quite the contrary, he taught that the apostasy must occur first and that the man of sin must first be revealed (2 Thess. 2:3)" (emphasis Rosenthal's). Rosenthal, *The Pre-Wrath Rapture of the Church*, 249.

31　The prewrath position allows for the Rapture to possibly occur near the Second Coming as the first phase of that event. However, that leaves little time for the "Day of the Lord" outpouring of wrath between the Rapture phase and the

Second Coming, in which the seven trumpets and seven bowls of wrath occur in Revelation. Therefore, on this point, prewrath is weaker that posttribulation as a model.

32 Cf. Pentecost, *Things to Come*, 206–07.

33 For debate on this issue, see Blaising, et al., *Three Views on the Rapture* (2010), 206–207, 233, 251–252, 267–269. See also Brown and Keener, *Not Afraid of the Antichrist*, 152–153.

CHAPTER 7

Posttribulation Position

Immediately after the tribulation of those days the sun will be darkened, and the moon will not give its light; the stars will fall from heaven, and the powers of the heavens will be shaken. Then the sign of the Son of Man will appear in heaven, and then all the tribes of the earth will mourn, and they will see the Son of Man coming on the clouds of heaven with power and great glory.

Matthew 24:29–30 NKJV

+ + ◆ ◆ ◆ + +

Will Christians go through the Tribulation period? It is not an easy question to answer because there is no place in the Bible where we are explicitly told *when* the Rapture of the church will occur. We are certainly told that it will occur! However, the timing of that event in relation to the Tribulation period is difficult to pin down. We are examining the strengths and weaknesses of the three prominent theories on the subject. We have processed the pretribulation and midtribulation models. In this chapter, we will explore the posttribulation position.

Strengths of the Posttribulation Position

Greek Terms

The identification of the Rapture with the Second Coming in this model best explains why a specific timing for the Rapture is not stated in the New Testament. This one issue is almost decisive in favor of the posttribulation position. In chapters 5 and 6, we found that the New Testament writers used all three Greek terms for the coming of the Lord to refer to *both* the Rapture and the Second Coming. If the timing of those two events were markedly different, we would expect them to avoid doing that or at least provide a clearer separation of the events.

Let me illustrate what I'm saying this way. My daughter, Karol, lives in San Clemente, California, near Los Angeles. Suppose I sent an email yesterday telling her that I have bought a flight ticket to Los Angeles and will arrive on March 30. Today I send another email saying I will pick up my baggage at the United Airlines baggage area. I do not specify what day that will happen. What would be my daughter's assumption about the timing of the baggage pickup? In the absence of me specifying something different, she would assume that baggage pickup happens on the same day already given, March 30. Unless I specify a different date, she would assume that new detail happens in conjunction with my arrival as already stated.

Jesus told us plainly that he would come back at the end of the Tribulation period. In Matthew 24:29–30 he said, "Immediately after the tribulation of those days the sun will be darkened, and the moon will not give its light; the stars will fall from heaven, and the powers of the heavens will be shaken. Then the sign of the Son of Man will appear in heaven, and then all the tribes of the earth will mourn, and they will see the Son of Man coming on the clouds of heaven with power and great glory." He clearly tells us when he is coming back to the earth. Scholars in all three camps generally agree on that.

Later we receive a letter from Paul about the coming of the Lord. In 1 Thessalonians 4, he gives details about the Rapture/Resurrection of Christians. He does not specify the timing. What should be our assumption about the timing? If the timing is the same as what Jesus has already told us, then there is no need to specify it. If the timing is radically different, one would expect him to indicate the different time in order to avoid confusion.

There is no passage in the Bible that specifically tells us when the Rapture occurs. That is one reason this analysis is necessary. We can point to symbols that might indicate something about that, but in the process of interpreting those symbols and metaphors, we could easily be wrong. If Jesus or the apostles were pretribulationists or midtribulationists, it would be natural for them to state the distinction between the timing of the Rapture and the Second Coming. Instead, we find no direct statement indicating a different timing for the two. On the contrary, we find them using the same terms interchangeably in reference to the Rapture and the Second Coming.

Forty years ago, I looked unsuccessfully for a word distinction in the New Testament that would set the Rapture apart from the Second Coming. My assumption was that *parousia* was used for the Rapture and *apokalupsis* for the Second Coming. But even back then, I discovered that both terms were used for both the Rapture and the Second Coming. That left me somewhat tentative about the pretribulation theory. I was seeing this argument for posttribulationism in my own study of Scripture before reading it the writing of others. However, I had been taught pretribulationism and continued to lean in that direction, even though I entertained some reservations.

In this study, I have realized the weight of this argument. It does not conclusively lead one to a posttribulation position. But this is the most compelling argument in the whole debate. The default position from Scripture should be that the Rapture and the Second Coming are descriptive of *one* return of the Lord Jesus Christ. To take a different position, we need at least one statement in the New Testament telling us they come at significantly different times. I am unable to find it. I can give rationale for why the timing might be different. I can interpret symbolism to support a different timing. But the only timing that is clearly stated is the Second Coming at the end of the Tribulation period. This is almost a conclusive argument for posttribulationism.[1]

In chapter 5, we demonstrated how the New Testament writers used the Greek words (*parousia, apokalupsis,* and *epiphaneia*) to refer to *both* the Rapture and Second Coming without distinguishing between the two events. In the pretribulation theory, those two events are separated by seven years and are major temporal markers. This distinction between Rapture and Second Coming are so unique and separated in that theory that we have found it necessary to identify the first event as "Rapture" and the second event as "Second Coming" in order to avoid confusion in our eschatological communication. Why didn't the writers of the New Testament feel such a need? Probably because they did not espouse that seven-year gap in their eschatology. Probably because they viewed the Rapture and the Second Coming as one event. While it is not outside the realm of possibility that they held a pretribulational view, it is doubtful they would have failed to distinguish these two crucial events.

The reader may not see the significance of this argument for posttribulation on first reading because the issue rests on how people use language. Language evolves to distinguish things, especially important things, so that concepts and ideas are communicated clearly. For example, a different word is used in English for orange than the one used for apple. That happened in order for the speaker/writer to clearly communicate what he or she is talking about. It is simply not logical that the Rapture event and the Second Coming event would be referred to with the same Greek word interchangeably if they were two separate events, one marking the beginning of the Tribulation period and the other marking the end of the period. Granted both oranges and apples are referred to as fruit when a major category of food is the subject. It is possible that in the many passages using the Greek words, the New Testament writers could have been speaking in such general terms that they meant the whole seven years as the coming of the Lord. However, that is not very likely.

Therefore, the burden of proof is on the pretribulationists and midtribulationist to demonstrate by Scripture that the New Testament writers deviated from the normal use of language. I find no convincing support for such a deviation. This issue should not be taken lightly since it is at the heart of understanding biblical revelation in our study. The way the New Testament writers used words matters.

2 Thessalonians

Second Thessalonians seems to tell us the Rapture will occur at the time of the Second Coming. We have dealt with these passages to some extent in chapters 5 and 6. But this is a significant strength for the posttribulation position. It is significant because the basis for our position must rest primarily on what the Bible says. And these passages seem to tell us the Rapture will not be prior to the Tribulation.

In 2 Thessalonians 1, Christians are given rest in the same event that means destruction to their enemies. The Second Coming is clearly in view in this passage but notice how the rescue is linked with that coming. Paul recognized the suffering these Christians were experiencing, then says in verses 6–8, "since it is a righteous thing with God to repay with tribulation those who trouble you, and to give you who are troubled rest with us when the Lord Jesus is revealed from heaven with His mighty angels, in flaming fire taking vengeance on those who do not know God, and on those who do not obey the gospel of our Lord Jesus Christ." You may recall from chapter 5 how we focused on the word "when" in that passage and how that seems to place the Rapture with the Second Coming.[2]

In 2 Thessalonians 2, we are given two events that will occur before the Rapture: a great apostasy and the revelation of the Antichrist. These two events occur during the Tribulation period. Scripture plainly tells us that the revelation of the Antichrist does not happen until the Tribulation period. The language in verse 4 points to the abomination of desolation which occurs at the middle of the Tribulation period.

Second Thessalonians 2:1 introduces the subject: "Now, brethren, concerning the coming of our Lord Jesus Christ and our gathering together to Him." Most scholars agree that the phrase *our gathering together to him* is a reference to the Rapture. The *coming of our Lord Jesus Christ,* and *our gathering together to him* are closely linked in that verse as one event.[3]

Then Paul continues, "we ask you, not to be soon shaken in mind or troubled, either by spirit or by word or by letter, as if from us, as though the day of Christ had come. Let no one deceive you by any means; for that Day [a reference to verse 1] will not come unless the falling away comes first, and the man of sin is revealed, the son of perdition, who opposes and exalts himself above all that is called God or that is worshiped, so that he sits as God in the temple of God, showing himself that he is God" (2 Thess. 2:1–4). On the one hand, we don't have a verse specifically telling us the Rapture occurs before the Tribulation period, which would support pretribulationism. On the other hand, this passage seems to be telling us the Rapture happens *after* these Tribulation events. That lends proof for posttribulationism. Paul's teaching in 2 Thessalonians provides powerful support for the posttribulation position.

Olivet Discourse

The Olivet Discourse seems to communicate a posttribulation position. Jesus's teaching recorded in Matthew 24, Mark 13, and Luke 21 is foundational to understanding end-time prophecy. The general structure is laid out in that discourse, and our eschatology must be based on it. For that reason, we will examine it closely in the next section. At this point, we simply list it as a strength for the posttribulation position and will explore that more fully later.

Bride of Christ

This theory provides a seven-year refinement period preparing the church, the bride of Christ, for her groom. As we concluded in chapter 6, this is not a very strong argument for the model because it would only address the last generation, and the final preparation of the bride is her glorification that occurs at the Resurrection of the Just. The refinement and maturing of the church during the Tribulation is presented as a significant argument for midtribulationism and posttribulationism. However, the strength of the argument fades under close examination.

Perseverance

Posttribulation teaching tends to prepare Christians for handling persecution and suffering that would occur during the Tribulation period. Is the average Christian adequately prepared to stand firm if his or her faith is severely attacked and tested during the end-time Tribulation? Probably not.

If the assumption is made that we will be raptured out and exempted from all that trouble, and that turns out to be wrong, there are going to be some very disillusioned Christians. A pretribulation theory could leave Christians very off balance if it turns out to be wrong. On the other hand, a posttribulation theory braces Christians for the impact of persecution. If that turns out to be wrong, they are happily surprised by the Rapture. Posttribulationist Mike Bickle expresses concern that believers be equipped now "so that they are not *offended* by Jesus' leadership, *deceived* by the enemy, *seduced* by the culture, or *fearful of* and *confused by* what will occur in the end times" (emphasis Bickle's).[4]

In his book, *The Nations Rage*, David Sliker identified three storms that will characterize the last days: the storm of revival (Joel 2:28–32), the storm of rage (Ps. 2), and the judgments of the Lord (Rev. 17–19). From our perspective, revival may not seem like a storm, but it certainly will for the world. It will disrupt their plans in the same way Jesus was perceived as a threat to the leaders' plans in Judea. We know how Herod and the Jewish leaders responded to that.[5] We also know from the Acts account that when the early church moved in the power of the Holy Spirit reaching multitudes with the gospel, it sparked a response of rage from the ungodly. The end-time revival prophesied in Joel 2:28–29 will provoke a reactive storm of rage. But in the end, God's judgments will prevail. Jesus will return destroying the enemies of God and establishing his righteous millennial rule in the earth.[6]

The concern we must consider is for people who are relying upon superficial rituals and token religion as a preparation for those events.[7] If posttribulationists are right, Christians must be grounded in their faith to withstand the coming deception (Matt. 24:4,11, 24). They must be abiding in Christ, receiving his strength to stand in the face of persecution. Furthermore, they must be walking in the Spirit so that they are able to participate in the last-days harvest of souls (Rev. 7:9–14). The danger with the pretribulation position is that Christians would see the easy Rapture exit as a signal that none of those preparations are necessary. A strength of posttribulationism is that it confronts Christians with a call to prepare for those things *now* so that they are equipped to face the potential challenges and opportunities.

Corri ten Boom shared, "I have been in countries where the saints are already suffering terrible persecution. In China the Christians were told, 'Don't worry, before the tribulation comes, you will be translated—Raptured.' Then came a terrible persecution. Millions of Christians were tortured to death. Later I heard a Bishop from China say, sadly, 'We have failed. We should have made the people strong for persecution rather than telling them Jesus would come first.' Turning to me he said, 'You still have time. Tell the people how to be strong in times of persecution, how to stand when the tribulation comes—to stand and not faint.'"[8]

This is a practical concern that should be seriously considered by all. It should not be a decisive argument because pretribulationists should be teaching Christians to brace for tribulation and persecution anyway. It is par for the course for every generation of Christians. Jesus flatly told us that in this world we would have tribulation (John 16:33). However, the pretribulation model can easily lend itself to escapism, leaving believers ill-equipped for end-time revival and the hardships of Tribulation-period persecution. There is too much uncertainty about the Rapture's timing to teach a Polly Anna mindset about what lies ahead.

Overall, the first three strengths listed here are very compelling. In the chapters that follow, we will see more biblical support for the posttribulation position in the Olivet Discourse. However, there are some weaknesses in the model that must be considered.

Weaknesses of the Posttribulation Position

Purpose of Rapture

The purpose of the Rapture is obscured by a quick up-and-down event at the end of the Tribulation period. We know from 1 Thessalonians 4:17 that at the time of the Rapture, living Christians will be caught up (*harpazō*) to meet the Lord in the air. That verse says, "Then we who are alive and remain shall be caught up together with them in the clouds to meet the Lord in the air. And thus we shall always be with the Lord." If the posttribulation theory is right, we would expect the last sentence to say something like, "And we will return with Him in glory." The language does not seem to support an immediate return with him.

We also know from Scripture that raptured/resurrected saints will return with him at his Second Coming. Revelation 19:12–14 describes the

Second Coming: "Now I saw heaven opened, and behold, a white horse. And He who sat on him was called Faithful and True, and in righteousness He judges and makes war. His eyes were like a flame of fire, and on His head were many crowns. He had a name written that no one knew except Himself. He was clothed with a robe dipped in blood, and His name is called The Word of God. And the armies in heaven, clothed in fine linen, white and clean, followed Him on white horses."

It might be argued that *the armies in heaven* are just angels.[9] But just a few verses earlier, the bride of Christ is described in exactly the same way as the armies in heaven are described. In Revelation 19: 8 the church is described as "arrayed in fine linen, clean and bright." Then, in verse 14, the armies with the Lord are described as "clothed in fine linen, white and clean." Additionally, Jude quotes Enoch specifically telling us that the Lord is coming with his saints. Jude 1:14–15 says, "Now Enoch, the seventh from Adam, prophesied about these men also, saying, 'Behold, the Lord comes with ten thousands of His saints, to execute judgment on all, to convict all who are ungodly among them of all their ungodly deeds which they have committed in an ungodly way, and of all the harsh things which ungodly sinners have spoken against Him.'"

So, what we have with the posttribulation theory is the church going up and coming right back down. At the very least, it seems strange.

Judgment Seat of Christ

This theory leaves one wondering how the Judgment Seat of Christ and the Marriage of the Lamb fit in the chronology of events. In both the pretribulation and midtribulation models, those events happen in heaven after the Rapture and before the Second Coming. John's placement of those events in Revelation 19 suggests they happen before the Second Coming.

The description of the bride in Revelation 19:7–8 suggests post-resurrection and post-judgment of Christian works. That passage says, "'Let us be glad and rejoice and give Him glory, for the marriage of the Lamb has come, and His wife has made herself ready.' And to her it was granted to be arrayed in fine linen, clean and bright, for the fine linen is the righteous acts of the saints." The implication is that her works have been evaluated, have survived the fire described in 1 Corinthians 3:12–15, and she is clothed with her righteous acts. That all fits with the pretribulation model and the midtribulation model.[10] But it is hard to see when and how it happens in the posttribulation model. The posttribulation answers to these questions are not convincing.[11]

Overlap of Church Age

The seven-year overlap of the church age with the 70th week of God's program for Israel raises difficult questions. Pretribulationism provides a logical, orderly transition from the church age back to the final seven years of God's program for Israel. We must remember that the church was not a part of Daniel's 69 weeks in Daniel 9:24–27 of God's program for Israel. It logically follows that the church would not be a part of the 70th week. Chafer writes, "If the church was in the 483 years, she may be expected to appear in the last 7; but inasmuch as she was not in the 483 years, she could not be in the 7, and no Scripture ever relates the Church to the seven years of tribulation."[12] This was presented as a strength of pretribulationism in chapter 4 and a weakness of midtribulationism in chapter 6.

However, Gundry provides a satisfactory answer to this concern. First, he demonstrates how the transition into the church age involved some overlap. During his ministry, Jesus trained the apostles who became the foundation of the church (Eph. 2:20). During those years, Jesus also provided teaching for the church. For example, in Matthew 18 He gave instruction for church discipline. While the Day of Pentecost (Acts 2) marked the beginning of the church, only 120 were baptized in the Spirit that day. We know from Acts that other believers came into that experience after the Day of Pentecost. Acts 9:1–7 is an example of that. The temple sacrifices continued until 70 AD. Since that kind of overlap occurred at the beginning of the church age, it is not unreasonable to expect some overlap at the conclusion of the church age.[13]

The overlap during the Tribulation period makes sense in the light of the following insight from Gundry: "The regenerate Jewish remnant will belong to the Church then [converted during the Tribulation period] as now (Rom. 11:5) and will be Raptured at the posttribulational advent of Christ. That unconverted part of the Jewish nation who by God's special protection will physically survive the Tribulation (Rev. 7:1–4) will repent, believe, and be saved as they see their Messiah descending. But they will have missed the Rapture. Instead, they will enter the millennium as the natural-bodied subjects of the restored Davidic kingdom."[14]

Gundry's understanding of the Jewish sacrificial system during the Tribulation period not only makes sense in the light of Scripture but also in the light of the current condition of Israel today. The conclusion of the exile (Luke 21:24) began in 1948 and continues to this day. But as a nation Israel is in her homeland in unbelief. The nation as a whole has not accepted her Messiah. Her state of unbelief as a nation will continue through the Tribulation period up to the Second Coming. The nation of Israel is not the evangelistic force during the Tribulation period. The church, which includes believing Jews, will be evangelizing the nations and completing the great commission (Matt. 24:14).[15]

The conversion of Israel nationally occurs at the Second Coming (Zech. 12:1–14:8; Rom. 11:26). Gundry writes, "*But the reinstitution of the Mosaic system in Israel during the tribulation will not enjoy divine sanction.* General unbelief will still characterize Israel. God will not approve of Judiastic practices then any more than he approved of them during the period from the crucifixion of Christ to the destruction of the temple in AD 70. Worship in the temple will receive its sanction, not from God, but from the Antichrist, who 'will make a firm covenant' with the Jews only to break it by putting 'a stop to sacrifice and grain offering' (Dan. 9:27)" (emphasis Gundry's).[16] With this insight, we must set aside this as a weakness since the posttribulationists adequately explain it.[17]

Populating the Millennium

A better explanation of how the Millennium is populated is needed in the posttribulation model. When the Rapture takes place, according to 1 Corinthians 15 and 1 Thessalonians 4, all living believers are changed into glorified bodies. Furthermore, the common understanding of the judgment of the sheep and goats (Matt. 25:31–46) is that it occurs at Christ's Second Coming to determine who of those living at the time will enter the Millennium, and only believers will enter. Highlighting the weakness of posttribulationism on this matter, Charles Ryrie explains how pretribulationism provides the population for the Millennium, then writes,

In contrast [to pretribulationism], stands the posttribulational picture. The church, of course, will live through the Tribulation. Though some will be martyred, many will be protected and survive. The 144,000 Jews and the great multitude of Revelation 7 are included in the church. At the end of the Tribulation all living believers will be raptured, given resurrection bodies, and return immediately to earth in the single event of the Rapture and Second Coming. This would seem to eliminate all redeemed, resurrected people from the earth at that point in time so that there will be no one left to begin to populate the kingdom. If the wicked survivors are either killed or consigned to hades at the end of the Tribulation, then there will be no one left in An unresurrected body to enter the Millennium.[18]

We know the Millennium will be populated with people in mortal bodies (Isa. 65:21–25). So where do they come from? In the pretribulation model, those saved during the Tribulation period become the procreators of the millennial population. But in the posttribulation model there is no provision for that. John Walvoord writes:

If the translation takes place after the Tribulation, the question facing the posttribulationists is a very obvious one. Who is going to populate the earth during the Millennium? The Scriptures are specific that during the Millennium saints will build houses and bear children and have normal, mortal lives on earth. If all believers are translated and all unbelievers are put to death at the beginning of the Millennium, there will be no one left to populate the earth and fulfill the Scriptures. . . . The posttribulation position leads logically to an abandonment of the premillennialism altogether, or requires such spiritualization of the Millennium that it becomes indistinguishable from an amillennial interpretation.[19]

Some of the answers to this dilemma proposed by posttribulationists are not very convincing.[20] For example, Gundry populates the Millennium using the 144,000. But his reasoning is based on inferences and is strained.[21] As we continue this study, especially in chapter 12, we will revisit this issue.

Imminence

Posttribulationism may be weak on the issue of imminence. Pretribulationists say the recognizing of any signs to be fulfilled weakens the many verses that tell us we do not know when the Lord will return and to stay ready for him to come at any moment. But as we saw in the previous chapter, this issue is complex. It is very challenging to reconcile all the verses on this subject. Some passages give us signs of his coming, while others warn us that he will come "at an hour you do not expect" (Luke 12:40). Our starting point should not be the word imminence meaning "at any moment."[22] We must begin with Scripture and develop our concepts from the varied truths communicated on the subject. Doing that seems to modify the "at any moment" with biblical exhortation to be alerted by the signs that signal his soon return.

In Matthew 24:44, Jesus warns, "Therefore you also be ready, for the Son of Man is coming at an hour you do not expect." Then He gave the parable of the servant who said in his heart, "My master is delaying his coming." With that thinking, the evil servant began "to beat his fellow servants, and to eat and drink with the drunkards" (Matt. 24:48). That parable is immediately followed by two more parables indicating possible delay: The parable of the ten virgins, and the parable of the talents (Matt. 25:1–30). So, there we find a tension between immediacy and delay.

In chapter 6, we examined the distinction Paul made in 1 Thessalonians 5 between the world being surprised at his coming versus believers who are walking in the light not being caught off guard. Verses 2–3 describe his coming as a thief taking the ungodly by surprise. Then, in verse 4, he writes, "But you, brethren, are not in darkness, so that this Day should overtake you as a thief." So, there is a difference in the surprise element of his coming between the godly versus the ungodly. That must be taken into consideration when forming our doctrine on this subject. Certainly, there is ongoing caution for Christians to stay spiritually alert and ready.

For those of us schooled in modern, rationalistic thinking, we easily struggle with the tension between the "at any moment" possibility and a potential long delay. We struggle with the tension between the existence of signs and the possibility of Christ coming "at an hour you do not expect" (Luke 12:40). George Ladd suggests that our frustration may be due to our modern intolerance for paradoxical tension. God may have built into the revelation enough uncertainty about the timing that we simply need to continually stay ready. Ladd writes, "The predominating emphasis is upon the uncertainty of the time, the light of which people must always be ready."[23] He quotes Oepke saying, "The tension between imminence and delay in the expectation of the end is characteristic of the entire biblical eschatology."[24]

When we consider all the passages calling us to stay spiritually alert, (watching for and passionately desiring our Lord's return) with the possibility that He could come *at an hour you do not expect*, we are left with a biblical concept that is characterized by enough *uncertainty* that we must continually stay prepared.[25] Perhaps this is one reason the timing of the Rapture is not more clearly stated in Scripture (Deut. 29:29). But our concept of imminency must be tempered with a watchfulness that discerns the times and seasons (1 Thess. 5:1–10).[26]

We get a sense of how imminence will play out in Christ's return by examining what happened at the First Advent. Signs had been given in the Old Testament, but very few discerned the fulfillment of those signs. Most were so occupied with their daily lives that they did not see what was happening (Matt. 24:37–39). The priests and Pharisees studied the scriptures on the subject. Yet, they did not discern the signs either. Only a remnant of sincere, dedicated people was in tune enough with God to be in the know.

A carpenter named Joseph and a teenage girl named Mary were discerning events. A priest named Zachariah and his wife Elizabeth (Luke 1) were in that inner circle. Two prayer warriors, Simeon and Anna, knew as well (Luke 2:25–40). In contrast, the religious leaders in Israel, with all their study of the Bible, did not discern the first coming. There can be signs given, but we must walk in the Spirit to rightly interpret and apply them.

One sign that was given at the end of Malachi was the coming of Elijah. Even the disciples did not see John the Baptist as a fulfillment of this sign until Jesus later explained it to them. In Matthew 17:10, they asked, "Why then do the scribes say that Elijah must come first?" Jesus answered, "Indeed, Elijah is coming first and will restore all things. But I say to you that Elijah has come already, and they did not know him but did to him whatever they wished. Likewise the Son of Man is also about to suffer at their hands'" (Matt. 17:11–12). Matthew then comments, "Then the disciples understood that He spoke to them of John the Baptist" (Matt. 17:23). A biblical sign does not necessarily mean everyone will discern its fulfillment and know what is happening. In fact, the evidence is that most will not see it for what it is; most will be in the dark about what's going on even though signs have been given in Scripture (Luke 12:56). Only those in communion with God will understand the fulfillment of signs pointing to Christ's return.

I began this study thinking the doctrine of imminence to be a paramount concern in determining which Rapture theory is correct. Embracing a one-sided, "at any moment" understanding of Christ's return, I saw this as a significant issue favoring the pretribulation theory. I now think the biblical call to readiness is extremely important, but it can happen under any of the three models. Therefore, I now put far less weight on this issue.

Wrath

The posttribulation position on 1 Thessalonians 5:9 is criticized by the other two camps. First Thessalonians 5:9 says, "For God did not appoint us to wrath, but to obtain salvation through our Lord Jesus Christ." The pretribulation and midtribulation positions find in that verse the promise of a Rapture before God pours out his wrath upon the earth, especially during the second half of the Tribulation period.

Posttribulationists have three arguments countering this criticism. One is that God is just talking about *eternal* wrath. The context argues against that. Paul is talking about eschatological wrath. Another is that it is just promising exemption for the wrath poured out on the last day of the Tribulation period at the Second Coming, i.e., the one day that Christ returns. To support that argument "the day of the Lord" in verse 2 must mean only Christ's descent at the Second Coming. But the next phrase in verse 3 argues against that: "For when they say, 'Peace and safety!' then sudden destruction comes upon them, as labor pains upon a pregnant woman." That language indicates "the day of the Lord" should be interpreted more broadly, thus beginning with the Tribulation period.[27] Neither of those two posttribulation arguments is convincing.

However, the third argument is not as easily dismissed. It recognizes the context of 1 Thessalonians 5:9 as eschatological wrath poured out during the Tribulation period but understands the promise to be exclusion from God's wrath while still on earth. The opposite of wrath in the verse is salvation. The verse does not explicitly promise a Rapture out of it. The Greek word translated salvation (*sōtēria*) is used in various ways depending on the context. It can mean "deliverance, preservation, safety, salvation"[28] depending on the context. Therefore, it could just as easily mean preservation *in the midst* of the wrath as a Rapture *out of* the wrath. It could mean either one.[29] This is a strong argument in defense of the posttribulation position.

In the Old Testament we have examples of God saving his people by preserving them through something in some cases and in other cases taking them out before the wrath is poured out. There seem to be more cases of preservation than of taking out. Lot is an example of God taking him out of Sodom before the judgment was poured out. Enoch was raptured out before the great flood and therefore missed that judgment. However, Noah was preserved through it. The flood was poured out over the whole earth, but God preserved Noah in the ark. The three Hebrew children were preserved through the fiery furnace. These stories can be used to illustrate either form of salvation.

Perhaps the strongest Old Testament verse in favor of this posttribulation defense is Isaiah 26:20–21. It is particularly relevant because the context is end-time judgment. In fact, scholars refer to Isaiah 24–27 as the Apocalypse of Isaiah. In that passage the deliverance or salvation comes in the form protection. Isaiah 26:20–21: "Come, my people, enter your chambers, And shut your doors behind you; Hide yourself, as it were, for a little moment, Until the indignation is past. For behold, the Lord comes out of His place To punish the inhabitants of the earth for their iniquity; The earth will also disclose her blood, And will no more cover her slain."[30]

I entered this study thinking the wrath issue to be a strong argument for the other two positions and a crucial weakness in the posttribulation model. I no longer see it that way. God has not appointed his people to wrath. On the cross Jesus bore the wrath of God in our behalf. We will never experience it in any shape or form. But exclusion from that wrath could just as easily come by way of protection (as in the case of Noah) as being taken out (as in the case of Lot). Since either is equally tenable, this is not much of an argument against posttribulationism.

Conclusion

We have examined some of the major strengths and weaknesses of the three Rapture theories. We have tried to objectively process this subject with an open mind to learn what we can. [31] In the next section we will consider the Olivet Discourse of Christ and let it inform our thinking on this subject. The importance of that discourse in understanding end-time prophecy cannot be overstated. It is crucial to sound eschatology. There are exegetical challenges in interpreting it, but the benefits of diligently studying the material will be evident.

Most American Christians are bored, apathetic, and ill-equipped. They often come to church preoccupied with the things of this world, wanting to hear something that does not require much thought. The Sunday service becomes a gentle rest from a demanding workweek. It's not hard to understand how easily that happens. But that produces lukewarm Christianity. Life in Christ is a call to passionate discipleship. We must stir ourselves up in that and encourage others as well.

How do we keep our Christian lives vibrant and engaging? We do it by:

1. Learning: aggressively seeking wisdom from God's word
2. Serving: investing in the lives of others, and
3. Evangelizing: engaging the world with the good news of Jesus Christ.

When we're growing and on mission, Christianity is interesting and exciting.

Endnotes: Chapter 7

1. For a fuller discussion of this argument, see Blaising, et al., *Three Views on the Rapture* (2010), 100–22, 194–201; Brown and Keener, *Not Afraid of the Antichrist*, 126–30.

2. Rev. 20:4–6 divides the Resurrection into two parts: the Resurrection of the Just and the Resurrection of the Unjust. It is possible that John is speaking in general terms concerning the Resurrection of the Just—that he is not detailing divisions of that event. But the more natural reading is that the Resurrection of the Just occurs at this point in prophetic history which would tend to place it at the end of the Tribulation period. Since the Rapture is clearly connected with the Resurrection of the Church, that would tend to put the Rapture at that point in time. This is not conclusive evidence for the posttribulationism but does add support for that position.

3. Cf. Kittel and Friedrich, *Theological Dictionary of the New Testament*, vol. 7, s.v. "*episunagōgē*," by Wolfgang Schrage, 842.

4. Bickle, *Studies in the Book of Revelation*, 7.

5. Cf. John 11:48. Sliker points out the significance of ungodly people, especially leaders, feeling threatened that their position of power or lifestyle would be changed by God's revival intervention in the situation. This perceived threat is often the igniter of persecution against the people God is using. Sliker, *The Nations Rage*, 69-133.

6. Sliker, *The Nations Rage*, 69–121.

7. The distorted message of cheap grace that is popular in churches today will leave the listeners ill-equipped for end-time revival and end-time persecution. Christians navigate those realities well only out of a rich relationship with God, which is not cheap but is exorbitantly valuable. Bonhoeffer distinguishes between the "costly grace" taught in Scripture, in contrast to "cheap grace" that does not result in biblical discipleship. Dietrich Bonhoeffer, *The Cost of Discipleship*, trans. R.H. Fuller, (1937; rev. ed., New York: Macmillan, 1960), 30.

    Billy Graham warned professors of Christianity about the deception inherent in "easy believism." He wrote, "It should not be surprising if people believe easily in a God who makes no demands, but this is not the God of the Bible. Satan has cleverly misled people by whispering that they can believe in Jesus Christ without being changed, but this is the devil's lie. The Bible teaches that belief in Him changes a person." Billy Graham, *The Reason for My Hope: Salvation* (Nashville, TN: W Publishing of Thomas Nelson, 2013), 118.

8. Corri ten Boom as quoted by Jim McKeever, *Christians Will Go through the Tribulation: And How to Prepare for It*, 1978, Medford, OR: Omega Publication, 1980 [1978]), 5. In the mid-1970's I heard a leader from China tell how many

Christians denied the faith during that terrible persecution. He too warned American Christians to adopt a more biblical mindset toward suffering.

9 We know from Matthew 16:27; 24:29–31; 25:31; 2 Thess. 1:7–10 that the angels will also be with him.

10 Cf. Pentecost, *Things to Come*, 206, 220, 226–28.

11 Cf. Gundry, *The Church and the Tribulation*, 163–71. Ladd's answer to this weakness, although not entirely convincing, deserves consideration. His contention that "Revelation 19:6–9 is a *prophetic* hymn of the marriage supper of the Lamb and not an actual portrayal of the event (emphasis Ladd's)" has merit. The way the passage is introduced in 19:6 lends itself to Ladd's interpretation. Ladd, *The Blessed Hope*, 99–104.

12 Chafer, *Systematic Theology*, vol. 4, 340.

13 Cf. Gundry, *The Church and the Tribulation*, 19–24. Also see Robert H. Gundry, *First the Antichrist: A Book for Lay Christians Approaching the Third Millennium and Inquiring Whether Jesus Will Come to Take the Church out of the World before the Tribulation* (Grand Rapids: Baker Books, 1997), 134–40.

14 Gundry, *The Church and the Tribulation*, 24. In his comments about the 144,000 Jews, Van Kampen writes, "These 144,000 will become the firstfruits of unsaved Israel (Rev. 14:4), not saved until the Rapture occurs—which is why they will not be Raptured with the saints—and soon become the inhabitants of the Millennial Kingdom on earth over which Christ will rule." Van Kampen, *The Rapture Question Answered*, 155 (see also pp. 53–54). However, it is difficult to say these 144,000 are "not saved until the Rapture occurs" when the text speaks of them as redeemed and having the "Father's name written on their foreheads," and following "the Lamb wherever He goes" (Rev. 14:1–5).

15 For Gundry's understanding of the 144,000 Jews referred to in Rev. 7:1–8; 14:1–5, see Gundry, *The Church and the Tribulation*, 26–27.

16 Gundry, *The Church and the Tribulation*, 25.

17 In the pretribulation model, the heavenly visions in the book of Revelation seem to fall into place more chronologically than in posttribulationism. In the posttribulation model we are forced to explain them as interludes with little or no chronological significance; John is simply sharing the visions in the sequence received. This is a viable explanation, but the order in which events are recorded in Revelation should be interpreted as chronological unless other factors compel us to do otherwise.

18 Charles C. Ryrie, *What You Should Know about the Rapture* (Chicago: Moody Press, 1981), 76–77. Cf. Blaising, "A Case for the Pretribulation Rapture" in *Three Views on the Rapture* by Blaising, et al. (2010), 68; George N. H. Peters, *The Theocratic Kingdom*, vol. 2 (Grand Rapids: Kregel, 1952), 374–75; Archer, "The Case for the Mid-Seventieth-Week Rapture Position" in *Three Views on the Rapture* by Archer, et al. (1996), 116, 120–122.

19 Walvoord, *The Rapture Question*, 86–87.

20 See Feinberg, "The Case for the Pretribulation Rapture Position," in *Three Views on the Rapture* by Archer, et al. (1996), 72–79 for a critiquing of this debate.

21 Cf. Gundry, *The Church and the Tribulation*, 81–83. This issue is processed more fully in chapter 12 of this book.

22 The concept of "at any moment" imminence seems to be only one side of the biblical revelation. When we begin there and force everything else in Scripture to fit it, we may fail to arrive at a proper balance in the full revelation on the subject. Are we beginning at the right place in our view of imminence? Shouldn't the development of our theology on this subject begin with an inductive study of Scripture and allow that to define the theological concept?

23 Ladd, *A Theology of the New Testament*, 210. Cf. *The Blessed Hope*, 154–56.

24 A. Oepke, StTh 2 (1949–50), 145 as quoted in Ladd, *A Theology of the New Testament*, 210. Cf. Ladd, *The Blessed Hope*, 105–19. Moore writes, "It can, therefore, be expressed only obliquely. This accounts for the variety of the New Testament expressions for the nearness and for the use of terms which are either ambiguous or flexible. It accounts, too, for the otherwise irreconcilable juxtaposition of exhortations to watch expectantly beside warning to patient endurance in face of the possibility of a delay." A. L. Moore, *The Parousia in the New Testament* (Leiden, Netherlands: E. J. Brill, 1966), 173.

25 Of course, there is no uncertainty about the fact that Christ will come. The uncertainty is about the timing.

26 Gundry provides an extensive study of Bible passages on this subject. His insight leaves the reader careful about applying an excessively rigid understanding of imminence. Moo's analysis is equally stimulating. Walvoord's rebuttal of Gundry's analysis is not entirely convincing. To deal with this subject we should not begin with a concept of imminence and impose it on Scripture. Instead, we should analyze the tension of truth communicated in Scripture on this subject and incorporate that into our eschatology. Cf. Gundry, *The Church and the Tribulation*, 29–43; Moo, "A Case for the Posttribulation Rapture" in *Three Views on the Rapture* by Blaising, et al. (2010), 235–39; Walvoord, *The Rapture Question*, 165–69.

27 For debate on the meaning of "the Day of the Lord," see Blaising, et al., *Three Views on the Rapture* (2010), 29–34, 189, 201–206, 246–251, 268–269.

28 Joseph Thayer, *Thayer's Greek Lexicon* (Originally published by Harper & Brothers, New York in 1896) s.v. "NT: 5183." Accessed in Electronic Database: Biblesoft, Inc. 2010.

29 Cf. Ladd, *The Blessed Hope*, 84–85.

30 Michael Brown provides a competent defense of the posttribulation position concerning wrath in Brown and Keener, *Not Afraid of the Antichrist*, 81–96.

Cf. Hultberg, "A Case for Prewrath Rapture" in *Three Views on the Rapture* by Blaising, et al. (2010), 192–94; Ladd, *The Blessed Hope*, 120–29.

31 Any of us can get stuck in the way we view a passage or a subject in Scripture. David Sliker defines the problem this way: "Ideas or interpretations become lodged in a person's mind, and it can be problematical for them to think of Bible verses differently." David Sliker *End-Times Simplified: Preparing Your Heart for the Coming Storm* (Kansas City, MO: Forerunner Books, 2005), 5. We need the Holy Spirit to help us take a fresh, objective look at passages, rather than simply defending what we think we already know. We need a willingness to test our assumptions by what the Bible is saying.

SECTION III

OLIVET DISCOURSE

CHAPTER 8

Matthew 24:1–14: Conditions During Church Age

And this gospel of the kingdom will be preached in all the world as a witness to all the nations, and then the end will come.

Matthew 24:14 NKJV

In this chapter, we will begin an analysis of the Olivet Discourse. The Olivet Discourse is Jesus's prophetic message recorded in Matthew 24, Mark 13, and Luke 21. It is the most important teaching on end-time prophecy. In this discourse Jesus provides the overall structure of how history will unfold as it progresses toward the Second Coming. We will concentrate on Matthew's account since it has the most end-time material.

Challenges in Interpreting the Olivet Discourse

Before we launch into this study, we must acknowledge some of the challenges in interpreting this portion of Scripture. It is one of the most difficult sections of Scripture. Yet, it is absolutely essential to understanding biblical prophecy. D. A. Carson says, "Few chapters of the Bible have called forth more disagreement among interpreters than Matthew 24 and its parallels in Mark 13 and Luke 21."[1] Why is that so?

Prophetic Genre

The prophetic nature of the material allows for dynamics that we don't find in the less ambiguous genres like epistles. In prophetic material, we often have "the law of double reference" at work. We talked about that in chapter 1. In prophecy, there is often a partial fulfillment as a foreshadowing of the complete fulfillment in the future.[2]

In Acts 2:16, Peter quotes Joel 2:28–32 and identifies the events on the Day of Pentecost as a fulfillment of Joel's prophecy. But it was only a partial fulfillment. Joel 3:1–2 continues the prophecy: "For behold, in those days and at that time, When I bring back the captives of Judah and Jerusalem, I will also gather all nations, And bring them down to the Valley of Jehoshaphat; And I will enter into judgment with them there On account of My people, My heritage Israel, Whom they have scattered among the nations; They have also divided up My land." That part of the prophecy has not been fulfilled. Peter rightly points to the prophecy as predictive of the Acts 2 event. However, Acts 2 was not the final, complete fulfillment. In his discussion of this, Gundry writes, "The fulfillment of Pentecost must therefore be the first or precursive part of a double fulfillment."[3]

We have a similar pattern in Jesus's prediction of the abomination of desolation (Matt. 24:15). Its ultimate fulfillment will happen in the middle of Daniel's seventieth week at the end of the age. Paul deals with the event in 2 Thessalonians 2:3–4, and John deals with it in Revelation 13. However, there was a portend to this ultimate event in 70 AD when the temple was destroyed. The destruction of the temple foreshadowed events that would occur at the end of the age. While the destruction of the temple is addressed in the Olivet Discourse, the thrust of the narrative moves toward the final consummation. Matthew's focus is on the abomination of desolation that occurs three and a half years before Christ's Second Coming.[4]

This double application in the discourse must be understood for an accurate interpretation. Gundry identifies Payne's failure to do this as a fundamental error in that commentary. Gundry writes, "Yet, Payne must disjoin these verses from the end of the age in order to maintain that the fall of Jerusalem exhausted them and at the same time escape the fact that Jesus did not return 'immediately after' AD 70 . . . we should say that 'the tribulation of those days,' 'immediately after' which Jesus returns, has to do with a period of persecution and upheaval connected with a yet future abomination of desolation and only foreshadowed by the events during AD 66–70."[5] The double application of some of the Olivet material makes the passage challenging to exegete.

Uncertainty of Timing

Another factor affecting our interpretation of this discourse is the fact that Jesus himself did not know the day of his return. We tend to read the passage as if that were not the case. However, Jesus plainly told us this fact in Matthew 24:36: "But of that day and hour no one knows, not even the angels of heaven, but My Father only." Mark 13:32 is more specific. "But of that day and hour no one knows, not even the angels in heaven, nor the Son, but only the Father." That tells us something about the full humanity of Christ in his incarnation. But even more relevant, it tells us that Jesus gave this prophecy not knowing the timing of his return. That is why his predictions in this sermon are communicated with an element of uncertainty. He is subject to the Father and will return at the Father's command, no sooner and no later. Just as Jesus embraced that uncertainty in his submission to the Father, we embrace it and submit to our Lord's command to "be ready, for the Son of Man is coming at an hour you do not expect" (Matt. 24:44). Because of uncertainty about the time of his return, Jesus spoke to his immediate hearers with the urgency of being prepared at all times.

One of the hotly debated verses in Matthew 24 is Jesus's statement in verse 34: "Assuredly, I say to you, this generation will by no means pass away till all these things take place." Unfortunately, preterists hang their interpretation of this discourse on the insistence that Jesus has to be referring exclusively to his first century audience.[6] So, they claim everything in Matthew 24 was fulfilled when the temple was destroyed in 70 AD. That usually forces them to allegorize or spiritualize the coming of Christ and the events surrounding the Parousia. This is particularly disconcerting when the literal, visible, physical return of Christ promised in Matthew 24:30 is dismissed as a spiritual, invisible coming. The blessed hope of Christianity is Christ's literal return.

Mounce understands "the events of the immediate period leading up to the destruction of Jerusalem portend a greater and more universal catastrophe when Christ returns in judgment at the end of time." He agrees with Gundry's (p. 491) assessment that the double fulfillment "involves an ambiguity that needs to be accepted as fact rather than objected to on literary grounds." Mounce puts this in perspective when he writes, "The discourse began with two questions: the first asked when the temple would be destroyed, and the second, what would be the sign of Jesus' coming (24:3). The answer to the first is that it will take place in the lifetime of the present generation. The answer to the second is that the events connected with Jesus' return (vv. 5–29) are like the budding of a fig tree that indicates the arrival of summer. The exact time, however, (**that day or hour**), is known by no one (**not even the angels in heaven, nor the Son**), but only the Father (v. 36)" (emphasis Mounce's).[7]

Jesus prophesied in this discourse without knowing the time of his return. If the Father's time had been in the first century, the Parousia would have occurred in that generation. But the ambiguity of the prophecy also allows for that to only be a portend of a future fulfillment chosen by the Father. Baising points to this reality as an explanation for the way the discourse is expressed.[8]

Douglas Moo takes a similar position concerning Jesus's uncertainty as to when the Parousia would occur (Matt. 24:36). He writes, "He [Jesus] therefore addresses his followers as if they themselves might be present for all climatic eschatological events. Of course, they were not. . . he [Jesus] does not predict that they will be present for the eschatological climax but simply suggests that they might be. This way of presenting the Parousia, as an event that could take place in any generation (what we have called 'imminence' above), is found throughout the New Testament."[9]

We see Paul speaking in a similar fashion when he includes himself and his generation among those who may be raptured. Notice his use of the first-person plural in 1 Corinthians 15:51–52: "Behold, I tell you a mystery: We shall not all sleep, but we shall all be changed — in a moment, in the twinkling of an eye, at the last trumpet. For the trumpet will sound, and the dead will be raised incorruptible, and we shall be changed." Did Paul give a false prophecy in that text? No, he spoke with the biblical mindset of imminency. He does the same thing in 1 Thessalonians 4: 16–17: "For the Lord Himself will descend from heaven with a shout, with the voice of an archangel, and with the trumpet of God. And the dead in Christ will rise first. Then we who are alive and remain shall be caught up together with them in the clouds to meet the Lord in the air. And thus we shall always be with the Lord."

So, we must read Matthew 24 with this understanding of biblical imminency. Jesus would not have told his hearers that he did not know the day or hour of the Parousia if it were not relevant to their interpretation of his prophecy.

Redaction by Gospel Writers

The redaction of Jesus's discourse by the *inspired* writers of the gospel accounts must also be considered when interpreting this passage.[10] This adds a layer of analysis that cannot be ignored. I only mention this now. We will talk about it in more depth as we get into the teaching. I will only address one more exegetical challenge before getting into the text.

Addressees

Jesus speaks this message to his disciples (Matt. 24:3–4). But the exegetical question must be answered: Who do the disciples represent: Israel, the church, or both? These men were Jews, so it is possible that they represent the Jewish remanent. Of course, that remanent is particularly important during Daniel's seventieth week. Matthew wrote to his fellow Jews with the idea of affirming Jesus as the Messiah. Therefore, we would expect to see, and we do see, a strong Jewish orientation in his gospel.[11] But was Matthew writing only to Jews? Did the disciples represent only ethnic Jews? Many of us who are studying his gospel today are Gentiles. Is the message of this discourse relevant to us today?

As Jesus spoke to the disciples, He was shaping them as the foundation of a new community that would be known as the church (Eph. 2:20). That context is important for answering our question. The primary readers of Matthew's gospel (manuscript) would be Christians with the distinction of Jew versus Gentile erased during the church age (Gal. 3:28).

But many pretribulation dispensationalists take Matthew 24 as being spoken to the Jews and not to the church.[12] This conveniently answers certain difficulties that can be encountered in the passage. For example, Jesus says to his hearers in Matthew 24:15, "Therefore when you see the *'abomination of desolation.'*" With the pretribulation model, Christians would not see that event. If Christians are already raptured when the abomination of desolation occurs, it does not make sense for Jesus to talk about them seeing it. But if this discourse is only for Jews, Jesus's statement presents no challenge to the pretribulation theory.

If we take the position that the Olivet Discourse is only for the Jews, what do we do with the Sermon on the Mount and other discourses spoken to the disciples and other members of the Jewish nation? It would be inconsistent to apply the Sermon on the Mount to followers of Christ in the church, but not apply the Olivet Discourse to them. The early church considered Matthew's gospel as written for them and included it in the New Testament canon. We should not exclude the church from being part of the intended audience for this discourse.

On the other hand, Replacement Theology would say God is finished with Israel as a nation, and this prophecy is *only* for Christians.[13] We cannot agree with that position either because it allegorizes and spiritualizes much of the prophecies to the nation of Israel, in effect nullifying a literal fulfillment of those promises. The Olivet Discourse contains instruction to the Jews; that is evident in the statement, "then let those who are in Judea flee to the mountains" (v. 16). It also speaks to Christians as is evident in the warning, "and you will be hated by all nations for My name's sake" (v. 9) and in the promise in verse 14, "And this gospel of the kingdom will be preached in all the world as a witness to all the nations, and then the end will come" (Matt. 24:9–16).

So do the disciples represent the Jewish remnant or do they represent the church. I would suggest that they are representative of both, and we should read the passage with that perspective.[14] With that grounding, we will now begin our study of the Olivet Discourse.

Israel's Rejection of Messiah

To get Matthew 24 in context, we go back to Matthew 23. In that chapter Jesus pronounced eight woes on the Jewish leadership. As the official representatives of the nation, those leaders had rejected Messiah. Except for a small remnant, the common people will confirm this rejection when they demand Christ's crucifixion at his trial (Mark 15:11–14). The offer of Messiah to the nation of Israel has been rejected by the time we get to Matthew 23. Everything prophesied in Matthew 24 flows out of that reality.

Matthew 23:37 gives us a sense of the emotion Jesus felt over this rejection and the consequences of their decision: "O Jerusalem, Jerusalem, the one who kills the prophets and stones those who are sent to her! How often I wanted to gather your children together, as a hen gathers her chicks under her wings, but you were not willing!" If Israel had received her king, Jesus would have led them into the millennial blessing promised in the Old Testament. He would have gathered them under the safety and care of his leadership like a mother hen gathers her chicks under her wings. But they "were not willing!" We feel a little bit of what Jesus experienced when we present the gospel and people turn it down. We feel it when our children insist on going in a direction that will most certainly be harmful to them. Israel's rejection of Messiah was painful for him. It will be painful for the nation in the days ahead.

In Matthew 23:38, Jesus addresses Israel's current situation of pending judgment. Then he contrasts that with the different attitude they will have toward him when he returns at his Second Coming: "See! Your house is left to you desolate; for I say to you, you shall see Me no more till you say, 'Blessed is He who comes in the name of the Lord!'" (Matt. 23:39). He was telling the nation that they would not see him again until they are ready to receive him. The trouble that Israel will experience, especially in those last three and a half years before Christ's return, is not just punishment. It is a preparation for receiving Messiah. It is designed to work such repentance that they welcome Messiah at his Second Advent.[15] "For I say to you, you shall see Me no more till you say, 'Blessed is He who comes in the name of the Lord!'" That is a messianic quote from Psalm 118:26. The crowds had echoed it a few days earlier at his triumphant entry into Jerusalem (Matt. 21:9), but that proved to be a shallow, uncommitted celebration on their part. The Great Tribulation and the extreme distress prophesied in Zechariah 14 will prepare the nation to wholeheartedly receive Jesus as Messiah. At Jesus's Second Advent, Israel will say, "Blessed is He who comes in the name of the Lord!" The prophecies in Matthew 24 point toward that climactic day: Christ's Second Coming in power and glory. With that in mind, we proceed to Matthew 24.

Jesus's Prediction of the Destruction of the Temple

In Matthew 24:1–2, Jesus predicts the destruction of the temple. "Then Jesus went out and departed from the temple, and His disciples came up to show Him the buildings of the temple. And Jesus said to them, 'Do you not see all these things? Assuredly, I say to you, not one stone shall be left here upon another, that shall not be thrown down.'" We know from history that this prophecy was fulfilled in 70 AD when the Roman general Titus destroyed Jerusalem.[16]

We can only understand the conversation that follows when we know how central the temple was to the Jewish faith. They were awed by the beauty and majesty of the structure. But beyond that, the temple represented the presence of God and his favor on their nation. It is hard for us to grasp the significance of the predicted destruction of this center of Jewish worship. The disciple's response to the prophecy proceeds from that Jewish mindset.

Disciples' Questions in Response to Jesus's Prediction

These disciples respond by asking two questions in Matthew 24:3: "Now as He sat on the Mount of Olives, the disciples came to Him privately, saying, 'Tell us, when will these things be? And what will be the sign of Your coming, and of the end of the age?'"

In their minds, the destruction of the temple surely meant *the end of the age*. They had no clue that 2000 years would separate the destruction of the temple and the end of the age. So, they ran all this together in these two questions. The second question is a compound question. So, we could understand it as three questions:

1. "When will these things be?" What things do they have in mind? They are responding to the destruction of the temple that Jesus just prophesied.
2. "And what will be the sign of Your coming"
3. "and of the end of the age?"

Matthew does not record Jesus's answer to the first question in the straight-forward way that Luke does. Matthew only alludes to the destruction of Jerusalem as a foreshadowing of the greater, end-time event. For that reason, we will examine the answer to question one using Luke's account. Luke 21:7 records the question this way: "So they asked Him, saying, 'Teacher, but when will these things be? And what sign will there be when these things are about to take place?'" Luke is more focused on the destruction of the temple than Matthew.[17]

We need all three gospel accounts of the Olivet Discourse for our understanding of the message. Each writer has an inspired theological agenda for his gospel. The material included best serves that author's purpose.[18] For example, both Mark (13:3) and Matthew (24:3) specify this discourse as happening on the Mount of Olives and the questions being asked in private. This is absent in Luke's account.[19] The way Matthew handles Jesus's answer to the first question allows him to present a broad chronology of the prophetic future without undue attention to the 70 AD event. Luke redacted the discourse to fit his theological message. Matthew shared the prophecy in a way that suited his inspired purpose. Matthew focused on the questions, "And what will be the sign of Your coming, and of the end of the age?'" (Matt. 24:3). This distinction between Matthew's redaction and Luke's redaction will become more evident as we look more closely into the accounts.

So, what was Jesus's answer to their question concerning the temple? We find that clearly stated in Luke 21:20–24:

> But when you see Jerusalem surrounded by armies, then know that its desolation is near. Then let those who are in Judea flee to the mountains, let those who are in the midst of her depart, and let not those who are in the country enter her. For these are the days of vengeance,

that all things which are written may be fulfilled. But woe to those who are pregnant and to those who are nursing babies in those days! For there will be great distress in the land and wrath upon this people. And they will fall by the edge of the sword, and be led away captive into all nations. And Jerusalem will be trampled by Gentiles until the times of the Gentiles are fulfilled.

So, the sign that the temple was about to be destroyed was "when you see Jerusalem surrounded by armies."

Jesus goes on to tell them what to do when that sign (Jerusalem surrounded by armies) appeared. He tells them to get out of Jerusalem: "let those who are in Judea flee to the mountains" (Luke 21:21). That was contrary to the thinking in the day. When armies appeared on the scene, it was customary for everyone to flee into the walled city for protection. But here, Jesus tells them to go from Jerusalem into the more remote areas. The historian Eusebius tells us that in 68 AD many Christian Jews fled to Pella on the other side of the Jordon River and were spared.[20]

One way we know this passage was fulfilled in 70 AD is the prophecy in Luke 21:24: "And they will fall by the edge of the sword, and be led away captive into all nations [that is the Jewish exile]. And Jerusalem will be trampled by Gentiles until the times of the Gentiles are fulfilled."[21]

The city of Jerusalem would be controlled by Gentiles "until the times of the Gentiles are fulfilled." That is exactly what has happened for almost 2000 years. Then, as a result of the 1967 war, Jerusalem was recaptured by Israel. That was an astonishing prophetic event, moving the world closer to the end. Gentiles still trample Jerusalem. The Muslim Dome of the Rock is still there. But history is rapidly progressing toward the conclusion of *the times of the Gentiles*. We live in amazing times.

Signs Leading to the Great Tribulation

Now let us see how Jesus answered the compound question asked in Matthew 24:3: "And what will be the sign of Your coming, and of the end of the age?'" Jesus began his answer in Matthew 24: 4–14:

And Jesus answered and said to them: "Take heed that no one deceives you. For many will come in My name, saying, 'I am the Christ,' and will deceive many. And you will hear of wars and rumors of wars. See that you are not troubled; for all these things must come to pass, but the end is not yet. For nation will rise against nation, and kingdom against kingdom. And there will be famines, pestilences, and earthquakes in various places. All these are the beginning of sorrows. Then they will deliver you up to tribulation and kill you, and you will be hated by all nations for My name's sake. And then many will be offended, will betray one another, and will hate one another. Then many false prophets will rise up and deceive many. And because lawlessness will abound, the love of many will grow cold. But he who endures to the end shall be saved. And this gospel of the kingdom will be preached in all the world as a witness to all the nations, and then the end will come."

In those verses, Jesus is prophesying the conditions in the world leading up to the Tribulation period. What are the clues that tell us that? In verse 6 Jesus interjects this statement: "See that you are not troubled; for all these things must come to pass, but the end is not yet." Wars, pestilence, earthquakes can seem like the end of the world. I have never been in a level eight earthquake, but at least momentarily, it would be easy to think the end has surely come. However, as Jesus lists these signs, his statement is: "The end is not yet." Verse 14 also indicates the possibility of an extended time when these things are going on, prior to the end. Matthew 24:14: "And this gospel of the kingdom will be preached in all the world as a witness to all the nations, and then the end will come." That is our primary concern in this current church age: "preaching the gospel in all the world" (Mark 16:15). So, in 4–14 Jesus describes what will be happening from the time of this discourse up to the end time.

However, in Matthew 24:8 He says, "All these are the beginning of sorrows." The Greek word translated sorrows is *ōdin*. It more specifically means birth pains.[22] That is why the NIV is a better translation of this verse: "All these are the beginning of birth pains." This labor pain metaphor was also used in 1 Thessalonians 5:3: "For when they shall say, Peace and safety; then sudden destruction cometh upon them, as travail upon a woman with child; and they shall not escape" (KJV). The NIV says, "as labor pains on a pregnant woman." Of course, the emphasis there is on the inevitability of what will follow. But the metaphor of labor pains also implies something else. Every mother knows that labor pains grow in intensity and frequency the closer one gets to the end.

All these signs Jesus lists in Matthew 24:4–11 will be happening during the church age. But they will be building in frequency and intensity. In keeping with the birth pain metaphor, we will see them become much more intense as the Tribulation period begins in Revelation 6. Jesus lists 14 signs in this portion of Matthew 24 that will be characteristic of the church age. It is tempting to comment on each one, but we want to get an overview of the chapter and not get too bogged down in the details. I do want you to be aware of the warnings against deception in this passage and be aware that the Bible predicts an increase in deception and apostasy (2 Thess. 2:3) as we move toward the end. Here are the 14 signs:

1. Deception (vv. 4–5, 11)
2. False Christs (v. 5)
3. Wars and rumors of wars (v. 6–7)
4. Famines (v. 7)
5. Pestilences (v. 7)
6. Earthquakes (v. 7)
7. Persecution of Christ's followers (v. 9)
8. Offenses (v. 10): The Greek word here is *skandalizō*. We get our English word scandal from it. It means to trip someone up. One definition is "to cause to fall away."[23]
9. Betrayals (v. 10)
10. Hatred toward one another (v. 10)
11. False prophets (v. 11)
12. Lawlessness abounding (v. 11)
13. Love growing cold (v. 11)
14. World evangelism (v. 14):[24] While all kinds of negative things will be going on, the gospel will be going forth, and many will come

to Christ. With the massive increase in communication through television and the internet, this is happening on a scale never before experienced. So, what is the evidence that we are moving toward the end? It is not the existence of these realities; it is the increased frequency, intensity, and universality of them that points to the end.

In Revelation 6, we see these signs/activities released during the Tribulation period with such magnitude that one-fourth of the world's population is killed (Rev. 6:8)! Do you remember our discussion of the restrainer in 2 Thessalonians 2? Something or someone is holding back the Antichrist until God's timing for the Tribulation period. We are not told who or what the restrainer is. Because it has to be something or someone powerful enough to hold back Satan's plan, my best guess is that it is a reference to the Holy Spirit, but not necessarily through the church. Pretribulationists contend that the Holy Spirit in the church is restraining the manifestation of the Antichrist, and when the church is raptured, Revelation 6:1 can happen. That is a possibility, but it cannot be proven from the text. At any rate, the restraint on the Antichrist is removed, and in Revelation 6:2 he comes to the forefront.

Each of the four horsemen in this passage represents the Antichrist and his activities. These first four seals probably happen in the first half of the Tribulation period. Revelation 6:1–2: "Now I saw when the Lamb opened one of the seals [notice the restraint on this is removed as Christ opens the seal]; and I heard one of the four living creatures saying with a voice like thunder, 'Come and see.' And I looked, and behold, a white horse. He who sat on it had a bow; and a crown was given to him, and he went out conquering and to conquer." This depiction of the Antichrist looks so much like Christ that some teachers think it is representing Christ.[25] He is riding a white horse, like Jesus does in Revelation 19. But this is the Antichrist coming with deception. He conquers without firing a shot. He has a bow, but he needs no arrows because at this phase his weapon is deception and intimidation.

Revelation 6:3 releases the next phase of his activities. "When He [Christ] opened the second seal, I heard the second living creature saying, 'Come and see.' Another horse, fiery red, went out. And it was granted to the one who sat on it to take peace from the earth, and that people should kill one another; and there was given to him a great sword." The red horse represents war and bloodshed. And there will be a lot of it.

With verse 5 comes the black horse. "When He opened the third seal, I heard the third living creature say, 'Come and see.' So I looked, and behold, a black horse, and he who sat on it had a pair of scales in his hand. And I heard a voice in the midst of the four living creatures saying, 'A quart of wheat for a denarius, and three quarts of barley for a denarius; and do not harm the oil and the wine'" (Rev. 6:5). A denarius was a day's wages.[26] The black horse represents famine. A person would work all day to barely earn enough for one person to eat. The scales in the hands of the Antichrist probably represent rationing by the government. The Antichrist will measure out what people get, and because of all the wars, the resources will be scarce.

The pale[27] horse in Revelation 6:7–8 represents death, widespread death from disease, pestilence, and various causes represented at the end of verse 8. "When He opened the fourth seal, I heard the voice of the fourth living creature saying, 'Come and see.' So I looked, and behold, a pale horse. And the name of him who sat on it was Death, and Hades followed with him. And power was given to them over a fourth of the earth, to kill with sword, with hunger, with death, and by the beasts of the earth."

When the fifth seal is opened in verse 9–11, we see the result of the persecution of God's people during this first half of the Tribulation period. Whether they are Christians or Tribulation saints depends on whether you are a pretribulationist or posttribulationist. But they are people martyred during this Tribulation period. We know that because "their murderers still live in the earth."[28] Revelation 6:9–11: "When He opened the fifth seal, I saw under the altar the souls of those who had been slain for the word of God and for the testimony which they held. And they cried with a loud voice, saying, 'How long, O Lord, holy and true, until You judge and avenge our blood on those who dwell on the earth?' Then a white robe was given to each of them; and it was said to them that they should rest a little while longer, until both the number of their fellow servants and their brethren, who would be killed as they were, was completed." So, there is the end-times intense persecution that Jesus prophesied in

Matthew 24. This table will help you visualize the parallel of Matthew 24 with Revelation 6.

COMPARISON OF REVELATION 6 WITH MATTHEW 24

Rev. 6 verse	Seal	Imagery	Matt. 24 verses
V. 2	#1 White horse	Deception	V. 4–5, 11
V. 4	#2 Red horse	War	V. 6–7
V. 5	#3 Black horse	Famine	V. 7
V. 7	#4 Pale horse	Death	V. 7
V. 9	#5 Martyrs	Persecution	V. 9–10

Table 3. Comparison of Revelation 6 with Matthew 24

Conclusion

We have seen in Matthew 24, events that would follow Christ's crucifixion and intensify as history moves into the Tribulation period. Now Jesus mentions an event that serves as a milestone in prophetic history: the abomination of desolation. We know, from previous studies, that event occurs in the middle of the seven-year Tribulation period (Dan. 9:27).[29] In Matthew 24:15–21, Jesus said, "Therefore when you see the 'abomination of desolation,' spoken of by Daniel the prophet, standing in the holy place" (whoever reads, let him understand), then let those who are in Judea flee to the mountains . . . For then there will be great tribulation, such as has not been since the beginning of the world until this time, no, nor ever shall be."

In the next chapter, we will continue our study of the Olivet Discourse with this event which Jesus referred to as the abomination of desolation. It is a key time marker in the end times.

Endnotes: Chapter 8

1   D. A. Carson, *Matthew, Mark, Luke,* The Expositor's Bible Commentary, vol. 8, F. E. Gabelein and J. D. Douglas, eds. (Grand Rapids: Zondervan, 1984), 488. Cf. Wilkins, *Matthew,* 788; Douglas J. Moo, "Posttribulation Rapture Position" in *The Rapture* by Archer, et al. (1984), 190.

2   George Ladd talks about the way a historical event in both Amos and Zephaniah foreshadows an eschatological event. He writes, "The divine judgments in history are, so to speak, rehearsals of the last judgment and the successive incarnations of antichrist are foreshadowings of the last supreme concentration of the rebelliousness of the devil before the end." Ladd, *A Theology of the New Testament,* 199.

3   Gundry, *The Church and the Tribulation,* 196. Kaiser and Silva use this same passage to make the point. They write, "'Prophetic perspective' occurs quite frequently in the Old Testament prophets. It is the phenomenon of blending together both the near and the distant aspects of the prediction in one and the same version." Kaiser and Silva, *An Introduction to Biblical Hermeneutics* 143–144. Cf. Klein, Blomberg, Hubbard, Jr., *Introduction to Biblical Interpretation,* 305.

4   Cf. Fredrick Dale Bruner, *Matthew: A Commentary,* rev. ed., 1990, The Churchbook Matthew 13–28, vol. 2 (Grand Rapids: Eerdmans, 2004), 518–19.

5   Gundry, *The Church and the Tribulation,* 199. Cf. Payne, *The Imminent Appearing of Christ.* Mounce writes, "It is not uncommon for prophetic material to move between type and antitype without calling attention to exactly what is happening. Predictions of the future were of necessity couched in language taken from the prophet's own setting. The coming destruction of Jerusalem was an anticipation of the end of the age. The same essential principles are in play. To speak of the end of history in terms taken from the impending crisis was quite natural." Robert H. Mounce, *Matthew,* 1985, New International Biblical Commentary, W. W. Gasque, ed. (Peabody, MA: Hendrickson, 1991), 222.

6   There is an exegetical basis for taking this position. Bauer understands it this way in the Matthew 24:34 text. Fredrick William Danker, ed., *A Greek–English Lexicon of the New Testament and Other Christian Literature,* 3rd ed., based on Walter Bauer's *Wörterbuch zu den Schriften des Neuen Testaments und der fröhchristlichen Literatur,* sixth edition (Chicago: University Press of Chicago, 2000) s.v. *"genea,"* 191. However, he also recognizes the fact that this term is sometimes used to indicate "**those exhibiting common characteristics, race, kind** gener., as in **Luke 16:8**. . . ." Nolland also understands the term to be referring to "a single human generation," but also acknowledges that Matthew's "use of the term has a range of emphasis." John Nolland, *The Gospel of Matthew: A Commentary on the Greek Text,* The New International Greek Testament

Commentary, I. H. Marshall and D. A. Hagner, eds, (Grand Rapids: Eerdmans, 2005), 988–89.

Scofield acknowledges the common use of the term in Scripture for those living at one time but says it "could not here mean those alive at the time of Christ, as 'these things'—i.e., the world-wide preaching of the kingdom, the tribulation, the return of the Lord in visible glory, and the regathering of the elect—occurred then." He continues, "The expression 'this generation' here (1) may mean that the future generation which will endure the tribulation and see the signs, will also see the consummation, the return of the Lord; or (2) it may be used in the sense of *race* or *family*, meaning the nation or family of Israel will be preserved 'till all these things be fulfilled,' a promise wonderfully fulfilled to this day." C. I. Scofield, ed., *The New Scofield Reference Bible*, 1909 (London: Oxford University Press, 1967), 1035. Chafer (vol. 4, 316) and Pentecost (281) understand it in Scofield's second sense (*race* or *family*). In the light of Old Testament promises to Israel (like Jer. 31:37) and the satanically-inspired antisemitism seen, for example, during WWII, this could be the thrust of the promise.

In his commentary on Luke, Marshall surveys the many conflicting interpretations of the Olivet statement and identifies three that he thinks are most likely correct. I. Howard Marshall, *The Gospel of Luke: A Commentary on the Greek Text*, 1978, The New International Greek Testament Commentary, I. H. Marshall and D. A. Hagner, eds. (Grand Rapids: Eerdmans, 1989), 780––781. Given the diversity of interpretations of this statement (Matt. 24:34) it would seem unwise to base one's whole understanding of the discourse on this one verse. Gundry writes, "The emphasis on visibility and universality in vv 21–23 contrasts with false reports of a secret coming in vv 21–23 and rules out the positing of a spiritual coming shortly after A.D. 70." Robert H. Gundry, *Matthew: A Commentary on His Literary and Theological Art* (Grand Rapids: Eerdmans, 1982), 491.

7   Mounce, *Matthew*, 228.

8   See Blaising, "A Case for the Pretribulation Rapture" in *Three Views on the Rapture* by Blaising, et al. (2010), 39 – 40.

9   Moo, "A Case for the Posttribulation Rapture" in *Three Views on the Rapture* by Blaising, et al. (2010), 217. Cf. Archer, "The Case for the Mid-Seventieth-Week Rapture Position" in *Three Views on the Rapture* by Archer, et al. (1996), 116–17.

10   Redaction criticism is a "critical [analytical] method for the study of biblical texts. Redaction criticism regards the author of the text as editor of his or her source materials. . . . it focuses on how the redactor has shaped and molded the narrative to express his theological goals." "Definitions for Redaction Criticism," *Definitions*. Accessed at https://www.definitions.net/definition/redaction%20 criticism.

11 "There is a 'Jewishness' about this Gospel, as we see, for example, in Matthew's emphasis on the fulfillment of what is written in Scripture." Leon Morris, *New Testament Theology* (Grand Rapids: Zondervan, 1986), 115.

12 Cf. Chafer, *Systematic Theology,* vol. 5, 114–17.

13 Gundry also argues that the disciples represent only the church and not Israel. Cf. Gundry, *The Church and The Tribulation*, 133–34.

14 Cf: Blaising, et al., *Three Views on the Rapture* (2010), 112–15, 217–22; Archer, "The Case for the Mid-Seventieth-Week Rapture Position," in *Three Views on the Rapture* by Archer, et al. (1996), 123.

15 Ladd writes, "This is a saying that anticipates the repentance of Israel so that when he comes at the end of history to carry out God's judgment and final redemption, a repentant Israel will welcome him." Ladd, *A Theology of the New Testament*, 201. See Isa. 66:7–8; Zech. 12:10–13:1; Rom. 11:25–29.

16 Josephus, Flavius, "The Wars of the Jews, Book VI" in *Josephus Complete Works*, trans. by William Whiston,, (Grand Rapids: Kregel, 1981), 570–88. The phrase "not one stone shall be left here upon another" (Matt. 24:1) is hyperbolic indicating utter destruction. Cf. Craig S. Keener, *The IVP Bible Background Commentary: New Testament* 111–12.

17 However, Bock says, "The plural *tauta* is also significant, since it shows that, although the temple's fall is the question's focus, it is not the only topic." Certainly, in verses 27–31 Jesus addresses end-time events. This fact is important to our understanding of Matthew 24 because the same term is used in the question stated in Matthew 24:3. Therefore, even if Jesus did not address the destruction of Jerusalem directly in Matthew's account, it is alluded to there, and Luke's account deals with it in detail. Darrell L. Bock, *Luke*, Baker Exegetical Commentary on the New Testament, vol. 2, Moises Silva, ed. (Grand Rapids: Baker Books, 2004), 1663.

18 "They [the gospel writers] select events of Jesus' life and his teachings, guided not by comprehensiveness but by their purpose in writing. They arrange material not always on the basis of sequential order but with a view to impress upon the readers certain specific truths." Kaiser and Silva, *An Introduction to Biblical Hermeneutics*, 107.

19 Cf. Marshall, *The Gospel of Luke: A Commentary on the Greek Text*, 759. For a brief explanation of redaction criticism see Grant R. Osborne, "Redaction Criticism" in *New Testament Criticism & Interpretation*, Black and Dockery, eds., 197–224.

20 Eusebius, *Ecclesiastical History* 3.5.3. Cf. Gundry, *The Church and the Tribulation*, 133.

21 Green writes (p. 739), ". . . 'the times of the Gentiles' would mark a temporary season in which the Gentiles would occupy center stage in God's purpose, after which the spotlight would return to Jerusalem. On the other hand, with v 25

Jesus' eschatological discourse turns not to consider the place of Israel in God's plan but to the end time, marked by the coming of the Son of man." In our study we focus on the Matthew account. So, we will not explore the structure in Luke 21, which is provided by Joel B. Green in *The Gospel of Luke*, The New International Commentary on the New Testament, N. B. Stonehouse, F. F. Bruce, and G. D. Fee, eds. (Grand Rapids: Eerdmans, 1997) 731–32. Leon Morris notes, "There are some puzzling exegetical problems, notably those posed by the fact that part of the address seems to apply to the end of all things and part to the destruction of Jerusalem." Leon Morris, *The Gospel According to St. Luke*, 1974. The Tyndale New Testament Commentaries, R. Tasker, ed. (Grand Rapids: Eerdmans, 1980), 295. Cf. Pentecost, *Things to Come*, 315–16.

22   Kittel and Friedrich, *Theological Dictionary of the New Testament*, vol. 9, s.v. "ōdin," by Bertram, 667–674. See also Archibald T. Robertson, *Word Pictures in the New Testament*, 6 vols., s.v. "Matt. 24:8." Originally published by Harpers, New York in 1930. Accessed in electronic data: Biblesoft 2000. The labor pain metaphor is used in the Apocalypse of Isaiah (Isa. 26:17).

23   Strong, *New Exhaustive Strong's Numbers and Concordance*, s.v. "NT: 4624."

24   Alexander Reese sees support for posttribulationism in Christ's promise to be with his followers "even to the end of the age" (Matt. 28:20). Reese understands "end of the age" to indicate the time up to the beginning of the millennial golden age of Christ's reign on earth. During this age his followers would encounter fierce opposition, but he promises to be with them and empower them to fulfill the Great Commission. Reese writes, ". . . the fact that He said, 'I am with you always even unto the consummation of the age,' is proof that our Lord presupposed that His Church would not be removed from earth to heaven, several years or decades before the End. . . . according to Scripture the age that follows the present one is that of the kingly rule of Messiah. Moreover, Matthew xxiv. 3 shews that the consummation of the Age is Christ's Advent in glory and power to establish that Kingdom." Reese, *The Approaching Advent of Christ*, 108–09.

25   Cf. Ladd, *A Theology of the New Testament*, 674.

26   Smith, William, *Smith's Bible Dictionary*, (Peabody, MA: Hendrickson, 1990) s. v. "denarius." Originally published in London in 1863. Accessed in electronic data base: Biblesoft 2010. Cf. Matthew 20:2.

27   The color *chlōros* is "pale or yellowish like the grass when dried up in the heat." Zodhiates, *The Complete Word Study Dictionary*, 1477. Bauer has it as "***pale, greenish gray*** . . .as the color of a pers. in sickness contrasted with the appearance in health . . . " (emphasis Bauer's). Danker, ed., *A Greek-English Lexicon of the New Testament*, 1085.

28   Criswell, *Expository Sermons on Revelation*, vol. 3, 102.

29 See chapters 1 and 2 in this book. The classical interpretation of Daniel 9:27 is to see Antiochus Epiphanes's defilement of the temple in about 167 B.C. as the fulfillment of Daniel 9:27. But that is negated by the fact that in Matt. 24:15 Jesus speaks of this abomination of desolation, "spoken of by Daniel," as a *future* event. The event in 167 B.C. was a type of the ultimate fulfillment prophesied by Jesus in our text, to be followed by "great tribulation, such as has not been since the beginning of the world until this time, no, nor ever shall be" (Matt. 24:21). Hayford, ed., *The New Spirit Filled Life Bible*, s.v. "Dan. 9:26-27, One who makes desolate" by Coleman Phillips, 1136.

CHAPTER 9

Matthew 24:15–30: The Great Tribulation

So when you see standing in the holy place 'the abomination that causes desolation,' spoken of through the prophet Daniel. . . . For then there will be great distress, unequaled from the beginning of the world until now—and never to be equaled again.

Matthew 24:15–21 NIV

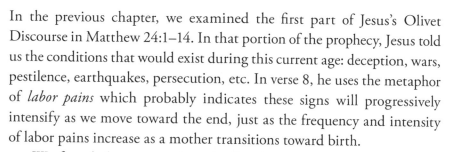

In the previous chapter, we examined the first part of Jesus's Olivet Discourse in Matthew 24:1–14. In that portion of the prophecy, Jesus told us the conditions that would exist during this current age: deception, wars, pestilence, earthquakes, persecution, etc. In verse 8, he uses the metaphor of *labor pains* which probably indicates these signs will progressively intensify as we move toward the end, just as the frequency and intensity of labor pains increase as a mother transitions toward birth.

We found these same signs in Revelation 6. In that passage the restraint is lifted (2 Thess. 2:6), and the four horsemen of the Apocalypse are released. As a result, the *severity* of these signs increases dramatically, so much so that one-fourth of the world's population is killed (Rev. 6:8). Try to imagine almost two billion people dying within a few years?[1] Between 70 and 85 million people died during World War II. That includes deaths by disease, famine, and other civilian casualties as well as military personnel. It was the deadliest military conflict in human history.[2] But in comparison to the devastation caused by the Antichrist, World War II was a minor skirmish. The World War II deaths are *only 4 percent* of what will be killed in Revelation 6, not to mention the multitudes who will die later during the Tribulation period (Rev. 9:18).

Abomination of Desolation

In Matthew 24:15, Jesus prophesied the abomination of desolation: "So when you see standing in the holy place 'the abomination that causes desolation,' spoken of through the prophet Daniel—let the reader understand" (NIV). That is an end-time pivotal event. It is the height of human arrogance and rebellion against God. It triggers an outpouring of God's wrath like this world has never seen.

We know from our study of Daniel 9:27 that this event happens in the middle of the seven-year Tribulation period.[3] "He [Antichrist] will confirm a covenant with many for one 'seven.' In the middle of the 'seven' he will put an end to sacrifice and offering. And at the temple he will set up an abomination that causes desolation, until the end that is decreed is poured out on him" (NIV). This is the abomination of desolation that Daniel prophesied.[4]

When Antichrist breaks his covenant with Israel and desecrates the sanctuary, he will unleash an unprecedented attack on the Jews.[5] His betrayal will be sudden and unforeseen by the Jews. They will be unprepared for the assault, and the only thing they can do is run. And that is exactly what Jesus tells them to do: "Then let those who are in Judea flee to the mountains. Let no one on the housetop go down to take anything out of the house. Let no one in the field go back to get their cloak. How dreadful it will be in those days for pregnant women and nursing mothers! Pray that your flight will not take place in winter or on the Sabbath. For then there will be great distress, unequaled from the beginning of the world until now—and never to be equaled again" (Matt. 24:1–21 NIV).

The language here is very similar to that used by Luke in his instructions for responding to the first-century crisis. This is one reason interpreters get the events confused. Both Matthew and Luke are quoting from Jesus's Olivet Discourse. But Luke is focused on the first-century destruction of the temple, and Matthew focuses on the abomination of desolation that occurs during the Tribulation period.[6] As we have said, the first-century event is a portend of the end-time event. For that reason, there are many similarities.[7] And in both cases, those in Judea will be unprepared for its coming. Therefore, in both cases, a speedy exit is the only means of survival.

In this discourse Jesus spoke in terms that his immediate audience would understand. Coming down off the housetop, for example, was directly applicable to the first century setting in Judea.[8] Everything Jesus says here makes sense to those who are listening to his sermon. But the message is this: make a hasty exit because the persecution will unfold rapidly. You will not have time to gather your things. Just get out as quickly as you can. That advice is applicable to the first-century Jews who fled Jerusalem in the first century, and it is applicable to those in Judea when Antichrist breaks his treaty during the Tribulation period.[9]

This is an example of how redaction criticism is necessary for interpreting this discourse.[10] We must understand that Luke quotes portions of the Olivet Discourse to communicate his message, and Matthew employs quotes from Jesus's prophecy to communicate the message God is giving through his gospel. If we just view the gospel writers as mere historians, we will have difficulty sorting this out. Why do we have three synoptic gospels instead of only one? God is giving us revelation in different ways through Matthew, Mark, and Luke. If that were not the case, God could have just given it in one gospel. What are the implications of this? It means Luke is not giving exactly the same message as Matthew. Each one is giving truth that the Holy Spirit directs for that author. Redaction criticism is valid because we recognize that the gospel writers were under the *inspiration* of the Holy Spirit in the selection of how they would present their message.[11]

So, Luke uses these quotes from Jesus to communicate the urgency of the situation in the first century, and Matthew uses quotes from the discourse to communicate the urgency that will exist in Judea in the middle of the Tribulation period. When we examine the differences between Matthew's account and Luke's account, this distinction becomes evident.[12]

Differences between Matthew's and Luke's Accounts

Consider the following differences between Matthew's account and Luke's account.[13]

Introduction of Scenario

Matthew and Luke introduce the subject differently. Luke 21:20 begins, "When you see Jerusalem being surrounded by armies, you will know that its desolation is near" (NIV). In contrast, Matthew 24:15 begins, "So when you see standing in the holy place 'the abomination that causes desolation,' spoken of through the prophet Daniel" (NIV).

In each case, the observation is to trigger the quick response. But armies surrounding Jerusalem is very different from the abomination of desolation in the holy place. Consider this: If Luke's readers in the first century had waited until they saw a desecration of the holy place, they would have been killed. It would have been too late to flee. We know that from the historical accounts. The first-century desecration happened *after* the people had been slaughtered and the temple was burned. Tasker and others point to Titus's soldiers carrying the Roman ensigns with the image of the emperor into the temple as the desecration.[14] Josephus says, "There did they offer sacrifices to them."[15] But observing that event as a sign for first-century Jews to flee would have been no help at all. The warning would have been meaningless. Commenting on this incident, John Nolland writes, "The nearest thing to a Roman profanation of the temple that Josephus reports happened quite late on, when the city and the temple were in flames."[16]

So, in verses 21:20–24, Luke is not talking about the end-time abomination of desolation that Matthew 24:15 references. He is talking about the destruction of the temple in 70 AD, which only served as a harbinger of the greater judgment that would come during the end-time Tribulation period. The events are introduced differently by the gospel writers.

Reference to Daniel

Matthew and Mark include the exhortation, "let the reader understand,"[17] which is absent in Luke. In Luke, there is no need for this exhortation to study the abomination of desolation in Daniel since that author is not making a direct reference to that. On the other hand, to put the abomination of desolation in proper context of future developments during the Tribulation, one needs to understand Daniel's prophecy.[18] For example, we know from Daniel 9:27 that the abomination of desolation happens in the middle of the seven-year Tribulation period. Therefore, both Matthew and Mark refer the reader back to Daniel, using the statement: "Let the reader understand" (Matt. 24:15; Mark 13:14 NIV).

The Time of Punishment

Matthew does not have the explanation recorded in Luke 21:22: "For this is the time of punishment [vengeance (KJV)] in fulfillment of all that has been written" (NIV). In His lament over Jerusalem, Jesus prophesied over that city: "Look, your house is left to you desolate" (Matt. 23:38 NIV). The destruction in 70 AD is a fulfillment of that prediction concerning the time of punishment (KJV: the days of vengeance), a prediction made prior to the Olivet Discourse. Luke revealed why this destruction came on the city in Luke 19:41–44: "As he approached Jerusalem and saw the city, he wept over it and said, 'If you, even you, had only known on this day what would bring you peace—but now it is hidden from your eyes. The days will come upon you when your enemies will build an embankment against you and encircle you and hem you in on every side. They will dash you to the ground, you and the children within your walls. They will not leave one stone on another, because you did not recognize the time of God's coming to you'" (NIV).[19]

Times of the Gentiles

Luke 21:24 includes the condition that follows the fall of Jerusalem: "They [those in Judea, especially Jerusalem] will fall by the sword and will be taken as prisoners to all the nations. Jerusalem will be trampled on by the Gentiles until the times of the Gentiles are fulfilled" (NIV).

That prophesies the exile of the Jews that began in the first century and has continued through the centuries during the church age. During that time, "Jerusalem will be trampled on by the Gentiles." Jerusalem will be controlled by Gentile nations.[20] How long will this go on? Luke says, "until the times of the Gentiles are fulfilled" (Luke 21:24 NIV). This statement would not properly follow Matthew's prediction of the abomination of desolation because there the exile and the times of the Gentiles is approaching its end, not its beginning. This is a significant clue that Luke is addressing the 70 AD event, and Matthew is addressing the end-time event.[21]

Great Tribulation

Matthew also marks the timing of his account with the statement in 24:21: "For then there will be great distress [tribulation], unequaled from the beginning of the world until now—and never to be equaled again" (NIV). "For then [that is the time marker: following the abomination of desolation event described in verses 15–20] there will be great distress [tribulation]."[22] Was there tribulation in the 70 AD event? Yes, Josephus tells us that 1,100,000 people were killed during the siege.[23] Horrific suffering accompanied that event.[24] But it was not a "great distress [tribulation], unequaled from the beginning of the world until now—and never to be equaled again."[25] Compared to the deaths of one-fourth of the world's population predicted in Revelation 6:8, the 70 AD destruction is relatively incidental, less than one percent! It was a local calamity highly significant to the Jewish people. But there have been events of greater tribulation since and will be even greater during the end-time Tribulation period. Matthew and Mark are using the abomination of desolation as a signal to indicate the beginning of the intense tribulation that would follow during the last three and a half years prior to Christ's Second Coming.[26]

Days Shortened

Luke does not include the statement found in Matthew 24:22: "If those days had not been cut short, no one would survive, but for the sake of the elect those days will be shortened." In the first century, the nations did not have the capacity to annihilate all humanity. That ability came with the development of nuclear weapons. Now and during the end time, the potential that "no one would survive" is very real.[27] Luke was not addressing such a time. In Luke's gospel the times of the Gentiles would *follow* the destruction of Jerusalem.

As Lightening from East to West

In his Olivet Discourse account, Matthew includes this vivid description of Christ's return: "For as lightning that comes from the east is visible even in the west, so will be the coming of the Son of Man" (24:27 NIV). Luke does not include that in his Olivet Discourse. Instead, he places that quote in Jesus's prediction of the Parousia in Luke 17:24.[28] This is a subtle difference between the accounts, but it is by no means accidental.

Immediate Return of Christ Following the Great Tribulation

Maintaining the chronological sequence of events, Matthew places the time of cosmic signs in the heavens and the coming of Christ *immediately* after the Great Tribulation.[29] Notice how Matthew 24:29 begins with the timing of these events. "Immediately after the distress of those days 'the sun will be darkened, and the moon will not give its light; the stars will fall from the sky, and the heavenly bodies will be shaken.' Then will appear the sign of the Son of Man in heaven. And then all the peoples of the earth will mourn when they see the Son of Man coming on the clouds of heaven, with power and great glory" (NIV).

In contrast, Luke simply states the future event in 21:25–27: "There will be signs in the sun, moon and stars. On the earth, nations will be in anguish and perplexity at the roaring and tossing of the sea. People will faint from terror, apprehensive of what is coming on the world, for the heavenly bodies will be shaken. At that time they will see the Son of Man coming in a cloud with power and great glory" (NIV). In Luke's gospel, what lies between his detailed account of the temple's destruction in 70 AD and the Parousia? It is stated in Luke 21:24: "the times of the Gentiles."

The Second Coming of Christ

Luke does not give details concerning the end-time Tribulation period the way Matthew and Mark do. But he does come along beside them in his description of the Parousia (Luke 21:25–27), which (in his gospel) comes *after* "the times of the Gentiles" (Luke 21:24).

Some preterists try to avoid the obvious implications of their erroneously identifying Matthew 24:15–22 with the destruction of the temple (70 AD) by spiritualizing/allegorizing the coming of the Lord described in Matthew 24:29–30 and Luke 21:25–27. They interpret the cosmic phenomena "symbolically as political disasters, and the gathering of the elect (Mk. 13:27) [according to their interpretation] refers to the mission of the church." They adopt the view developed by "J. M. Kirk (*Matthew Twenty-Four*, Philadelphia, 1948) and R. V. G. Tasker (*The Gospel according to St. Matthew*, 1961, 225–228) that in Mk. 13 (and Mk. 8:38; Mt. 10:28) parousia language is used symbolically to describe the fall of Jerusalem as the vindication of Jesus. . . ."[30] Using this allegorical method of interpreting the text, their view is that "the parousia took place in AD 70. . . ."[31]

The astronomical disturbances described in Matthew 24:29 will coincide with the Second Coming of Christ. "Immediately after the distress of those days 'the sun will be darkened, and the moon will not give its light; the stars will fall from the sky, and the heavenly bodies will be shaken" (NIV). The only reason to make that symbolical is that a literal interpretation defeats the preterist position. Everybody knows that those signs did not happen in 70 AD. Everybody knows that Jesus did not return in glory and power in 70 AD. So, you either abandon the preterist position, or you allegorize verses 29 and 30.

There is precedence for interpreting Matthew 24:29 literally. Look at the darkening of the sun when Jesus was crucified. All three synoptic gospels (Matt.27:45; Mark 15:33; Luke 23:44) tell us the sun was darkened that afternoon. It was not just symbolic; it literally happened. When the ten plagues fell on Egypt, Pharaoh responded because they were literally happening. There is no good reason to allegorize the coming of Christ in Matthew 24:30. There is no reason to allegorize the cosmic events surrounding his return either.[32] Of course, these physical manifestations reflect spiritual realities, just as the physical darkness did on the day of Jesus's crucifixion (Matt. 27:45). Gundry comments, "The falling of the stars refers to the shower of meteorites, and the shaking of the heavenly powers to God's displacing 'the spiritual forces of wickedness in the heavenly places (Eph. 6:12)."[33]

Matthew 24:29–30 says, "Immediately after the distress of those days 'the sun will be darkened, and the moon will not give its light; the stars will fall from the sky, and the heavenly bodies will be shaken.' Then will appear the sign of the Son of Man in heaven. And then all the peoples of the earth will mourn when they see the Son of Man coming on the clouds of heaven, with power and great glory" (NIV).[34] I have good news: That is really going to happen! John tells us in Revelation 1:7, "Look, he is coming with the clouds, and 'every eye will see him, even those who pierced him'; and all peoples on earth 'will mourn because of him.' So shall it be! Amen" (NIV).

In Acts 1:11, the two angels told the disciples, "'Men of Galilee,' they said, 'why do you stand here looking into the sky? This same Jesus, who has been taken from you into heaven, will come back in the same way you have seen him go into heaven'" (NIV). He ascended visibly in a glorified body. He will return "in the same way," in a glorified body. The King James Version says, "in like manner." The ascension was not an invisible, spiritual event. It was literal. It was visible. They saw him ascend. And the promise is, "This same Jesus, who has been taken from you into heaven, will come back in the same way you have seen him go into heaven" (Acts 1:11).

The language used in Matthew 24:30 is reminiscent of Daniel 7:13–14: "In my vision at night I looked, and there before me was one like a son of man, coming with the clouds of heaven. He approached the Ancient of Days and was led into his presence. He was given authority, glory and sovereign power; all nations and peoples of every language worshiped him. His dominion is an everlasting dominion that will not pass away, and his kingdom is one that will never be destroyed" (NIV). What a glorious day that will be![35] Now we will read Matthew 24:15–31, so we can appreciate the chronological flow of the text. It begins at the middle of the Tribulation period.

> So when you see standing in the holy place 'the abomination that causes desolation,' spoken of through the prophet Daniel—let the reader understand— then

let those who are in Judea flee to the mountains. Let no one on the housetop go down to take anything out of the house. Let no one in the field go back to get their cloak. How dreadful it will be in those days for pregnant women and nursing mothers! Pray that your flight will not take place in winter or on the Sabbath. For then there will be great distress [tribulation], unequaled from the beginning of the world until now— and never to be equaled again.

If those days had not been cut short, no one would survive, but for the sake of the elect those days will be shortened. At that time if anyone says to you, 'Look, here is the Messiah!' or, 'There he is!' do not believe it. For false messiahs and false prophets will appear and perform great signs and wonders to deceive, if possible, even the elect. See, I have told you ahead of time.

So if anyone tells you, 'There he is, out in the wilderness,' do not go out; or, 'Here he is, in the inner rooms,' do not believe it. For as lightning that comes from the east is visible even in the west, so will be the coming of the Son of Man. Wherever there is a carcass, there the vultures will gather (Matt. 24:15–28 NIV).

The King James Version erroneously translates *aetoi* as eagles. The NIV corrects that to vultures. This is a proverbial way of saying: It will be obvious! Verse 28 reinforces verse 27.[36] When you see a group of vultures circling in the air, you know there is a corpse at that location. You do not have to ask somebody where it is at or if it is there. You know! There may be an allusion to the millions killed at the battle of Armageddon. But the point is: Christ's coming will be an event that leaves no question that he has come. Jesus is making this clear, so people won't be deceived by false Christs. Now, in verses 29–31 of Matthew 24, we come to the end of the Tribulation period.

Immediately after the distress of those days 'the sun will be darkened, and the moon will not give its light; the stars will fall from the sky, and the heavenly bodies will be shaken.' Then will appear the sign of the Son of Man in heaven. And then all the peoples of the earth will mourn when they see the Son of Man coming on the clouds of heaven, with power and great glory. And he will send his angels with a loud trumpet call, and they will gather his elect from the four winds, from one end of the heavens to the other (NIV).

Warnings about Deception

Why does Jesus give the warning about deception in verses 23–28? It is a major concern in his mind. Remember in verses 4–14, he warned about deception during the church age. Like birth pains, deception will increase as history moves toward its conclusion. When the Antichrist comes in Revelation 6:2, he comes on a white horse with deception. That is the first thing he does.

Second Thessalonians 2:3 says, "Don't let anyone deceive you in any way, for that day will not come [the Parousia mentioned in verse 1] until the rebellion [falling away] occurs and the man of lawlessness [Antichrist] is revealed, the man doomed to destruction" (NIV). Now listen to the emphasis on deception in verses 9–12: "The coming of the lawless one will be in accordance with how Satan works. He will use all sorts of displays of power through signs and wonders that serve the lie, and all the ways that wickedness deceives those who are perishing. They perish because they refused to love the truth and so be saved. For this reason God sends them a powerful delusion so that they will believe the lie and so that all will be condemned who have not believed the truth but have delighted in wickedness" (2 Thess. 2:9–12 NIV).

Revelation 13 talks about the False Prophet who supports the Antichrist, the "first beast." Revelation 13:13–14 says, "And it [the False Prophet] performed great signs, even causing fire to come down from heaven to the earth in full view of the people. Because of the signs it was given power to perform on behalf of the first beast, it deceived the inhabitants of the earth. It ordered them to set up an image in honor of the beast who was wounded by the sword and yet lived [the Antichrist]" (NIV). Revelation 13 gives significant detail about the deception during the Tribulation period. When the Bible talks about end times, it consistently warns of deception.

We live in a day when deception has increased. There has always been deception. Ever since the serpent spoke to Eve in the garden, Satan has been persuading people with his lies.[37] But it is increasing rapidly. Anybody can be a prophet on the internet. The availability of false teaching has increased exponentially with the world wide web. That is one reason sound doctrine is so important in the hour we live. We must "contend for the faith that was once for all entrusted to God's holy people" (Jude 1:3). We do that primarily by faithfully proclaiming the truth.[38]

What is the greatest concern for our wellbeing in the days ahead? With the events that have occurred during the coronavirus pandemic, we are aware of plagues, shortages, and civil unrest. Some prudence needs to be exercised in managing natural resources. But when you weigh the massive amount of Scripture warning us against deception compared to making sure we have enough food on hand or making sure we are equipped to defend ourselves, without question the greatest concern is deception!

How do we avoid deception? We guard our hearts (Prov. 4:23). We do not allow place for any resentment or unforgiveness in our hearts toward others. We continually draw close to the Lord and follow him as our shepherd. We do not neglect this great salvation. We do not neglect gathering together unto the Lord.[39] We stay in prayer. We stay in the Word. We nurture a love for the truth. You are probably doing those things. But this is an encouragement to not grow weary in welldoing. Keep pressing into God. Keep feeding your spirit with his word. Keep worshipping God and praying. Keep seeking first his kingdom, and he will take care of you in any and every situation.

Endnotes: Chapter 9

1 The structure of the book of Revelation is debated among scholars. However, the statement made by martyrs during the fifth seal and the answer in 6:9–11 indicates that the first four seals occur before the end of the Tribulation with most expositors placing them in the first half of the Tribulation period. Cf. Pentecost, *Things to Come*, 187.

2 "World War II casualties," *Wikipedia*. Last edited June 22, 2021. https://en.wikipedia.org/wiki/World_War_II_casualties. Current world population is 7.8 billion. Using 1.5 billion deaths for his calculation back in 2002, Grant says, "That is more than all the wars in the last 200 years put together." And keep in mind that the deaths during the Tribulation period happen within a few years. The devastation is unimaginable! Grant R. Osborne, *Revelation*, Baker Exegetical Commentary on the New Testament, Moises Silva, ed. (Grand Rapids: Baker Academic, 2002), 283.

3 Interestingly, there is no mention of the Rapture of the church prior to Matt. 24:15. Considering the significance of the Resurrection of the Just, the absence of any reference to that event in those verses is telling and tends to support the posttribulation position.

4 See also Dan. 11:31; 12:11. Cf. Osborne, *Revelation*, 414.

5 Of course, Antichrist persecutes all followers of Christ, but the attention in Matt. 24:16–21 is on events in Judea.

6 Both Matthew and Mark focus on the abomination of desolation that occurs in the middle of the Tribulation period. To keep the presentation simple, we are concentrating on the comparison of Matthew and Luke.

7 In his commentary on Matthew, David Thomas writes, ". . . we have pre-delineated Two Great Days of Judgment. The one, which was to transpire in the destruction of Jerusalem and the utter abolition of the Old Hebrew Commonwealth; and the other, which was to take place at the end of the world, the termination of man's probationary career, and the irrevocable settlement of the destinies of the human race. One Day of Judgment was local, and the other is universal; the one has dawned and closed, and is a matter of history; the other still looms with a dark and terrible significance in the future." David Thomas, *The Gospel of Matthew: A Homiletical Commentary* (Grand Rapids: Kregel, 1979), 463.

8 Of course, Jesus would speak in the context of his day, and the gospel writers would do likewise. Applying the message in a future culture would be based on the principle being taught, in this case, leave immediately. Difficulties associated with the sabbath, mentioned in verse 20, would have relevance in modern Israel where the sabbath is observed. The shutting down of transportation opportunities on a sabbath day would make the flight more difficult. In Jesus's

day the roofs on the houses were flat and were used for various functions, like drying out vegetables, prayer, etc. "The staircase from the roof was on the outside of the house; one could descend without entering the house." Jesus was communicating urgency when He told them to not go back into the house to get anything (vs17). Keener, *The IVP Bible Background Commentary: New Testament,* 113. Bock insightfully points out that Luke does not quote Jesus's instruction to not go back into the house when he is speaking of the first-century destruction of Jerusalem (Luke 21:20) but does include it when he addresses the end-time crisis in Luke 17:31. Bock, *Luke,* vol. 2, 1678. Bock points out other contrasts between the Matthew/Mark accounts versus Luke's account as well (pp.1675–1682).

9   The instruction in Matt. 24:15–21 is given to people living in a specific region (Judea), whether living there in the first century or during the end-time Tribulation period. For that reason, this portion of Matt. 24 is of particular interest to Jews. However, the end-time abomination of desolation provoke consequences for God's wrath throughout the entire world.

10   Unlike higher criticism that undermines confidence in the authority of Scripture because of its false, naturalistic pre-assumptions, redaction criticism is a useful, necessary exposition tool. Cf. Klein, Blomberg, Hubbard, Jr., *Introduction to Biblical Interpretation,* 330; McQuilkin, *Understanding and Applying the Bible,* 30–32, 265–266; D. A. Hagner, "The New Testament, History, and the Historical-Critical Method" in Black and Dockery, eds., *New Testament Criticism & Interpretation,* 77–83. 199–226.

11   Failure to properly recognize the divinely inspired redaction by the gospel writers can easily result in misinterpretation due to *over-harmonizing* the synoptic gospels. Luke is zeroing in on the immediate crisis that will come in 70 AD. Matthew and Mark emphasize on the abomination of desolation that comes in the middle of the end-time Tribulation period.

12   After arriving at this conclusion through my own inductive study of Scripture, I was pleased to find others who came to the same insight. For example, Walvoord writes, "The portion of Christ's answer relating to the destruction of Jerusalem in A.D. 70 is found in Luke 21:20–24. The portion of Christ's answer dealing with the signs of His coming and the end of the age is given in Matthew 24:4–30 and includes the dramatic description of His Second Coming." Walvoord, *The Rapture Question,* 185.

Wilkins comes to a similar conclusion: "In this discourse we have historical and eschatological references, with Jesus prophesying both the fall of Jerusalem and his own Parousia. Luke focuses on historical details of the destruction of the temple and the fall of Jerusalem, events that happened in AD 70 (Luke 21:20–24), while Matthew and Mark give details that are difficult to see completely fulfilled with first-century events and thus point to a future fulfillment (cf. Matt.

24:15–22; Mark 13:14–20). Jesus does allude to the destruction of the temple in A.D. 70, but he uses these events to foreshadow end-time events." Wilkins, *Matthew*, 771. Cf. Ladd, *Theology of the New Testament*, 198.

Cranfield contends, "we must allow for a double reference, for a mingling of historical and eschatological." C. E. B. Cranfield, *The Gospel According to Mark*, Cambridge Greek Testament Commentary, C. F. D. Moule, ed. (1959; rev. and enl. ed., Cambridge: Cambridge University Press, 1972), 402.

13　These differences are so pronounced that G. Campbell Morgan thinks they are two different sermons. While that is possible, it is unlikely. Inspired redaction by the gospel writers is a more likely explanation of the differences. G. Campbell Morgan, *The Gospel According to Luke*, 1931 (Grand Rapids: Fleming H. Revell, 1992) 236.

14　This would be idolatrous and considered a desecration of the sanctuary. Cf. R. V. G. Tasker, *The Gospel According to St. Matthew*, Tyndale Bible Commentaries, vol. 1 (Grand Rapids: Eerdmans, 1961), 229.

15　Josephus, *Complete Works*, Book VI, 583.

16　Nolland, *The Gospel of Matthew*, 971. Caligula's plan to set up a pagan altar and standards is sometimes suggested as the first-century desecration, but that plan never got executed. Cf. Carson, *Matthew, Mark, Luke*, 500.

17　Matthew 24:15; Mark 13:14.

18　Cf. Moo, "The Case for the Posttribulation Rapture Position," in *Three Views on the Rapture* by Archer, et al. (1996), 190-92.

19　Bock comments, "Luke would probably suggest that the reason for the city's collapse was its failure to respond to the day of its visitation, that is, the coming of Messiah (Luke 19:41–44; 13:34–35)." Bock, *Luke*, vol. 2, 1679.

20　To discern the times, one must watch how history develops in the city of Jerusalem. It is easy for people to get focused on activity in their own nation or locality, but end-time prophecy revolves around Jerusalem and the nation of Israel.

21　This does not preclude the possibility that Luke is *alluding to* the end-time event and Matthew is *alluding to* the first century event. The destruction of the temple did foreshadow the end-time abomination. But the focus of each author is obviously very different. After discussing the terrible events that occurred in 70 AD, David Thomas writes, "Now, on the Great Final Day of Judgment, the attendant circumstances will be similarly terrible. Indeed, perhaps, the most terrible things which occurred in the destruction of Jerusalem are only faint shadows of what will occur at the end of the world." Thomas, *The Gospel of Matthew*, 471.

22　Matthew 24:21 NIV.

23　Josephus, *Complete Works*, Book VI, 587. From his limited first-century experience, Josephus identified the destruction of Jerusalem in 70 AD as the worst since the beginning of the world. But there is sorely inadequate support for identifying that event with the Matt. 24:21 statement. Josephus was a credible historian, but he was not inspired by the Holy Spirit, and he was wrong about it being the worst. Nolland quotes Josephsu: "Jos. *War* 1.12: 'Accordingly, it appears to me that the misfortunes of all people, from the beginning of the world, if they be compared to these of the Jews, are not so considerable as they were.'" Nolland, *The Gospel of Matthew*, 975.

When calamity strikes, people have historically jumped to the conclusion that it was the end of the age. Josephus seems to have made that erroneous judgment when the 70 AD event occurred. When the plague struck during the Middle Ages, many thought the end of the world had come. When the dust storms hit America during the depression, many thought the end had come. But events like that do not mean the end has come (Matt. 24:6). We know the end has come by the signs Jesus gave in Matthew 24:27–30. In Josephus's day 1.1 million Jews were killed. In Hitler's day six million Jews were killed.

24 For example, Josephus records a mother killing, roasting, and eating her child. Josephus, *Complete Works*, Book VI, 579.

25 Matthew 24:21.

26 Several commentators point out Mark's use of the masculine participle after the neuter abomination (13:14) as indication he is connecting the event with a person as Paul did in 2 Thess. 2. Matthew's use of the neuter participle may remind us it is an idolatrous object and event.

27 Matthew 24:22. Of course, the end of the human race could come through other means as well. But the Matt. 24:22 statement emphasizes the universality of the calamity, in contrast to the localized calamity in 70 AD. There is debate among scholars concerning the phrase: "but for the elect's sake those days will be shortened" (NIV). Some think that shortening has already been incorporated in the three and a half years designated between the abomination of desolation and the Parousia. Others inject the possibility that in mercy God might shorten the three and a half years. If that is the case, it adds another layer of uncertainty about the day and hour of Christ's return. Cf. Moo, "The Case for the Posttribulation Rapture Position," in *Three Views on the Rapture* by Archer, et al. (1996), 209.

28 Additionally, the warnings about deception that Matthew places in 24:26–28 records are also placed in Luke 17. Luke replaces the instruction in Matt. 24:17–18 with instruction to get out and stay out of the city (Luke 21:21). He places those instruction with his Parousia material in Luke 17:31.

29 "The main structure of the Olivet Discourse is quite clear. Matthew 24:4–14 describes the character of the age down to its end. Verses 15–28 describe the fearful events which will immediately attend the consummation of the age. They consist of three events: the emergence of Antichrist (v. 15), the Great Tribulation (vv. 16–26), and the glorious coming of Christ (vv. 27, 28). The following

paragraph (vv. 29–31) enlarges upon verse 27 to describe in greater detail the revelation of Christ when he shall come on the clouds of heaven with power and great glory. The rest of the chapter which contains the passages we are discussing gives the spiritual application, the main thrust of which is watchfulness." Ladd, *The Blessed Hope*, 112.

30 Those who confine this prophecy to the 70 AD event often point to hyperbolic language used by prophets in the Old Testament as justification for rejecting a literal fulfillment of Matt. 24:29–31. Indeed, examples of that can be found in the Old Testament. However, that does not automatically preclude literal fulfillment of events described in Matt. 24:29–31, which refer to the glorious, visible return of our Lord. It is not unreasonable to think there will be a cataclysmic convulsion of nature at the end of the age. Of course, nothing like that happened in 70 AD! For a scholarly defense of interpreting these events as prophetic hyperbole, see Jeffrey A. Gibbs, *Jerusalem and Parousia: Jesus' Eschatological Discourse in Matthew's Gospel* (Saint Louis, MO: Concordia Academic Press, 2000), 189–99.

31 Marshall, *The Gospel of Luke: A Commentary on the Greek Text*, 776–77. Marshall goes on to identify weaknesses of this view saying, "Nothing in the context leads us to believe that an unusual sense is to be found here; in fact the clear temporal sequence (Mk. 13: 24, 25) suggests that an event *after* the fall of Jerusalem is in mind" (emphasis Marshall's).

32 After grounding Matthew 24:29 in Old Testament imagery, especially Isa. 34:4, Donald Hagner writes, "The coming of the Son of Man, in short, will be attended by unusual phenomena in the sky." Donald A. Hagner, *Matthew 14–28*, Word Biblical Commentary, Vol. 33B, D. A. Hubbard and G. W. Barker, eds. (Dallas, TX: Word Books, 1995), 713. For Douglas Moo's three major arguments against the preterist view, see Moo, "A Case for the Posttribulation Rapture" in *Three Views on the Rapture* by Blaising, et al. (2010), 215. Cf. Revelation 6:12–14.

33 Gundry, *Matthew*, 487. Gundry attaches the following references to this statement: "Ezek 32:7–8; Joel 2:10, 31; 4(3):15; Hag 2:6. 21; Rev 6:12–13; *1 Enoch* 80:4; Esdr 5:4; As. Mos. 10:5." Mounce comments, "The 'heavenly bodies' (v. 29) are sometimes identified as astral divinities, but it is better to take the phrase in a more literal way." Mounce, *Matthew*, 226. Cf. Wilkins, *Matthew*, 782–83.

34 Various ideas have been proposed as to what "the sign of the Son of Man" (NIV) is in verse 30. Some have thought it to be the appearance of a cross in the sky. Others have suggested a flash of glory. But the most natural reading is to simply take it as a reference to "the Son of Man coming on the clouds" (Matt. 24:30) which all will see.

35 See also Zech. 14; 2 Thess. 1:6–12; Rev. 19:11–16.

36 "The readers are warned to disregard any such rumors of a Messiah who is already in the world, but hidden, for there will be no secrecy about the arrival of the Son of man. It will be as visible to all as lightening; unmistakable as a flood of vultures around a corpse." Francis Wright Beare, *The Gospel According to Matthew* (San Francisco, CA: Harper & Row, 1981), 470.

37 Cf. John 8:44; 2 Cor. 11:14; 1 John 2:18, 22–23.

38 Cf. 2 Tim. 4:1–4.

39 Cf. Heb. 2:3; 10:25.

CHAPTER 10

Matthew 24:31–44: Second Coming

So you also must be ready, because the Son of Man will come at an hour when you do not expect him.

Matthew 24:44 NIV

◆◆◆◆◆

Matthew 24 provides a chronological outline of events from the First Advent to the Second Advent. It is, therefore, an essential part of eschatological revelation. Our objective is to understand the main points in this discourse as a foundation for answering the question: Will Christians go through the Tribulation period? In this chapter, we will deal with some passages that scholars debate in determining the time of the Rapture.

Our last chapter concluded with the Second Coming as recorded in Matthew 24:29–31. To set this teaching in context, we will begin by reading those verses. "Immediately after the distress of those days [the Tribulation period] 'the sun will be darkened, and the moon will not give its light; the stars will fall from the sky, and the heavenly bodies will be shaken.' At that time the sign of the Son of Man will appear in the sky, and all the nations of the earth will mourn. They will see the Son of Man coming on the clouds of the sky, with power and great glory. And he will send his angels with a loud trumpet call, and they will gather his elect from the four winds, from one end of the heavens to the other" (NIV).

Gathering of the Elect (24:31)

Significant to our study is the debate on what is included in this gathering of his elect referenced in verse 31?[1] Who are the elect being gathered? Pretribulationists and posttribulationists differ as to the answer to that question.

Pretribulationist Dwight Pentecost interprets this verse as indicating the gathering of Israelites with no reference to the Rapture. He provides several statements by Old Testament prophets supporting God's promise to regather the Jews in the last days.[2] For example, Isaiah 43:5–7 promises the nation, "Do not be afraid, for I am with you; I will bring your children from the east and gather you from the west. I will say to the north, 'Give them up!' and to the south, 'Do not hold them back.' Bring my sons from afar and my daughters from the ends of the earth—everyone who is called by my name, whom I created for my glory, whom I formed and made" (NIV).[3]

John MacArthur does not identify the Rapture of the church with this verse either. He writes, "The gathering ones will include the 144,000 Jewish witnesses, their converts and the converts of the angelic preachers. They will include the Old Testament saints, gathered out of their graves and joined with their redeemed spirits. Those will all be assembled together before Christ and ushered into the glory of His eternal kingdom."[4] So pretribulationists usually see the gathering in our text as a fulfillment of God's promise to restore the scattered Jews to their homeland. They do not associate the text with the Rapture.

Posttribulation scholars see a reference to the Rapture of the church in Matthew 24:31.[5] Of course, this would include the Resurrection of the Just as well. Bruner explains, "This gathering is what the church calls the Rapture. Notice that the biblical Rapture occurs *after* the cosmic, public, and visible coming of the Son of Man. There is no such thing in Scripture as a secret Rapture before his coming. The coming and the Rapture happen *together* and, *in that order*, here and everywhere else in Scripture (cf., in addition to our vv. 30–31, also vv. 39–40 and 1 Thess. 4;16–17)" (emphasis Bruner's).[6] Commenting on the parallel verse in Mark 13:27, Ladd writes, "This appears to be the same event described by Paul as 'the Rapture' of the saints, when the dead in Christ are raised from the graves and the living saints shall be caught up (*rapiemur*) in the air to meet the returning Christ (1 Thess. 4:17).[7] Posttribulationists tend to include the final gathering of the Jews back to Palestine as part of the Matthew 24:31 event. But they also understand Matthew 24:31 as a reference to the Rapture.

Douglas Moo is probably right in saying this gathering is for *all* God's people.[8] This is the climactic event that concludes the current age. Therefore, God is not only fulfilling his promise to complete the regathering of national Israel to their homeland (in their mortal bodies) in preparation for the Millennium, but it is also resurrecting/rapturing the righteous Christians.

Certainly, such a conclusion involves some interpretation and is therefore subject to debate. However, it seems strange that Matthew would leave out such an important event as the Resurrection of the Just in his chronological account of coming events. A pretribulation Rapture would have fit it in before verse 15 in this chapter. If verse 31 includes the Rapture/Resurrection of the church, then it is posttribulational.

Before moving on, we will read Matthew 24:30–31 again to make sure we maintain the flow of thought. "At that time the sign of the Son of Man will appear in the sky, and all the nations of the earth will mourn. They will see the Son of Man coming on the clouds of the sky, with power and great glory. And he will send his angels with a loud trumpet call, and they will gather his elect from the four winds, from one end of the heavens to the other" (NIV).

Parable of the Fig Tree (24:32–35)

Immediately following those verses comes the parable of the fig tree. Matthew 24: 32–33: "Now learn this lesson from the fig tree: As soon as its twigs get tender and its leaves come out, you know that summer is near. Even so, when you see all these things, you know that it is near, right at the door" (NIV).

The point of this parable is that events will transpire that alert us to the soon coming of Christ. Some see the fig tree as representative of Israel. Other passages do teach us to watch events in Israel, particularly Jerusalem, as indicators of the times.[9] But in this passage, Jesus is not using the fig tree to teach us to look at Israel. How do we know that? Luke's version adds the phrase, "and all the trees." Trees in general bear leaves as summer is approaching. So, Luke 21:29–30 says, "He told them this parable: 'Look at the fig tree and all the trees. When they sprout leaves, you can see for yourselves and know that summer is near'" (NIV).

Jesus has just described the conditions that will develop near the end: the gospel will be preached in the whole world (Matt. 24:14); the Antichrist will break a treaty with Israel and set himself up in Jerusalem to be worshipped (Dan. 9:27; Matt. 24:15; 2 Thess. 2:4); there will be a time of tribulation such that the world has never seen, killing one fourth of the world's population first (Matt. 24:21; Rev. 6:8) and later one third of the population (Rev. 9:18); and cosmic disturbances will happen (Matt. 24:29). Jesus gave this parable to illustrate the fact that there will be indications that the end is near so that the children of light would not be caught off guard by his return but be fully prepared to meet him (1 Thess. 5:4–8).

Verse 34 is the most debated portion of the Olivet Discourse. It has been interpreted in a variety of ways.[10] "So you also, when you see all these things, know that it is near — at the doors! Assuredly, I say to you, this generation will by no means pass away till all these things take place" (Matt. 24:33-34). In this study, we can only deal with a few of the more popular explanations.

First Century Generation

Preterists rigidly identify *this generation* as the people living at the time Jesus spoke the Olivet Discourse. In favor of this interpretation is the fact that it usually means that in Matthew (11:16; 12:41–42; 17:17). However, we have seen some of the serious problems associated with that interpretation.[11] It leads to allegorizing the events in verses 29–31. A fundamental flaw in the preterist position is the insistence that "this generation" (*gena autē*) in 24:34[12] refers to those living in the first century when that interpretation simply does not fit the literal interpretation of the surrounding context; then forcing the context to fit that exegetical decision. The problem lies in the uncertainty of the antecedent for "this generation." It could refer to those living in 70 AD. If the context of the events described (especially vv. 29–31) fit that interpretation, we might be inclined to agree with understanding "this generation" as referring to those living in 70 AD. But they simply do not. And the only way to make them fit is to allegorize the context.

While acknowledging the uncertainty of determining "the antecedent in the author's mind," Wallace instructs, "*houtos* regularly refers to the *near* object ('this'), while *ekeinos* regularly *refers* to the far object ('that')" (emphasis Wallace's).[13] The nearest antecedent is the generation that sees "all these things" in verse 33. While some earlier generations may see *some* of these things (as the first century experienced), there is only one end-time generation that will see *all* these things. Debunking the preterist interpretation, Vanlaningham writes, "to assign **to this generation** the referent 'those living in the disciples' day who survive until AD 70 is somewhat ungainly in light of the contextually-immediate discussion of the events associated with the end (especially vv. 30-31, **all these things** in vv. 33 and 34)" (emphasis Vanlaningham's).[14] This exegetical mistake forces preterists to symbolize verses 29–31.

Even worse than allegorizing verses 29–31 is the conclusion drawn by some liberal theologians that Jesus simply gave a false prophecy. Obviously, the destruction of Jerusalem in 70 AD was not tribulation (*thlipsis*) "unequaled from the beginning of the world until now-and never to be equaled again" (Matt. 24:21 NIV). Obviously, Jesus did not return "on the clouds of the sky, with power and great glory" for all the world to see him (Matt. 24:30 NIV). Since, these scholars contend, *this generation* in verse 34 must—absolutely must—mean exclusively those in the first century, then they surmise that Jesus thought he would return then, but he was wrong. He gave a false prophecy![15] Could anything be more contradictory to the message of the New Testament? If Jesus was wrong in Matthew 24:34, then what else was he wrong about? What can we rely on? But in the next verse, Jesus says, "Heaven and earth will pass away, but my words will never pass away" (24:35 NIV). It is interesting that these erroneous teachers put all the emphasis on verse 34 but do not show the same confidence in verse 35. In verse 36 Jesus does say, "No one knows about that day or hour, not even the angels in heaven, nor the Son, but only the Father." But there is a vast difference between not knowing while knowing you don't know, versus making a false prediction. The idea that *this generation* can only be those in the first century simply does not fit with the rest of the discourse.

Uncertain Generation

Another explanation is that Jesus was speaking in terms of imminence in much the same way Paul spoke in 1 Corinthians 15:51–52 and 1 Thessalonians 4:17. This interpretation of verse 34 has considerable merit. Since we discussed it in chapter 8, we only mention it here.

Jewish Race

Some understand *genea* (generation) in Matthew 24:34 as a reference to a race, in this case the Jewish race.[16] This is a possibility, especially when we consider Satan's tenacious efforts to exterminate the Jews.[17] However, the context makes this interpretation unlikely. Dale Allison writes, "But, given that our verse immediately trails the parable of the fig tree, surely the chronological sense of 'generation' is more natural."[18] There are competent theologians who teach this approach identifying *genea* with the Jewish race. But the weight of evidence is against it.

Generation Living When Signs Appear

Perhaps the best interpretation is to understand *this generation* as a reference to those living at the time all these signs appear. After all, that is the context in which Jesus is making the statement. He gives the metaphor of the fig tree for watching events as indicators of the end, then says in Matthew 24:33, "So you also, when you see all these things, know that it is near — at the doors!" The key to understanding verse 34 is "all these things" in verse 33. The *Moody Bible Commentary* says,

> **All these things** (vv. 33, 34) refers to the signs mentioned in vv. 4–31. When these signs begin to come to pass, the people alive at that time can be assured that they will see His second coming as well. . . . **All these things** probably

include the world-wide preaching of the gospel message followed by the end (v. 14), the future abomination of desolation (vv. 15), the unparalleled world-wide tribulation for which God limits the days (vv. 21–22), the increase of false messiahs (vv. 24), followed immediately by cosmic upheaval (v. 29), the militaristic sign of Jesus' coming (v. 30), and then, presumably, His second coming which follows hard on the heels of these signs (v. 30; probably v. 33). The near-demonstrative pronoun **this** often refers to that which is near in the mind of the writer or speaker . . ." (emphasis Vanlaningham's).[19]

This is simply the most natural reading in the context. Commending this view, Darrell Bock writes, "What Jesus is saying is that the generation that sees the beginning of the end, also sees its end. When the signs come, they will proceed quickly; they will not drag on for many generations. It will happen within a generation."[20]

Warning about the Uncertainty of Timing (24:36–41)

In Matthew 24:36, Jesus begins warning his followers about the uncertainty of the timing of his return.[21] He provides signs to watch, but then pivots to the fact that even he does not know the day or hour. This creates a tension between watching the signs on the one hand and recognizing an element of uncertainty on the other. Our understanding of imminence must include both sides of this tension of truth.

As we examine verses 32–41, watch for this tension. "Now learn this lesson from the fig tree: As soon as its twigs get tender and its leaves come out, you know that summer is near. Even so, when you see all these things, you know that it is near, right at the door. I tell you the truth, this generation will certainly not pass away until all these things have happened. Heaven and earth will pass away, but my words will never pass away" (Matt. 24: 32–35 NIV).

Jesus has given us instruction for watching the development of events so that we are properly prepared for his coming. Now in the next few verses, he balances that with the fact that the day and hour will be unknown so that we should always stay ready. Verses 36–41: "No one knows about that day or hour, not even the angels in heaven, nor the Son, but only the Father. As it was in the days of Noah, so it will be at the coming of the Son of Man. For in the days before the flood, people were eating and drinking, marrying and giving in marriage, up to the day Noah entered the ark; and they knew nothing about what would happen until the flood came and took them all away. That is how it will be at the coming of the Son of Man. Two men will be in the field; one will be taken and the other left. Two women will be grinding with a hand mill; one will be taken and the other left" (Matt. 24:36–41 NIV). Verses 40–41 are particularly relevant to our study on the Rapture. Scholars differ as to whether the ones *taken* are taken in salvation or taken in judgment.

Pretribulationist John Walvoord argues they are taken in judgment. He writes, "In the illustration from 'the days of Noah,' those who are taken away by the flood are the ones who are drowned, and the ones who are left are the ones who are left in safety in the ark."[22]

Posttribulationist Robert Gundry concedes this is the context but gives reasons the ones taken are taken in salvation. He points out the difference in the Greek word (*airō*) used for taken in verse 39 and the Greek word (*paralambanō*) used in verses 40 and 41. He says, "The same word could easily have been employed had an exact parallel between the two takings been intended. Instead, we have the employment of another word which only two days later describes the Rapture (John 14:3)."[23] John 14:3: "And if I go and prepare a place for you, I will come back and take [*paralambanō*] you to be with me that you also may be where I am" (NIV).

These men are representative of their respective camps. Both scholars recognize Matthew 24:40–41 as happening at the Second Coming. Walvoord sees those taken as Christ's enemies destroyed at his coming and those left will be godly people in their natural bodies who enter into the blessings of the Millennium.[24] Gundry sees Matthew 24:40–41 as a description of the Rapture/Resurrection of the Just that occurs at the Second Coming.[25]

The suddenness of the event and the immediate separation of the godly from the ungodly should not be overlooked. These people in the days of Noah (vv. 37–39) and described in verses 40–41 are simply going about their daily business. They are not sitting on a mountain somewhere waiting for Christ's return. They are occupied with the things of this world to the neglect of the watching Jesus is calling for in this discourse. Bruner points out how similar two people were at work (vv. 40–41) and how dissimilar at the judgment! The wheat and tares may stand side by side up until the day of the Lord (Matt. 13:24–30). But on that day the godly will be saved, and the ungodly will be destroyed. We must not miss the main point Jesus is making. "The most obvious meaning of our text," Bruner writes, "is the *surprise* of the last day and the *incalculability* of that day's coming. The day of the Lord is both a surprising day and a separating day (Henry, 361)" (emphasis Bruner's).[26]

Exhortation to Stay Ready (24:42–44)

In verses 42–44, Jesus drives home the primary point of his sermon: Stay spiritually alert and ready for his return. It is foolish to try to calculate the days and somehow beat God at his own game. The signs will point us to his coming. But the primary admonition is to simply live in a way that keeps you prepared to welcome him.

In Matthew 24:42–44, Jesus gives the response necessary to everything he has said: "Therefore [in the light of what has been said, this is what you must do] keep watch, because you do not know on what day your Lord will come. But understand this: If the owner of the house had known at what time of night the thief was coming, he would have kept watch and would not have let his house be broken into. So you also must be ready, because the Son of Man will come at an hour when you do not expect him" (NIV).

The exhortation to "keep watch" draws on the image of a watchman at his post.[27] It is essential that a watchman stay alert and fulfill his assigned duty. If we are obediently doing the assignment the Lord gives us, we will be ready for his return. We are not to abandon our natural responsibilities; we are not to retreat and isolate ourselves from the harvest field. We are to be light and salt (Matt. 5:13–16). We are to be about our Father's business.[28] We are to be fulfilling the Great Commission given to us by the Lord (Matt. 28:19–20).

In Titus 2:11–14, Paul describes the way we are to wait for the blessed hope of Christ's coming. He writes, "For the grace of God that brings salvation has appeared to all men. It teaches us to say 'No' to ungodliness and worldly passions, and to live self-controlled, upright and godly lives in this present age, while we wait for the blessed hope—the glorious appearing of our great God and Savior, Jesus Christ, who gave himself for us to redeem us from all wickedness and to purify for himself a people that are his very own, eager to do what is good" (NIV). If we live in that mode, we will be ready for his appearing. Keep your hand to the plow and your eye toward heaven. Your redemption draws nearer every day!

Endnotes: Chapter 10

1   The word translated elect (*eklektos*) is the same word used in 24:22 and 1 Pet. 1:1. The reader's decision as to whom the disciples represent as Jesus's audience for the Olivet Discourse influences one's interpretation of the *elect* in 24:31. If Jesus is speaking to the disciples as representatives of the Jewish remnant, the elect will probably be understood as Jews being regathered to their homeland with no reference to a Rapture. If the disciples represent all Christ's followers including the church, then the inclusion of the Rapture in verse 31 is a possibility. See chapter 8, "Matthew 24:1–14: Conditions During Church Age," in this book for a discussion of whom the disciples represent as Jesus's audience for this discourse.

    Moo reasons, "Moreover, Jesus has not many days previously pronounced this judgment upon Israel: 'Therefore I tell you that the kingdom of God will be taken away from you and given to a people who will produce its fruit' (Matt. 21:43). It is unlikely he would then turn around and refer exclusively to ethnic Jews as the 'elect.'" Moo, "A Case for the Posttribulation Rapture," in *Three Views of the Rapture* by Archer, et al. (1996), 194–95. Cf. Ladd, *A Theology of the New Testament*, 226.

2   Cf. Pentecost, *Things to Come*, 425, 504–05.

3   In Deut. 30:4 God promises Israel: "Even if you have been banished to the most distant land under the heavens, from there the LORD your God will gather you and bring you back" (NIV).

4   John MacArthur, *Matthew 24–28*, The MacArthur New Testament Commentary (Chicago: The Moody Bible Institute, 1989) 58. *The Moody Bible Commentary* takes a similar position on this verse. While conceding the possibility this refers to a Rapture, that commentary says: "The phrase **WILL GATHER** (*episynago*) is used in the LXX in Ps 105:47 (English translation 146:2) for the regathering of the Jewish people to the Holy Land following God rescuing them (also the point of the sounding of the trumpet in Is 27:13, cited by Matthew in v. 31). In the OT, this gathering was not a 'Rapture' in which God's people would receive their resurrected, glorified bodies but appears to be an event experienced in natural bodies in which God gathers them into the millennial kingdom" (emphasis Vanlaningham's). Rydelnik and Vanlaningham, eds., *Moody Bible Commentary*, 1501.

5   The verb, *episunagō*, in Matthew 24:31 is the same Greek noun, *episunagōgē*, in 2 Thessalonians 2:1.

6   Bruner, *Matthew: A Commentary*, 514. Keener comments, "The gathering here is probably understood as 'a Rapture to heaven' as in 1 Thess. 4:17, but employing language from Jewish eschatology (Davis and Allison 1997: 364)." Craig S. Keener, *A Commentary on the Gospel of Matthew* (Grand Rapids: Eerdmans, 1999), 587. Cf. Ladd, *The Blessed Hope* (Grand Rapids: Eerdmans, 1956), 73.

7   Ladd, *A Theology of the New Testament*, 205. Cf. Wilkins, *Matthew*, 785.

8   Cf. Moo, "A Case for the Posttribulation Rapture," in *Three Views on the Rapture* by Blaising, et al. (2010), 222.

9   For example, the abomination of desolation (v. 15) occurs in Jerusalem.

10   For a history of interpretation of "this generation," see Bruner, *Matthew: A Commentary*, 519 cites Martin Künzi, *Das Naherwartungslogion Matthäus 10:23: Geschichte seiner Auslegung* (1970), 213–24. For a summary of the major views see Dale C. Allison, Jr., ed., *Matthew: A Shorter Commentary*, (New York: T & T Clark International, 2004, 432–33.

11   See chapter 9: "Matthew 24:15–30: The Great Tribulation." Cf. Brunner, *Matthew A Commentary*, 518–19.

12   *Autē* is the nominative feminine singular of *houtos*.

13   Daniel B. Wallace, *Greek Grammar Beyond the Basics: An Exegetical Syntax of the New Testament with Scripture, Subject, and Greek Word Indexes* (Grand Rapids: Zondervan, 1996), 325–26. While these points are a bit technical, they are so crucial to the interpretation of this discourse they must be addressed.

14   Rydelnik and Vanlaningham, eds., *Moody Bible Commentary*, 1502.

15   For example, McNeile comes to this conclusion. Cf. A. H/ McNeile, *Matthew* (1952 [1915]) 355 as quoted by Bruner, *Matthew: A Commentary*, 519.

16   Cf. William Hendriksen, *Exposition of the Gospel According to Matthew* (Grand Rapids: Baker Book House, 1973) 868; Chafer, *Systematic Theology*, vol. 4, 316; W. Farrar, *The Gospel According to St. Luke in Greek: with Maps, Notes and Introduction* (Cambridge: Cambridge University Press, 1910) 364; Morris, *The Gospel According to St. Luke*, 301.

17   For example, we see a diabolical effort to destroy the Jewish race, followed by God's protection of them in Esther 3–9. Hitler's attempt to exterminate the race is another example. Additionally, Dan. 12:1 predicts a similar conflict: "At that time Michael, the great prince who protects your people, will arise. There will be a time of distress such as has not happened from the beginning of nations until then. But at that time your people— everyone whose name is found written in the book— will be delivered" (NIV). God does promise to preserve the Jewish people.

18   Dale C. Allison, Jr., ed., *Matthew: A Shorter Commentary*, (New York: T & T Clark International, 2004), 433. Carson responds to interpreting "this generation" as the Jewish race or some other group identification by saying, "Such broad senses, even if they were lexically possible [I contend that they are lexically possible], would offer no help in response to the disciples' question 'when.'" Carson, "Matthew" in *Matthew, Mark, Luke*, 930.

19   Rydelnik and Vanlaningham, eds., *Moody Bible Commentary*, 1501–02. MacArthur writes, "Matthew 24:34 is an explanation of the parable of the fig tree. The idea is that, just as the budding fig leaves means it is not long until

summer, so the generation alive when the signs occur will not have long to wait for Christ's appearance." MacArthur, *Matthew 24–28*, 85.

20 Bock, vol. 2, 1691–1692.

21 "While believers should have Christian certainty on the central topics of the faith, *debatable end-time knowledge* is not one of those central topics. The true orthodoxy here is sanctified ignorance" (emphasis Bruner's). Bruner, *Matthew A Commentary*, 523.

22 John Walvoord, *The Rapture Question*, 188.

23 Gundry, *The Church and the Tribulation*, 138. Cf. Reese, *The Approaching Advent of Christ*, 214–15.

24 Witherington associates these verses (40–41) with Noah's experience rather than Jesus's statement in verse 31. He says, "The 'taken ones' are the unfortunate ones, swept away by judgment." Ben Witherington III, *Matthew*, Smyth & Helwys Bible Commentary, M. K. Elroy, ed. (Macon, GA: Smyth & Helwys Publishers, 2006), 455. Cf. MacArthur, *Matthew 24–28*, 75.

25 "But *one is taken*, to share in the blessings of being with the Lord (it is possible to understand *taken* in the sense 'taken for punishment,' but this seems less likely)" (emphasis Morris's). Leon Morris, *The Gospel According to Matthew* (Grand Rapids: Eerdmans, 1992), 614. France writes, "*Taken* is the same verb used, e. g., in 1:20; 17:1; 18:16; 20:17; it implies to take someone to be with you, and therefore here points to the salvation rather than the destruction of the one 'taken.' No indication is given of where they are 'taken' to; the point is simply the sharp division which the parousia will entail" (emphasis France's). R. T. France, *Matthew*, Tyndale New Testament Commentaries (Grand Rapids: Eerdmans, 1985), 348.

26 Bruner, *Matthew: A Commentary*, 527.

27 Keener, *A Commentary on the Gospel of Matthew*, 592.

28 Cf. Luke 2:49; John 4:34–35.

CHAPTER 11

Matthew 24:45–25:30: Watching for the Return

Therefore keep watch, because you do not know the day or the hour.

Matthew 25:13 NIV

◆◆◆◆◆

In this chapter, we continue to learn from the Olivet Discourse lessons about the coming of the Lord and how we are to respond to it. We concluded chapter 10 by noting the primary point Jesus is making in this sermon. He is exhorting all his followers to maintain an ongoing readiness for his return! In Matthew 24:42–44, he explicitly commands, "Therefore keep watch, because you do not know on what day your Lord will come. But understand this: If the owner of the house had known at what time of night the thief was coming, he would have kept watch and would not have let his house be broken into. So you also must be ready, because the Son of Man will come at an hour when you do not expect him" (NIV).

Importance of Personal Application

We can study biblical prophecy from the beginning of the Bible to the end. However, if we fail to obediently apply Jesus's instruction as stated in this discourse, it is all in vain. Are you living in continued readiness for his coming? Would his return today catch you unprepared or would it be exactly what you are living for?

The word *therefore* in verse 42 is a signal that this is Jesus's application of the teaching. This is the response required: "keep watch." The word translated "keep watch" is *grēgoreō*. In the Greek it is placed at the beginning of the sentence for emphasis. If this is what we must do, it is important to understand what the word means. The fact that it is in the present imperative tense indicates "constant vigil."[1] In the next few verses, we will see the importance of consistency—the importance of continuing in the faith. The fundamental meaning of the word is to stay awake.[2]

Paul's use of the word in 1 Thessalonians 5:6 is enlightening:

> For you know very well that the day of the Lord will come like a thief in the night. While people are saying, "Peace and safety," destruction will come on them suddenly, as labor pains on a pregnant woman, and they will not escape. But you, brothers and sisters, are not in darkness so that this day should surprise you like a thief. You are all children of the light and children of the day. We do not belong to the night or to the darkness. So then, let us not be like others, who are asleep, but let us be awake [*grēgoreō*] and sober. For those who sleep, sleep at night, and those who get drunk, get drunk at night. But since we belong to the day, let us be sober, putting on faith and love as a breastplate, and the hope of salvation as a helmet. For God did not appoint us to suffer wrath but to receive salvation through our Lord Jesus Christ (1 Thess. 5:2–9 NIV).

The contrast Paul is making is between the godly and the ungodly. Wicked people live in a kind of stupor—unaware of the reality around them, like a person that is asleep. The deceitfulness of sin is making them insensitive to the times and seasons. They are saying, "peace and safety" when "sudden destruction" (KJV) is right around the corner. In contrast, God's people are to know the times and seasons and live in a way that keeps them prepared for what is ahead.[3] The moral nature of this call to alertness is evident in the description Paul gives in verse 8: "let us be sober, putting on faith and love as a breastplate, and the hope of salvation as a helmet" (1 Thess. 5:8 NIV).

The exhortation in Revelation 16:15 reinforces this concept. "Look, I [Jesus] come like a thief! Blessed is the one who stays awake [*grēgoreō*] and remains clothed, so as not to go naked and be shamefully exposed" (NIV). It is not sitting on a mountain looking at the sky. It is being clothed in righteousness and living a life of purity.

This call to stay spiritually alert dominates the rest of Matthew 24 and all of chapter 25. We will make a quick survey of those verses since they are a part of the Olivet Discourse. In the remainder of Matthew 24, Jesus gives the parable of the unfaithful servant, warning us to stay faithful and prepared for his coming. Then, in chapter 25, he gives two more parables and a description of the judgment that follows his Second Coming. All this material revolves around the call to be ready for his return at all times. Each parable highlights a specific aspect of the way we are to watch for his coming.[4] In this chapter, we will deal with the three parables, and in the next chapter we will examine the judgment of the sheep and goats. Although we must segment Matthew 24 and 25 in this study, we should remember this is all one sermon. We must keep the flow and connection of the whole message in mind.

Parable of the Unfaithful Servant (Matt. 24:45–51)

In Matthew 24:45–51, Jesus illustrates his exhortation to be vigilant and ready with a story about a servant who failed to do that. The illustration alerts us to the danger of not continuing in welldoing.[5] Jesus introduces the parable with a question. "Who then is the faithful and wise servant, whom the master has put in charge of the servants in his household to give them their food at the proper time? It will be good for that servant whose master finds him doing so when he returns. Truly I tell you, he will put him in charge of all his possessions. But suppose that servant is wicked and says to himself, 'My master is staying away a long time,' and he then begins to beat his fellow servants and to eat and drink with drunkards. The master of that servant will come on a day when he does not expect him and at an hour he is not aware of. He will cut him to pieces and assign him a place with the hypocrites, where there will be weeping and gnashing of teeth" (NIV).

First, in verse 45, he uses two words to describe the servant who is ready: "*faithful and wise.*" The word translated faithful is *pistos*. In this context, it means being trustworthy, faithful, and dependable.[6] Jesus uses this term eight times in the next chapter when he gives the parable of the Talents. To the servants who increased the talents entrusted to them, Jesus says, "Well done, good and faithful servant! You have been faithful with a few things; I will put you in charge of many things. Come and share your master's happiness!" (25:21,23 NIV).[7]

The second word used to describe the watchful servant is *phronimos*, translated wise. It could be translated sensible, thoughtful, or prudent.[8] It is the same word used to describe the wise (*phronimos*) virgins in the parable of the ten virgins. So, if we want to know what Jesus means when he tells us to be ready for his return, these two descriptive terms should characterize the behavior of the watchful, prepared servant.

The main point Jesus is making in this parable is that we must persevere in welldoing. We must continue to live godly lives. This parable is sometimes called the parable of the faithful and unfaithful servant. However, that title can be misleading since there is only one servant in the story. It is the story of a servant who starts out right, but then forsakes that path, "and he then begins to beat his fellow servants and to eat and drink with drunkards" (Matt. 24:49). "The word '*that*' in the phrase '*that wicked servant*' certifies that we are dealing with the *same* servant, the one who was good in the preceding verses (Alfons Weiser, *Die Knechtsgleichnisse*, 1971, 5), and is therefore a warning: 'Watch out, 'good servant,' for you can turn bad very quickly' (cf. Davies and Allison, 3:386)" (emphasis Bruner's).[9]

Perseverance is essential for salvation. Both Calvinists and Arminians recognize that biblical fact. If a professor of the faith fails to persevere in welldoing, Calvinists take that as an indication that the person was never genuinely converted in the first place. Arminians recognize that possibility but also know the person could have been saved but turned from the truth.[10] The point Jesus makes in this story is that a person must not just begin well. The person must continue doing the will of the Father. Paul wrote to the Christians in Colosse, "Once you were alienated from God and were enemies in your minds because of your evil behavior. But now he has reconciled you by Christ's physical body through death to present you holy in his sight, without blemish and free from accusation— if you continue in your faith, established and firm, and do not move from the hope held out in the gospel" (Col. 1:21–23 NIV). "If" is a small word in Scripture, but we dare not ignore it. Earlier in this discourse, Jesus talked about the persecutions Christians would experience in this age (Matt. 24:9–10). Then he made this simple statement: "But the one who stands firm to the end will be saved" (Matt. 24:13 NIV). The evil servant in this parable did not stand firm to the end.[11]

God taught Israel this principle in Ezekiel 33:12–16:

> Therefore, son of man, say to your people, 'If someone who
> is righteous disobeys, that person's former righteousness
> will count for nothing. And if someone who is wicked
> repents, that person's former wickedness will not bring
> condemnation. The righteous person who sins will not be
> allowed to live even though they were formerly righteous.'
> If I tell a righteous person that they will surely live, but
> then they trust in their righteousness and do evil, none
> of the righteous things that person has done will be
> remembered; they will die for the evil they have done.
> And if I say to a wicked person, 'You will surely die,' but
> they then turn away from their sin and do what is just and
> right— if they give back what they took in pledge for a
> loan, return what they have stolen, follow the decrees that
> give life, and do no evil—that person will surely live; they
> will not die. None of the sins that person has committed
> will be remembered against them. They have done what
> is just and right; they will surely live (NIV).

Of course, we all like the part of this that offers forgiveness to the one who has sinned. But the other side of that is that one must continue living in obedience to the Lord.

Israel's response to this was somewhat predictable. Ezekiel 33:17–20: "Yet your people say, 'The way of the Lord is not just.' But it is their way that is not just. If a righteous person turns from their righteousness and does evil, they will die for it. And if a wicked person turns away from their wickedness and does what is just and right, they will live by doing so. Yet you Israelites say, 'The way of the Lord is not just.' But I will judge each of you according to your own ways" (NIV). God is not weighing the accumulation of righteous acts against the accumulation of unrighteous acts. Instead, he is looking on the heart and judging righteously.

The behavioral direction a person takes in life reveals that inner condition. The most important issue is not the merit points we accumulate through pious acts. It is what we ultimately become (Rom. 8:29)![12] In this parable, the servant's true heart condition was ultimately revealed.

The reason this servant turned from his faithful service was the perceived delay of the master's return. Matthew 24:48 provides insight into his thinking: "But suppose that servant is wicked and says to himself, 'My master is staying away a long time,' and he then begins to beat his fellow servants and to eat and drink with drunkards" (NIV).

Theme of Possible Delay and Unexpected Time of Return

All of these parables present the possibility of a *delayed* return. In the parable of the ten virgins, we read, "The bridegroom was a long time in coming, and they all became drowsy and fell asleep" (Matt. 25:5 NIV). The parable of the talents says, "After a long time the master of those servants returned and settled accounts with them" (Matt. 25:19 NIV).

What could possibly delay Christ's return? Jesus said, "And this gospel of the kingdom will be preached in the whole world as a testimony to all nations, and then the end will come" (Matt. 24:14 NIV). That must happen before the end can come.[13] It has been 2,000 years since Jesus spoke these words.

The delay has caused some people to even scoff at the promise. Peter addressed this when he wrote,

> Above all, you must understand that in the last days scoffers will come, scoffing and following their own evil desires. They will say, "Where is this 'coming' he promised? Ever since our ancestors died, everything goes on as it has since the beginning of creation." But they deliberately

forget that long ago by God's word the heavens came
into being and the earth was formed out of water and
by water. By these waters also the world of that time was
deluged and destroyed. By the same word the present
heavens and earth are reserved for fire, being kept for the
day of judgment and destruction of the ungodly. But do
not forget this one thing, dear friends: With the Lord a
day is like a thousand years, and a thousand years are like
a day. The Lord is not slow in keeping his promise, as
some understand slowness. Instead he is patient with you,
not wanting anyone to perish, but everyone to come to
repentance. But the day of the Lord will come like a thief.
The heavens will disappear with a roar; the elements will
be destroyed by fire, and the earth and everything done in
it will be laid bare Since everything will be destroyed in
this way, what kind of people ought you to be? You ought
to live holy and godly lives as you look forward to the day
of God and speed its coming. That day will bring about
the destruction of the heavens by fire, and the elements
will melt in the heat (2 Pet. 3:3–12 NIV).

Notice how Peter brings all this down to our lifestyle: "Since everything
will be destroyed in this way, what kind of people ought you to be? You
ought to live holy and godly lives as you look forward to the day of God
and speed its coming" (2 Pet. 3:11–12 NIV). The kind of watching Jesus
calls for and Peter confirms is to *live holy and godly lives*. It is a mindset in
which we "look forward to the day of God and speed its coming" (2 Pet.
3:12 NIV). That is how we stay prepared for Christ's return.

The possibility of the Lord's return taking us by surprise is taught in
the New Testament. It will certainly take the world by surprise. The only
way it doesn't take us by surprise is if we stay spiritually alert doing the
will of the Father. The warning in this parable is the timing of his return
is unknown and may come at an unexpected time. In this story, Jesus says,
"The master of that servant will come on a day when he does not expect
him and at an hour he is not aware of" (Matt. 24:50 NIV).

The metaphor of the thief coming in the night when the household is asleep is often used to communicate this.[14] Jesus used it right before this story. Matthew 24:43–44: "But understand this: If the owner of the house had known at what time of night the thief was coming he would have kept watch and would not have let his house be broken into. So you also must be ready, because the Son of Man will come at an hour when you do not expect him" (NIV). The suddenness of Noah's flood illustrates the point.[15] Jesus told the church at Sardis to repent. Then he said to them, "Remember, therefore, what you have received and heard; hold it fast, and repent. But if you do not wake up [again we have the command to watch], I will come like a thief, and you will not know at what time I will come to you" (Rev. 3:3 NIV). So, the lesson in this parable of the unfaithful servant is to *continue* in welldoing.

Parable of the Ten Virgins (Matt. 25:1–13)

Matthew 25 continues this theme of watchfulness with the parable of the ten virgins. The reader should read this parable and the parable of the talents if not already familiar with those stories.[16] Our purpose is to simply show how Jesus gave these two stories to reinforce the necessity of *watchfulness*.

In interpreting parables, we must be careful about making too much of the details. Often the details are simply part of the story. For example, the significance of the virgins is not their purity; it is their function and readiness to perform it.[17] In that culture unmarried friends of the bride fulfilled this role in the wedding, rather than married women.[18] They were simply unmarried girls who supported the bride by meeting the groom on his arrival and escorting him to the bridal place.[19]

Jesus states the point of the story in 25:13, "Therefore keep watch, because you do not know the day or the hour" (NIV). The NKJV says, "Watch therefore, for you know neither the day nor the hour in which the Son of Man is coming." In his book, *The Blessed Hope*, George Ladd provides an extensive discussion of the biblical concept of watching. From his analysis of the five Greek terms in the New Testament translated "keep watch," Ladd concludes, "the command to watch does not mean 'to look for' but 'to be wakeful.'"[20] The idea is that we would be spiritually awake and alert, filled with the Holy Spirit, and not overtaken by the cares of this life: that our lives would be characterized by seeking first the kingdom of God at all times.[21] The opposite of this is warned against in Luke 21:34–35: "Be careful, or your hearts will be weighed down with carousing, drunkenness and the anxieties of life, and that day will close on you suddenly like a trap. For it will come on all those who live on the face of the whole earth" (NIV).

In this parable, the foolish virgins made some preparation, but it proved to be inadequate. Either through human morality or religious ritual, many people think they are prepared for the Lord's return or for their own personal death. But in this story an "essential" was missing in the foolish virgins' preparation. So, the warning is to make sure you have made *full* preparation to meet the Lord.

The lengthy delay in the story (Matt. 25:5) was an unexpected factor. An initial profession of Christ is not enough. The sincerity of our commitment may be tested over time. As taught in the previous parable, perseverance is an essential element of salvation (Matt. 24:13).

All these virgins knew the groom was coming, and they understood the signs. For example, there would be a shout alerting them that he was almost there. They knew in general how his coming would take place. Yet, they were surprised by the timing.[22] There is a sense of urgency in Matthew 25:6: "At midnight [a time when all the virgins were drowsy] the cry rang out: 'Here's the bridegroom! Come out to meet him!'" (NIV). Midnight was an inconvenient time, for that time is typically used for sleep. In some respect, they did not expect the bridegroom to come at that hour. Even though we are given signs that the time may be drawing near, the warning here and elsewhere in the New Testament is that the timing may come as a surprise. Look again at the focus Jesus brings on this in Matthew 25:13. "Watch therefore, for you know neither the day nor the hour in which the Son of Man is coming."[23]

The fact that these foolish virgins were not given a second chance at the end is also sobering. Many assume God will soften in the end and give them a second chance to get matters right. The Catholics offer purgatory as a second chance. Hinduism offers reincarnation. But the Bible offers the gospel to whosoever will receive it on God's terms. The opportunity is offered, but once the door is shut, it remains shut.[24] Matthew 25:10–12: "But while they [the foolish virgins] were on their way to buy the oil, the bridegroom arrived. The virgins who were ready went in with him to the wedding banquet. And the door was shut. Later the others also came. 'Lord, Lord,' they said, 'open the door for us!' But he replied, 'Truly I tell you, I don't know you'" (NIV). They were saying, "Lord, Lord, open the door for us!" But he was saying, "I do not know you."

The preparation must be done *now*! And the preparation is found in doing the will of God. Satan has successfully destroyed millions with the simple suggestion that there is no hurry; the decision can be made later.[25] The urgency of serving God *now* is depicted metaphorically in this poem.

> The clock of life is wound but once,
> And no man has the power
> To say just when the hands will stop:
> At late or early hour.
>
> Now is the only time we own
> To do His precious will,
> Do not wait until tomorrow;
> For the clock may then be still.[26]

Parable of the Talents (Matt. 25:14–30)

In the parable of the talents, we get additional insight into what it means to *wait* for Christ's return. In this story, the three servants were entrusted with bags of gold: one with five, one with two, and one with one bag (*talanta*). A *talanta* (translated "talent" in KJV) was a large sum of money, perhaps 6,000 days' wages.[27] The talent simply represents what the master entrusts to the servant for stewardship.

What prepared these servants for their master's return? It was the faithful fulfillment of their assigned tasks. The way we *wait* for Christ's return is to get up each day doing what he has assigned for us to do.[28] Some of the Christians at Thessalonica did not understand this. In their anticipation of Christ's return, they stopped working and sat waiting for the event. Paul had to correct this misunderstanding, instructing them to carry on their daily responsibilities.[29]

The master's condemnation of the one–bag servant focused on his failure to do what he was assigned to do. In Matthew 25: 26, he is referred to as a "wicked, lazy servant" (NIV). In the parable of the unfaithful servant at the end of Matthew 24, the emphasis was on sins of *commission*. That servant "begins to beat his fellow servants and to eat and drink with drunkards" (Matt. 24:49 NIV). In this parable, the emphasis on sins of *omission*.[30] This servant did not put the resources to good use. He produced no increase. The failure to bear fruit is often condemned in Scripture as it is here. Jesus emphasized this in the parable of the fig tree (Luke 13:6–9). Jesus told the Jewish leaders in Matthew 21:43, "Therefore I tell you that the kingdom of God will be taken away from you and given to a people who will produce its fruit" (NIV). A similar judgment is pronounced on the lazy servant in this parable.

Theme of Eternal Consequences

The severity of judgment in all these parables, as well as in the judgment of the sheep and goats, tells us Jesus is not distinguishing between committed Christians versus nominal Christians. The distinction is between those who enter the kingdom and those who do not enter the kingdom. Consider these judgments:

1. In Matthew 24:50–51, "The master of that servant will come on a day when he does not expect him and at an hour he is not aware of. He will cut him to pieces and assign him a place with the hypocrites, where there will be weeping and gnashing of teeth" (NIV). "The weeping and gnashing of teeth represent 'inconsolable grief and unremitting torment.'"[31]
2. The door is shut to the five foolish virgins in Matthew 25:10, and the Lord's answer to their request to open it is "Truly I tell you, I don't know you" (Matt. 25:12 NIV).[32] Matthew used similar language in 7:21–23 where Jesus condemns those who talk the talk but don't walk the walk. "Not everyone who says to me, 'Lord, Lord,' will enter the kingdom of heaven but only the one who does the will of my Father who is in heaven. Many will say to me on that day, 'Lord, Lord, did we not prophesy in your name and in your name drive out demons and in your name perform many

miracles?' Then I will tell them plainly, 'I never knew you. Away from me, you evildoers" (NIV). "I never knew you. Away from me" is fatal since Christ alone has the words of eternal life.[33]

3. The judgment on the unprofitable servant in Matthew 25:30 is: "And throw that worthless servant outside, into the darkness, where there will be weeping and gnashing of teeth" (NIV). God is light, and "the darkness" means the complete absence of God's presence. It is difficult to comprehend the horror of that since even the worst sinner in this life enjoys some of God's present mercies. Boice writes, "What a grim fate that is! *Darkness*, because it is life without God, who is the source of all light. *Outside*, because it is without God, who is the Creator and center of all things. In that darkness there is no hope, no joy, no love, no laughter. In that outside world there is only weeping and gnashing of teeth forever" (emphasis Boice's).[34]

4. The judgment pronounced over the ungodly in the judgment of the sheep and goats is *everlasting* punishment (25:46). The same word used to describe the unending bliss of the godly is used to describe the unending torment of the ungodly. In Matthew 25:41, Christ says to the ungodly, "Depart from me, you who are cursed, into the eternal fire prepared for the devil and his angels" (NIV).

The division in all these parables, as well as the judgment of the sheep and goats, is always heaven or hell, eternal life or eternal death. It's not a division between spiritual Christians and carnal Christians. You're either in or out![35] The contrast in all three parables is between *professors* of Christian faith versus *possessors* of Christian faith; between those who say, "Lord, Lord" but follow their own desires versus those who follow Christ and do the will of the Father.[36]

Theme of Watchfulness

The application of Jesus's sermon in Matthew 24 and 25 is: "Watch therefore, for you do not know what hour your Lord is coming" (Matt. 24:42). Jesus illustrates three key elements in our watching for his return by giving three parables.

1. We saw in the parable of the unfaithful servant that it means to *continue* in welldoing (Matt. 24:45–51). The servant in that parable did not persevere in the faith. He began well, but at some point turned from that and began "to beat his fellow servants and to eat and drink with drunkards" (Matt.24:49 NIV).

2. In the parable of the ten virgins, we learn to make *full preparation* to meet the bridegroom (Matt. 25:1–13). Do not assume you can ride the faith of others (v. 8); do not assume you will get a second chance (v. 11). Make the most of the opportunity you are given now!

3. In the parable of the talents, we learned that waiting for our master's return entailed *fulfilling the assignment* given to us (Matt. 25:14–30). Every one of us has been resourced by the Lord to advance his kingdom. When Christ returns, he should find us occupied with doing that. The biblical waiting is not passivity; it is doing what the Lord tells us to do.

We will see in the judgment of the sheep and goats that the *way we treat God's people* is extremely important (Matt. 25:31–46).[37] The judgment in that passage is based on that expression of our faith. The parable of the unfaithful servant taught that as well. He went from *serving* the household to *beating* his fellow servants. If we love God, we will love our neighbor and treat him or her right.

So, we are given a full picture of the kind of waiting and watching for the Lord's return that he wants from each of us. This lifestyle of love and service is the point of the Olivet Discourse.

Endnotes: Chapter 11

1   Cleon L. Rogers, Jr. and Cleon L. Rogers III, *The New Linguistic and Exegetical Key to the Greek New Testament* (Grand Rapids: Zondervan, 1998), 55. Cf. Kittel and Friedrich, *Theological Dictionary of the New Testament,* vol. 2, s.v. *"grēgoreō"* by Albrecht Oepke, 338.

2   Robertson comments, "Keep awake, be on the watch 'therefore' because of the uncertainty of the time of the Second Coming." Robertson, *Robertson's Word Pictures in the New Testament,* s.v. "Matt. 24:42." Accessed in electronic data base: Biblesoft, Inc. 2010. Jesus used this word twice in Matt. 26:40–41 in contrast to the disciples falling asleep when they should have been prayerful and spiritually alert. "Then he returned to his disciples and found them sleeping. 'Couldn't you men keep watch [*grēgoreō*] with me for one hour?' he asked Peter. '"Watch [*grēgoreō*] and pray so that you will not fall into temptation. The spirit is willing, but the flesh is weak'" (NIV). As in this verse, the word for watching is linked with prayerfulness in Colossians 4:2.

3   Paul opens 1 Thessalonians 5:1, recognizing his readers awareness of "the times and the seasons" (KJV). Cf. 1 Chronicles 12:32.

4   "The purpose of these four stories is to teach the practical ways 'to keep alert for the any-day coming of Christ' that was taught so powerfully in the preceding chapter." Bruner, *Matthew A Commentary,* 535.

5   Cf. Rom. 2:7; 1 Cor. 15:1–2; Gal. 6:9; 1 Tim. 4:16; 2 Pet. 2:20–22.

6   Danker, ed., *A Greek-English Lexicon of the New Testament and Other Christian Literature*) s.v. *"pistos,"* 820; Joseph Thayer, *Thayer's Greek Lexicon,* s.v. "NT: 4244."

7   "Faithfulness is the common denominator of all three Judgment Parables: faithfully feeding a household, faithfully bringing oil, faithfully working a talent." Bruner, *Matthew: A Commentary,* 557.

8   Danker, ed., *A Greek–English Lexicon of the New Testament,* 1066.

9   Bruner, *Matthew: A Commentary,* 539.

10 Cf. Heb. 6:1–8; 10:26–39; 2 Pet. 2:21–22.

11 In Ezek. 33:12–20 God taught Israel the necessity of continuing in obedience.

12 ". . . every time you make a choice you are turning the central part of you, the part of you that chooses, into something a little different from what it was before. And taking your life as a whole, with all your innumerable choices, all your life long you are slowly turning this central thing either into a heavenly creature or into a hellish creature. . . ." C. S. Lewis, *Mere Christianity* (London: C. S. Lewis Pre. Ltd., 1952) revised and amplified, New York: HarperCollins Publishers, 2001), 92.

13 Commenting on Matt. 24:15 Gundry writes, "The preceding paragraph [verses 3–14] detailed the noneschatological characteristics of the church age and closed

with the statement that the end will come only after the universal preaching of the gospel of the kingdom." Gundry, *Matthew*, 481.

14 Cf. 1 Thess. 5:2–4; 2 Pet. 3:10.

15 That generation had the prophecies of Enoch and the testimony of Noah. There were signs or indicators that this was coming. However, because of the hardness of their hearts, they ignored those signs and continued in their ungodliness. In that state, they were surprised by the judgment when it came.

16 It is recommended that Matthew 25 be read at this point, especially if the reader is unfamiliar with the passage.

17 Cf. Morris, *The Gospel according to Matthew*, 620.

18 In some contexts, *parthenes* is used with emphasis on purity. However, here, it is simply used as bridesmaids (NLT), the unmarried young women who were part of the celebration. Friberg's first definition of *parthenes* is "as an unmarried young woman *virgin, maiden, girl*" (emphasis Friberg's). Timothy Friberg, Barbara Friberg, and Neva F. Miller, *Analytical Greek Lexicon to the New Testament*, Baker Greek New Testament Library (Grand Rapids: Baker Books, 2000). Accessed in electronic data base: Bibleworks, version 6.0, 2003.

19 Alfred Edersheim, *The Life and Times of Jesus the Messiah*, Part II, 1971 (Grand Rapids: Eerdmans, 1984), 455.

20 Ladd, *The Blessed Hope*, 107.

21 Cf. 1 Thess. 5:1–8; Rom. 8:9; Eph. 5:18; Matt. 6:33. The signs given in Scripture of Christ's return are discerned by those abiding in Christ and walking in the Spirit. Carnal efforts to discern the times and season will not work any better than the Pharisees' failed effort to discern Messiah's first coming. Sliker insightfully writes, "Watching does not imply evaluating world events to obtain information: watching is intricately linked to a spirit of Prayer." Sliker, *Biblical Foundations of Eschatology*, 59.

22 "The phrase '*in the middle of the night*' suggests a surprise Return; the '*cry*' denotes its excitement; and the '*come!*' sees it privileges—meeting the Lord (emphasis Bruner's). Bruner, *Matthew A Commentary*, 547–48.

23 "They did not know exactly when the bridegroom was coming, so it made good sense to bring extra oil, just in case. If we think we know *exactly when* the critical meeting will occur—that it will be definitely *delayed* (as the wicked servant thought in the *preceding* parable, 24:48) or that it will definitely be *immediate* (as the foolish bridesmaids think in *this* parable, 25:3)—we will see no need to make any special preparations" (emphasis Brunner's). Bruner, *Matthew A Commentary*, 546–47.

24 Cf. Gen. 7:16; Isa. 55:6; Luke 13:23–28; John 6:44; Acts 26:28–29; 2 Cor. 6:1–2.

25 There is an old fable that illustrates this point well. In the fable three demons suggest ways to destroy people. The first suggests telling people there is no

God. The second suggests telling them there is no hell. Satan tells them their suggestions won't work because people know better. The third demon suggests telling people there is plenty of time. This is the strategy Satan commends. James Montgomery Boice, *The Gospel of Matthew, An Expositional Commentary: Vol. 2, The Triumph of the King Matthew 18–28* (Grand Rapids: Baker Books, 2001), 521.

26 Walter B. Knight, ed., *Knight's Master Book of New Illustrations*, 1956 (Grand Rapids: Eerdmans, 1979), s.v. "Waiting—For What?" (author unknown), 522.

27 There are several complications in defining the monetary value, but knowing the value is not very important for understanding the point of this story. Cf. Allison, Jr., *Matthew: A Shorter Commentary*, 448; Morris, *The Gospel according to Matthew*, 627.

28 "Watching is defined not so much as an attitude as a conduct, 'Blessed is that servant, whom his lord when he cometh shall find *so doing*' (vs. 43)" (emphasis Ladd's). Ladd, *The Blessed Hope*, 117. The church must never neglect the Great Commission (Matt. 28:18–20) for any reason.

29 2 Thess. 3:6–15. The reason they were not working is inferred from the context of teaching on the Parousia in both Thessalonian epistles, but it is not explicited stated. What is abundantly clear is that Christians must work and fulfill their daily responsibilities. "Waiting" on the Lord involves faithful stewardship of the resources and abilities our Lord has entrusted to us. Throughout history, many have been deceived into thinking it is withdrawal from those responsibilities in the name of super spirituality.

Morris comments on 1 Thessalonians 3:6, "The offenders are characterized as being 'disorderly' and as not following the 'tradition.' 'Disorderly' is the adverb from the same root as that which we examine in the note on 'the disorderly' in 1 Thess. 5:14. It shows us that the same people are in mind as in the former passage, and, as we saw there, their offence was idleness. In view of the nearness of the Parousia (as they thought) they were refraining from work." Morris, *The First and Second Epistles to the Thessalonians*, 251.

30 Spurgeon vividly comments, "His lord called this servant 'wicked.' Is it, then, a wicked thing to be unprofitable? Surely wickedness must mean some positive action. No. Not to do right is to be wicked; not to live for Christ is to be wicked; not to be of use in the world is to be wicked; not to bring glory to the name of the Lord is to be wicked; to be slothful is to be wicked." Charles H. Spurgeon, "The Unprofitable Servant" in *A Treasury of Spurgeon on the Life and Work of Our Lord*, vol. III, The Parables of Our Lord (Grand Rapids: Baker Book, 1979) 121–22. "For all the sad words of tongue or pen, the saddest are these: 'It might have been!'" John Greenleaf Whittier, *Maud Muller*, as quoted by MacArthur, *Matthew 24–28*, 96.

31 MacArthur, Jr., *Matthew 24–28*, 80.

32 Drawing on the works of Augustine, Jermias, and others, Bruner says, "'I don't know you' was a Semitic idiom, used especially by rabbis who dismissed certain students, meaning 'I don't want anything more to do with you." Bruner, *Matthew: A Commentary*, 550. Whether Matthew meant it this way or is implying a lack of relationship is of little consequence since the phrase, either way, means utter rejection.

33 Cf. John 6:68; Acts 4:12; 1 John 5:12; Tow, *Authentic Christianity*, 363–364.

34 Boice, *The Gospel of Matthew*, 537.

35 Cf. Ladd, *The Blessed Hope*, 117.

36 Having framed the Olivet Discourse as a message to the Jewish remnant, dispensationalists apply these parables to the remnant of Israel after the church has been taken in a pretribulation Rapture. Thus, it would have no direct relevance to today's Christian. In contrast, most scholars see this discourse as exclusively to the church (as a replacement of Israel) or a message to all those who would follow Christ. But applying this to *all* followers of Christ (Jew and Gentile) seems to be the best approach. Cf. Pentecost, *Things to Come*, 281–84; Chafer, *Systematic Theology*, vol. 4, 408–409.

37 While our immediate text focuses on the treatment of Christ-followers, other passages teach similar kindness to those who do not know God (Matt. 5:43–48; Luke 6:27–36; 10:30–37).

CHAPTER 12

Matthew 25:31–46: Judgment of Sheep and Goats

All the nations will be gathered before Him, and He will separate them one from another, as a shepherd divides his sheep from the goats.

Matthew 25:32 NKJV

+ ◆ ◆ ◆ ◆ ◆ +

In the previous chapter, we examined three parables that Jesus used to drive home the importance of being ready for his return. Each parable highlights an essential aspect of *watching* for his coming. In the first parable (Matt. 24:45–51) the emphasis was on *continuance*. In that story, the servant began well. But at some point, he turned from that and began "to beat his fellow servants, and to eat and drink with the drunkards." He did not persevere in the faith! In the parable of the ten virgins, the foolish bridesmaids made some preparation, but it was inadequate. They left out one essential, the additional oil to maintain the flame. The lesson there is that we must make *full preparation* to meet the Lord. The parable of the talents is a warning against sins of omission. In this story, preparation for the Lord's coming is found in *faithfully doing* what he has assigned for us to do. Waiting for the Lord is not passivity; it is serving in the assigned responsibility. It is putting our gifts and resources to work for the furtherance of the master's kingdom.

Now we will examine the judgment of the sheep and goats in Matthew

25:31–46. All three parables that precede it communicate the urgency and seriousness of our response to the kingdom. The Lord's return will result in a separation that is both radical and permanent. The final note of Jesus's sermon is stated in the last verse: "And these will go away into everlasting punishment, but the righteous into eternal life" (Matt. 25: 46). The message must not be taken lightly, for one's eternal destiny is at stake. Matthew 25:31–46 describes this judgment.

> When the Son of Man comes in His glory, and all the holy angels with Him, then He will sit on the throne of His glory. All the nations will be gathered before Him, and He will separate them one from another, as a shepherd divides his sheep from the goats. And He will set the sheep on His right hand, but the goats on the left. Then the King will say to those on His right hand, "Come, you blessed of My Father, inherit the kingdom prepared for you from the foundation of the world: for I was hungry and you gave Me food; I was thirsty and you gave Me drink; I was a stranger and you took Me in; I was naked and you clothed Me; I was sick and you visited Me; I was in prison and you came to Me."

> Then the righteous will answer Him, saying, "Lord, when did we see You hungry and feed You, or thirsty and give You drink? When did we see You a stranger and take You in, or naked and clothe You? Or when did we see You sick, or in prison, and come to You?" And the King will answer and say to them, "Assuredly, I say to you, inasmuch as you did it to one of the least of these My brethren, you did it to Me."

> Then He will also say to those on the left hand, "Depart from Me, you cursed, into the everlasting fire prepared for the devil and his angels: for I was hungry and you gave Me no food; I was thirsty and you gave Me no drink; I was a stranger and you did not take Me in, naked and

you did not clothe Me, sick and in prison and you did not visit Me."

Then they also will answer Him, saying, "Lord, when did we see You hungry or thirsty or a stranger or naked or sick or in prison, and did not minister to You?" Then He will answer them, saying, "Assuredly, I say to you, inasmuch as you did not do it to one of the least of these, you did not do it to Me." And these will go away into everlasting punishment, but the righteous into eternal life.

Pretribulation Compared to Posttribulation Interpretations

The majority view is that this judgment, sometimes called the judgment of the nations, is not a parable. However, it has parabolic qualities and depicts the final judgment in general, rather than a specific scene. The mistake often made when interpreting this passage is to identify it as a specific scene to be placed on an eschatological chart. This mindset forces the injection of assumptions that distort the message Jesus is giving. After all that he has said about this age and the end of the age, including all the trouble his followers will experience, he is now communicating the end of the matter. When all is said and done, "these [the ungodly] will go away into everlasting punishment, but the righteous into eternal life" (Matt. 25:46). The pericope is a warning to selfish sinners who may prosper temporarily and a comfort to Christ's followers who may endure persecution for a time.

Craig Keener calls this a parable with the message that the king (Jesus) will judge people based on how they responded to the gospel.[1] The judgment includes all of humanity; no one will be excluded. It has a significant bearing on how we answer our question: Will Christians go through the Tribulation period? For that reason, its interpretation is vital to the debate between pretribulationists, midtribulationists, and posttribulationists.

Pretribulationists see this as a judgment of mortal (rather than resurrected) Gentiles living at the time of Christ's Second Coming.[2] In that model, Israel has already been judged (Ezek. 20:33–38; Matt. 25:1–30). So, this judgment concerns Gentiles only, and the basis of the judgment is how they treated "My brethren" (Matt. 25:40).[3] Dispensationalists interpret *My brethren* to be a reference to Israelites preaching the gospel of the kingdom during the Tribulation period. Pretribulationism insists that this judgment not be confused with the great white throne judgment of the *resurrected* dead which occurs at the end of the Millennium (Rev. 20:11–15). As a result of the judgment in our text, the sheep (righteous Gentiles) enter the Millennium along with the godly remnant of Israel —all in their natural bodies. Therefore, this theory provides the mortal people who populate the Millennium.[4] In their argument, they point to posttribulationists' inadequate explanations of how the Millennium is populated with people in their mortal bodies.[5]

The dilemma facing posttribulationist can be stated as follows: Since posttribulationism proposes the Resurrection/Rapture of all the righteous at the Second Coming, all the righteous have glorified bodies at the beginning of the Millennium.[6] They cannot procreate the millennial population. Walvoord comments, "Pretribulationists have often pointed out that if every living saint is Raptured at the time of the Second Coming this would, in itself, separate all saints from unsaved people and would leave none to populate the millennial earth."[7] If the judgment of the sheep and goats is a specific event at the end of the Tribulation period and the wicked are killed as a result of judgment on them, the posttribulationists are left with no mortals to populate the Millennium.

Posttribulationist Gundry's solution to this dilemma is to identify this judgment of the sheep and goats with the Great White Throne Judgement in Revelation 20 and place it at the end of the Millennium rather than the beginning.[8] Therefore it is a judgment of resurrected people, not those in their natural bodies—not a judgment to determine whether they enter the Millennium. While there are strengths in Gundry's argument, there are problems with this approach as well. There are too many differences between the descriptions of these two judgments for them to be the same scene.

Pentecost argues against Gundry's position by pointing out those differences. The weakness in Pentecost's argument is that some of his stated differences are based on his own assumptions about the judgment of the sheep and goats, rather than clear biblical statements.[9] Perhaps the most serious problem with Gundry's explanation is the direct statement Jesus makes introducing this pericope in Matthew 25:31: "When the Son of Man comes in His glory, and all the holy angels with Him, then He will sit on the throne of His glory." According to that statement, this judgment would follow the Second Coming if a specific scene on the prophetic chart is being communicated.[10]

Interpretation of the Judgment of the Sheep and Goats

Neither pretribulationists, nor posttribulationists offer a fully satisfying explanation of this passage, although both sides provide helpful insights. Gundry correctly identifies the general nature of the judgment of the sheep and goats. However, he errs by placing the timing of the judgment of *all* humanity at the end of the Millennium and identifying it with that one scene.[11] The wicked will be judged at that time, but the Resurrection of the Righteous occurs before the Millennium (Rev. 20:4–6). Again, the mistake commonly made is to view this passage as a specific scene at a specific time, rather than a general statement of how it all ends. When all is said and done, the righteous will enter eternal bliss, and the unrighteous will enter eternal damnation.

Moo's explanation of Matthew 25:21–36 is the most satisfying. He interprets this passage as "a merging of the premillennial judgment (at Christ's coming) and the postmillennial judgment (the final judgment). Thus passages that describe a universal judgment along with Christ's return have as their purpose to specify the ultimately universal effects of Christ's victory; they do not require that *all* are judged *at the same time* (at the Parousia)" (emphasis Moo's). With that statement he adds, "Therefore these texts constitute no difficulty for the view that some unbelievers will enter the Millennium."[12]

Jesus is concluding his discourse with a general declaration about the ultimate judgment of humanity. He is making a broad statement that warns people concerning their accountability to God. Other passages in Scripture fill in the details of this broad statement. For example, Revelation 20:4–6 tells us the Resurrection of the Just occurs before the Millennium and the Resurrection of the Unjust occurs at the end of the Millennium. Jesus is not supplying that detail in this text. First Thessalonians 4:13–18 provides details about the Resurrection of the Just, and 2 Corinthians 5:9–10 gives details about the judgment of the godly. Revelation 20:11–15 supplies details concerning the judgment of the ungodly. Jesus is not depicting a specific scene; he is communicating eternal separation between the godly and ungodly in Matthew 25.

Jesus is using something familiar to his audience: the separation of sheep and goats. Keener writes, "Although sheep and goats grazed together, it is said that Palestinian shepherds normally separated sheep and goats at night because goats need to be warm at night while sheep prefer open air."[13] This parabolic scene made the abstract truth vivid in the minds of Jesus's first-century hearers. George Ladd says, "The dramatic picture of the judgment of the sheep and the goats . . . is not to be taken as a program of the eschatological consummation but as a parabolic drama of the ultimate issues of life."[14]

The theme in the Olivet Discourse has been watchful preparation for Christ's coming. It is the Second Coming that initiates the final judgment, which results in eternal life or eternal death (Matt. 25:46). Therefore, Matthew 25:31 begins with the time of Christ's return as King of Kings and Lord of Lords.[15] After he returns, "then He will sit on the throne of His glory."[16] More detail concerning *when* of his return and the *then* of him sitting on his throne would be helpful. But this passage does not supply that. We find those specifics elsewhere in Scripture.

The terminology in our text is the language of *eternal* bliss or damnation. The judgments declared are not temporal and are not specifically about which mortals enter the Millennium. Instead, the point Jesus is making is a word of comfort to persecuted followers of Christ and a word of warning to those who oppress them. The separation between the two will be extreme, irreversible, and everlasting! Gundry rightly identifies the eternal nature of what Christ is communicating here. However, equating it with the specific scene in Revelation 20:11–15 is too restrictive. This passage includes that judgment of the wicked, but it includes more. After all, our text portrays a judgment of the sheep and goats, not just the goats. Keener corrects the erroneous dispensational interpretation of this passage. He writes, "Because the passage explicitly declares that this judgment determines people's eternal destinies (25:46), it cannot refer to a judgment concerning who would enter the millennium, as in some old dispensational schemes (Ladd 1977: 38; cf. idem 1978b; 98–102)."[17]

This judgment of the sheep and goats is of *individuals* in all the nations. Some dispensationalists interpret this as a judgment of nations *as a group*. But the judgment of everlasting damnation (25:41, 46) on the goats excludes that possibility. God holds people individually responsible for their moral choices and does not send nations as a group to hell. Most dispensationalist follow Scofield's lead and acknowledge this.[18] Furthermore, Mounce writes, "The masculine *autous* ('them') in 32b following the neuter *ethnē* (nations) in 32a indicates that the separation will be between individual people rather than between nations."[19]

The Greek word translated nations is *ethnos*. It is sometimes used as a reference to Gentiles, to the exclusion of Jews. However, in this sweeping statement of judgment, it includes all (*pas*) nationalities, including Jews. Every human being is ultimately subject to the eternal judgment of heaven or hell. The universality of this judgment is found in the word all (*pas*) in verse 32. John Gill understands this as a judgment of Christian "professors only."[20] The merit in this interpretation is that Christian professors seem to be the subject of the three parables that precede it. However, the phrase in 25:32, *panta ta ethnē* (all the nations), seems to exclude that interpretation.

The basis of the judgment is on how they treated his *brethren*. Earlier in Matthew 12:50, Jesus defined his brethren when he said, "For whoever does the will of My Father in heaven is My brother and sister and mother." This would include anyone, Jew or Gentile, who lives in obedience to God.[21] Of course, doing the will of the Father requires regeneration and enablement by the Holy Spirit (John 3:3; Rom. 8:9; Heb. 11:6). In Matthew 28:10, Jesus refers to his followers as his brethren. The dispensationalist understanding of *My brethren* as only ethnic Jews living during the Tribulation period conflicts with the definition Matthew has already given in this gospel.

Additionally, we must not divorce Matthew's Olivet Discourse from his Great Commission, something the whole book (manuscript) moves toward.[22] The final point of Matthew's narrative is "Go therefore and make disciples of all the nations" (Matt. 28:19). To whom was that exhortation directed? Matthew's intended audience was the Christian community of his day. The manuscript was written in Greek. So, he was not speaking exclusively to ethnic Jews, although many in the early church were of Jewish origin. His audience (implied reader) was Christian followers of Jesus. That fact informs our understanding of the terms "nations" in Matthew 24:32 and "My brethren" in Matthew 24:40. The brethren are those sent out with the gospel, which theoretically includes all Christians. The nations are those people Christ's brethren take the gospel message to in all the world.[23]

The way people treat those who carry the message of Christ reflects their response to the gospel and Christ himself.[24] Rejection of the message accompanies rejection of the messenger.[25] And Jesus said to his disciples, "He who hears you hears Me, he who rejects you rejects Me, and he who rejects Me rejects Him who sent Me" (Luke 10:16). Rejection of Christ's message of salvation is damning to the soul (Matt. 25:41, 46) since he alone has the words of eternal life (John 6:68).

The treatment of Christ's brethren reflects the condition of the soul. This is not salvation by works. Instead, the behavior provides evidential proof of either receptivity to God or alienation against him (James 2:14–26).

Populating the Millennium under Posttribulationism

If this understanding of the judgment of the sheep and goats is correct, not all unbelievers are destroyed prior to the Millennium. Some enter the Millennium in their mortal bodies. The following explanation of how the Millennium is populated under the posttribulation position is offered for consideration.

First, Zechariah 14:12 describes the physical death that the Armageddon armies will experience at Christ's Second Coming: "And this shall be the plague with which the Lord will strike all the people who fought against Jerusalem: Their flesh shall dissolve while they stand on their feet, Their eyes shall dissolve in their sockets, And their tongues shall dissolve in their mouths." The brightness of Christ's glory will melt their flesh.[26] Verses 13–15 and other passages provide additional detail about the destruction of the Antichrist armies at Armageddon.

But Zechariah 14:16–19 indicates there will be Gentiles left alive who will go into the Millennium.[27]

> And it shall come to pass that everyone who is left of all
> the nations which came against Jerusalem shall go up

from year to year to worship the King, the Lord of hosts, and to keep the Feast of Tabernacles. And it shall be that whichever of the families of the earth do not come up to Jerusalem to worship the King, the Lord of hosts, on them there will be no rain. If the family of Egypt will not come up and enter in, they shall have no rain; they shall receive the plague with which the Lord strikes the nations who do not come up to keep the Feast of Tabernacles. This shall be the punishment of Egypt and the punishment of all the nations that do not come up to keep the Feast of Tabernacles.

Gundry points this out in his analysis.[28]

Secondly, some Jews will be converted immediately *after* the posttribulation Rapture when they see Christ's (Messiah's) scars at his Second Coming. This will be too late for the Rapture which occurs immediately prior to Christ's arrival on earth. These Jews will enter the Millennium in mortal bodies. Zechariah 12:10–13:1 describes this remarkable event:

> And I will pour on the house of David and on the inhabitants of Jerusalem the Spirit of grace and supplication; then they will look on Me whom they pierced. Yes, they will mourn for Him as one mourns for his only son, and grieve for Him as one grieves for a firstborn. In that day there shall be a great mourning in Jerusalem, like the mourning at Hadad Rimmon in the plain of Megiddo. And the land shall mourn, every family by itself: the family of the house of David by itself, and their wives by themselves; the family of the house of Nathan by itself, and their wives by themselves; the family of the house of Levi by itself, and their wives by themselves; the family of Shimei by itself, and their wives by themselves; all the families that remain, every family by itself, and their wives by themselves. In that day a fountain shall be opened for the house of David and for the inhabitants of Jerusalem, for sin and for uncleanness.

Gundry incorrectly identifies the 144,000 Jews mentioned in Revelation as those who go into the Millennium in mortal bodies. Instead, the 144,000 will be believers in Jesus as the Messiah and will be glorified in the posttribulation Rapture. It is the unbelieving Jews who repent when they see Messiah at his Second Coming who go into the Millennium in mortal bodies.[29] The universal impact of the Second Coming (Matt. 24:27, 29–30) suggests the possibility of many Gentiles responding in post-Rapture repentance. Therefore, under a posttribulation rapture position, the Millennium will be populated with (1) mortal Jews who believe on Christ at his Second Coming immediately after the Rapture, and (2) non-Christian Gentiles who have not received the mark of the beast and are not killed by the judgments during the Tribulation (Zech. 14:16-19).

Due to the judgments during the Tribulation period and at the Second Coming, the population on earth will be much less than it is now (Isa. 13:12). However, conditions during the Millennium will be conducive to rapid population growth (Isa. 65:20– 25; Zech. 9:10) so that the end of the Millennium will reflect a very large population (Rev. 20:7–8).

Conclusion

In this study, our primary interest in the Millennium is to determine whether each of the Rapture theories contain a reasonable account of how that period is populated with mortal beings after the Second Coming. The pretribulation theory and, to a lesser extent, the midtribulation theory do provide that. In this chapter, we have also found that the posttribulation model offers a viable explanation as well. Therefore, this is not a weakness in the posttribulation position, as I initially thought.

The posttribulation strengths discussed in chapter 7 are quite compelling, and it is probably the best alternative. Nevertheless, all three models depend on some inference. There is much we do not know. Therefore, it is wise to maintain a humble, teachable attitude as we continue to search the Scriptures on this subject. It is important to hear one another, respect one another, and learn from one another. May we all work together to hasten that glorious day! May we all be fully prepared to welcome our bridegroom when he returns!

Endnotes: Chapter 12

1 Keener, *A Commentary on the Gospel of Matthew*, 602, 605. Cf. Morris, *The Gospel According to Matthew*, 633.

2 Cf. Pentecost, *Things to Come*, 349.

3 Chafer understands the timing of their consignment to hell as happening at the close of the Millennium at the Great White Throne Judgment. Chafer, *Systematic Theology*, vol. 4, 410.

4 For a concise explanation of this dispensational interpretation, see Scofield, *The Scofield Reference Bible*, 1036–37.

5 See the previous discussion in chapter 7: "Posttribulation Position."

6 Cf. Archer, "The Case for the Mid-Seventieth-Week Rapture Position," in *Three Views on the Rapture* by Archer, Jr., et al. (1996), 121.

7 Walvoord, *The Blessed Hope and the Tribulation*, 52–53.

8 Cf. Gundry, *The Church and the Tribulation*, 163–71. Gundry limits the scope of the judgment articulated in Matt. 24:40–41 as part of his theory as well (pp. 137, 143). For a critique of Gundry's position, see Feinberg, "The Case for the Pretribulation Rapture Position," in *Three Views on the Rapture* by Archer, et al. (1996), 72–79.

9 Pentecost lists the many differences between the two judgments demonstrating the high probability they are not the same judgment. Cf. Pentecost, *Things to Come*, 425–26.

10 Dan. 12:11–12 adds an additional 30 days, then another 45 days to God's end-time program for Israel. Little explanation is given for this. However, in the pretribulationist model, this judgment may account for some of these additional days between the end of the tribulation and full entry into the millennial blessing. Cf. C. I. Scofield, *The Scofield Reference Bible*), 918; John MacArthur, *Matthew 24–28*, 114. For a more detailed suggestion of events during this 75–day period, from a posttribulationist perspective, see Sliker, *End-Times Simplified*, 116–20. For a prewrath perspective, see Rosenthal, *The Pre-Wrath Rapture of the Church*, 273–76.; Van Kampen, *The Sign*, 328–29, 331, 360, 389, 423. For a pretribulation critique of the prewrath position, see Showers, *The Prewrath Rapture View*, 84–92. Since all the Rapture positions place the Rapture prior to these events, a study of these 75 days is beyond the scope of this book.

11 Cf. Gundry, *The Church and the Tribulation,* 163.

12 Moo, "Response [to Archer]" in *Three Views on the Rapture* by Archer, et al. (1996), 163.

13 Keener continues, "Sheep were more valuable than goats, and characteristics like this may have influenced how these terms would be heard figuratively. . . . The right is the preferred side in ancient texts; in the few scenes of judgment where it occurs, the right side is for the righteous and the left for the wicked (e.

g., the Testament of Abraham recension A)." Keener, *The IVP Bible Background Commentary: New Testament*, 118. Cf. James M. Freeman, *Manners and Customs of the Bible* (Plainfield, NJ: Logos International, 1972), 379.

14   George Ladd, *A Theology of the New Testament*, 116. On page 206 Ladd writes, "This is not didactic eschatology but dramatic parable."

15   Cf. Revelation 19:16.

16   Matthew 25:31. Cf. Revelation 3:21.

17   Keener, *A Commentary on the Gospel of Matthew*, 604. Ladd also rejects the dispensational interpretation of Matthew 25:31–46 as determining which nations will enter the Millennium. He says, "The final issue of the judgment of the nations is not the millennial kingdom but is either eternal life or eternal punishment (Matt. 25:46). This is clearly the final judgment which depicts the eternal destiny of men." George Eldon Ladd, *A Commentary on the Revelation of John* (Grand Rapids: Eerdmans, 1972) 271.

18   Scofield, *The Scofield Reference Bible*, 1036. Walvoord comments, "They [the nations] will be judged individually, not as national groups." John F. Walvoord and Roy B. Zuck, *The Bible Knowledge Commentary: An Exposition of the Scriptures by Dallas Seminary Faculty*, New Testament edition (Wheaton, IL Victor Books, 1983), 80. Pentecost also says, "this must be an individual judgment to determine the fact of salvation." Pentecost, *Things to Come*, 420–21.

19   Mounce, *Matthew*, 235–36. Wallace confirms Mounce's understanding of this. Cf. Wallace, *Greek Grammar Beyond the Basics*, 400. Nolland points out the consistency of this with Matthew's use of the phrase "all the nations" (Matt. 25:32). He writes, "Taken literally, 'separate them from one another' should mean separate nations from one another, but the continuation of the present account is clearly focused on individuals, and in neither of the other Matthew references to 'all the nations' are the people dealt with as national groups." Nolland, *The Gospel of Matthew*, 1024–25.

20   "John Gill's Commentary of the Whole Bible: Matthew 25:32," *Good. Book. Free.* http://goodbooksfree.com/commentaries/gill/40025.html.

21   As Keener points out, "That the 'siblings' are here 'disciples' is the majority view in church history and among contemporary New Testament scholars, although those who hold 'siblings' to be disciples divide sharply over whether are specifically missionaries or poor disciples in general." Keener, *A Commentary on the Gospel of Matthew*, 606. The "brethren" should not be restricted to "missionaries" since all believers are to carry the witness of Christ to the world (Matt. 5:14–16). However, the reference may be particularly applicable to those who are actively doing that.

Gundry writes, "'These littlest brothers' can hardly denote an elite corps of Christian preachers in the church; for all those who do the will of the Father belong to the brotherhood (12:48–50) and 'the little ones' refers especially to obscure people in the church, who are easily despised and prone to stray but whose low position ecclesiastical leaders must themselves assume (18:1–14). Furthermore, all true disciples bear witness." Gundry, *Matthew*, 514. Of course, "brethren" in this text refers to male and female followers of Christ. Cf. Boice, *The Gospel of Matthew*, 542.

22 After criticizing scholarship for "the lack of a holistic treatment of the discourse," Jeffrey Gibbs writes, "This has been true regarding the place of the ED [Eschatological Discourse] within the context of the Gospel, and within the narrative of the Gospel" (emphasis Gibbs's). Gibbs, *Jerusalem and Parousia*, 15.

23 Cf. Gibbs, *Jerusalem and Parousia*, 213–22; Keener, *A Commentary on the Gospel of Matthew*, 604–606.

24 Cf. Ladd, *A Theology of the New Testament*, 206–207.

25 Cf. Matt. 10:14–15; Luke 10:10–16.

26 Second Thess. 2:8 references "the brightness of His [Christ's] coming," but is focused on the judgment of the Antichrist. Second Thess. 1:8 says Christ will come "in flaming fire taking vengeance on those who do not know God," then points to the eternal judgment they will experience by being excluded from God's presence forever.

27 See also Dan. 11:41: "He [the Antichrist] shall also enter the Glorious Land, and many countries shall be overthrown; but these shall escape from his hand: Edom, Moab, and the prominent people of Ammon."

28 Cf. Gundry, *The Church and the Tribulation*, 167. Bickle also projects "unsaved survivors of the Great Tribulation [Jew and Gentile], who will refuse to worship the Antichrist, even though they were not saved. . . . These will have an opportunity to be saved after Jesus returns to earth and will populate the millennial earth." Bickle, *Studies in the Book of Revelation*, 50.

29 Cf. Gundry, *The Church and the Tribulation*, 81–83.

CONCLUSION

For our citizenship is in heaven, from which we also eagerly wait for the Savior, the Lord Jesus Christ.

Philippians 3:20 NKJV

◆◆◆◆◆◆

We have weighed scriptural evidence concerning the timing of the Rapture in relationship to the end-time Tribulation period. In this process, we have examined strengths and weaknesses in each of the proposed models: pretribulationism, midtribulationism, and posttribulationism. The position each reader takes on the matter is probably influenced by the relative importance he or she places on each of those strengths and weaknesses. Unlike many of the foundational doctrines of the faith, there is not a clear, unequivocal answer to the question we have explored: Will Christians go through the Tribulation period? God has sovereignly left a degree of uncertainty as to the answer. He could have given us a verse that made the answer so clear that the current debate would be completely resolved. But there is some value in the uncertainty. That uncertainty keeps us dependent on him. It protects us from spiritual arrogance and self-sufficiency. Even with the signs of his soon coming, Jesus says to us, "Watch therefore, for you do not know what hour your Lord is coming" (Matt. 24:42).

The important takeaway for all of us is that we be spiritually alert and prepared for the days ahead whether that is Rapture or Tribulation followed by Rapture. The preparation is essentially the same! Whether we are raptured tomorrow or face increased persecution, right relationship with the Lord is the important thing. His grace is sufficient for us in any situation. When we are raptured, we want to be found pleasing to him. "Therefore we make it our aim, whether present or absent, to be well pleasing to Him" (2 Cor. 5:9). If we live in that attitude of heart, we will be ready for either situation. Regardless of the position one takes on the timing of the Rapture, it is essential that we live in an active, watchful state of service to our King.

Arriving at Tentative Conclusions

I began this hermeneutical cycle inclined in favor of pretribulationism. That position has some strong points which we have discussed. However, in the absence of a clear statement putting the Rapture prior to or in the middle of the Tribulation period, we are left with the probability that it will occur in conjunction with the Second Coming. We are plainly told in Scripture the Second Coming will occur at the end of the Tribulation period. That would seem to be the default position for the timing of the Rapture unless convincing evidence is present to contradict it. The apostles' terminology in the New Testament when referring to the Rapture seems to confirm, rather than contradict, a posttribulation Rapture. Our studies in the Thessalonian letters and the Olivet Discourse support a posttribulation model more than a pretribulation or midtribulation model. Primarily because of those considerations, I am left with an inclination in favor of posttribulationism. That may or may not be consistent with the reader's conclusions. And that is fine, for there will be additional examinations of this subject for all of us. My goal has not been to persuade readers toward a particular model. Instead, I have documented my own analysis of the subject as I have proceeded with this hermeneutical cycle. Hopefully, this has provided a useful template for readers doing their own analysis of the subject.

There is enough uncertainty about the Rapture's timing that we should humbly respect one another's conclusions. There is still much for all of us to learn. And there will always be some pieces of the puzzle that we do not have this side of glory. "The secret things belong to the Lord our God, but those things which are revealed belong to us and to our children forever, that we may do all the words of this law" (Deut. 29:29). With what we have been given, may each of us passionately follow the paths of righteousness, fulfilling the Great Commission together. "Even so, come, Lord Jesus!"

Making Personal Application of this Study

Bible study is of little eternal value *if* the student does not make application of the truths learned to his own personal lifestyle. While teaching about prophecy, Peter punctuated his instruction with this probing question: "Therefore, since all these things will be dissolved, what manner of persons ought you to be in holy conduct and godliness, looking for and hastening the coming of the day of God" (2 Pet. 3:11–12). Holy conduct should be the fruit of biblical inquiry. Moreover, godliness of character is the best equipping for navigating the days ahead.

We do not know the specific challenges and opportunities that will come our way as we progress toward the return of Christ. However, we have seen in our examination of Scripture that in the last days the church will experience a great falling away (1 Tim. 4:1; 2 Thess. 2:3). At the same time, there will be those who rise to the occasion by the grace of God, and multitudes will be saved. I sincerely want you and me to be among those overcomers who have drawn close to the Lord, know him intimately, and follow him wherever he leads. I want to participate in the last-days great harvest. I want to equip my brothers and sisters in Christ with the Word of God in such a way that they do not fall away, no matter what deception Satan throws at them. As each of us function in the gifts of God's grace, we want to strengthen and encourage one another to continue in the Lord, regardless of the trials and persecutions that may or may not come our way.

Our world is rapidly marching toward Armageddon. Deception is not *going to* happen; it *is* happening! Furthermore, it will likely grow worse. Just as Paul and those in the early church experienced divine empowerment when facing opposition (1 Cor. 16:9), we can expect the grace of God to be sufficient for every challenge. God has a way of supplying whatever strength is needed for those who love him and walk in obedience to him. In every generation, but perhaps especially in the last days, "the eyes of the Lord run to and fro throughout the whole earth, to show Himself strong on behalf of those whose heart is loyal to Him" (2 Chron. 16:9).

The best preparation we can make for tomorrow is to nurture a heart of loyalty toward our bridegroom—to love him with all our heart, soul, and mind (Matt. 22:37). Elijah did exploits during the ungodly reign of Ahab and Jezebel because his ear was open to the Lord, and he followed directions. By following directions, he walked into provision when it was needed. By following directions, he confronted the prophets of Baal successfully. He is a prototype of how we can navigate in the days ahead—not by political or military might, but by the leading and empowerment of the Holy Spirit.

However, there is a preparation *now* for doing that *then*. Soldiers don't wait until they're on the battlefield to prepare. They go to boot camp; they learn discipline; they toughen up to engage the enemy. Most of the Western church has not adequately prepared to be used by God in these last days. Do we know how to endure hardness as a good soldier of Jesus Christ (2 Tim. 2:3), or are we expecting to be carried into glory on a bed of ease?

My personal response to this study is to press into God more diligently than I have in the past—not because I am afraid of tomorrow, but because I want to be used by God and please him. We press into God by giving ourselves to personal and corporate prayer. We press into God by faithfully coming together and worshipping him with delight. We press into God by knowing and taking heed to his word. And we encourage one another in these disciplines.

APPENDICES

APPENDIX A: THE BOOK OF REVELATION

Blessed is he who reads and those who hear the words of this prophecy, and keep those things which are written in it; for the time is near.

Revelation 1:3 NKJV

+ + + + + +

The Rapture Question in the Book of Revelation

The book of Revelation is the most extensive prophecy of end-time events. Therefore, it should be diligently studied for the development of one's eschatology. However, this study focuses on the narrow question of when the Rapture occurs. At times in the study, we have interacted with Revelation. For example, at the beginning of chapter 3 we briefly explored the four basic approaches to interpreting that book. But our study of Revelation has been limited for three reasons.

1. Revelation is full of symbolism that must be interpreted. The more symbolic the language is, the greater the possibility of misinterpreting its meaning. For that reason, we should rest the weight of our eschatology first on straightforward statements in Scripture. If those passages are exegeted and understood, we are in a better position to interpret symbolism in other passages.
2. Revelation is the last inspired writing in the unfolding of progressive revelation.[1] Knowledge of previous revelation in

Scripture is necessary for accurate interpretation of the symbolism. A common mistake in understanding the book of Revelation is to interpret passages without grounding the interpretation in the firm foundation of previous revelation. The symbolism in Revelation is rooted in Old Testament truth.

The author, John, was a Jew familiar with Old Testament Scripture and the teachings of Jesus. Particularly important was the Olivet Discourse, which we dealt with extensively in the last section of this book. That discourse was foundational to John's understanding of eschatology and provides sound footing for us to interpret the visions recorded in the last book of the Bible.[2]

3. Most significantly, Revelation does not provide a clear, definitive statement about the timing of the Rapture. In our analysis of each position on the subject, we discussed how each camp uses symbolism in Revelation in defending their respective theories. But those arguments are weak because of the dependence on the expositor's interpretation of the symbols.

Revelation 20:4–5 makes a statement about the timing of the Rapture/Resurrection of the Just in relationship to the Millennium and the Resurrection of the Unjust. The posttribulationist contention is that this passage sets the Rapture at the end of the Tribulation. However, to argue this, one must admit the passage is not in chronological sequence since the binding of Satan in 20:1–3 precedes the passage in 20:4–5. This fact weakens the posttribulation use of those verses as support for their model.[3] That leaves us with very little proof in the book of Revelation about the timing of the Rapture. That is one reason Revelation is not emphasized more in this study. Once we have a sound eschatology based on less symbolic passages, we are in a good position to interpret John's visions.

The Structure of the Book of Revelation

An important challenge in understanding the book of Revelation is identifying the structure of the book. This is relevant to the subject of this study because there is a circular relationship between one's understanding of the structure of Revelation and conclusions about the timing of the Rapture. A person's belief on when the Rapture occurs can influence the structure chosen. The structure used to interpret Revelation can influence the understanding of when the Rapture occurs.

We saw this dynamic when analyzing the midtribulation position. For example, Norman Harrison supported his model of midtribulationism by identifying the Rapture with Revelation 11:15. In his framework of Revelation, that represents the middle of the Tribulation period. But some posttribulationists structure the book in a way that places Revelation 11:15 at the end of the Tribulation period.[4] Therefore, the structure used for interpreting Revelation should be considered carefully by students of that book.

In the futurist camp, the following two approaches to the structure of Revelation are prominent, although there are other variations. Most expositors agree on the structure of the first three chapters. Revelation 1:1–8 introduces the book; in the rest of chapter 1 John introduces and shares a vision of Christ. Chapters 2 and 3 consist of seven letters to specific churches that existed in John's day. Some believe they represent seven consecutive spiritual conditions that would exist during the church age, but that is by no means certain. The real challenge is to determine what framework John is using in the chapters that follow.[5]

1. One structure is to see the seven seals, seven trumpets, and seven bowls as addressing the same basic events. The trumpets and bowls are a reiteration of the seals. In this framework, "the reiteration always shows the previous vision in a new way, providing a close up of some specific aspect not evident before."[6] Proponents of this approach say the book follows the sequence in which John saw the *visions*, but that does not mean *events* are in chronological order since the trumpets and bowls are reiterating the seals.[7] Almost all expositors recognize parenthetical material in the book. In support of this view, Craig Keener writes, "Some writers have tried to make Revelation a continuous chronological account from beginning to ending, but that view is not widely held today. The dominant view, proposed by Victorinus in the late third century, is that the various series of judgments parallel one another rather than

following successively. Since each of these series of judgments seem to conclude with the end of the age (as noted above), this line of interpretation is almost certainly correct. The sort of events closing the seals, trumpets, and bowls cannot repeat unless the world as we know it can come to an end several times (these three reverences plus 19:11–21)."[8]

2. The other structure commonly used among futurists is to arrange the events chronologically, with some recognition of parenthetical chapters or interludes. Pretribulationist W. A. Criswell seems to follow this approach in his exposition of Revelation.[9] Many teachers using this structure see the visions as emerging "from one another like boxes within boxes, or like the graphic 'windows' some computer programs allow a user to open within other windows on a screen. . . ."[10] In this approach the "trumpets are *under* the seventh seal, it is commonly inferred, they refer to events or judgments subsequent to those of the seals" (emphasis Michaels's)[11] Likewise, the bowls flow out of and are under the seventh trumpet.

Posttribulationist Mike Bickle adopts this chronological structure of Revelation. He finds five chronological sections (chapters 6, 8–9, 11:15–19, 15–16, and 19–20) and five angelic explanations (chapters 7, 10–11, 12–14, 17–18, and 21–22).[12] In his explanation of the seven seals he writes, "The seven seals are *literal* (not symbolic), *future* (their fulfillment is still in the future), *progressive* (increasing in intensity), and *numbered* (released in a sequential order)" (emphasis Bickle's).[13] This would also be true of the trumpets and bowls. In general, these four adjectives provide a sound description of the events prophesied in Revelation. We should follow the chronology of the book unless there is a compelling reason to deviate from it.

The book of Revelation provides a wealth of detail concerning end-time events. It should be studied by every student of Scripture. And there is a specific blessing pronounced on those who do so (Rev. 1:3). Using the principle of the hermeneutical spiral discussed in the introduction of this book, students will adjust their view of the structure and symbols as they grow in their understanding of eschatology as a whole.

Endnotes: Appendix A

1 For a discussion of progressive revelation, see chapter 1: "Interpretation Method for Understanding End-Time Prophecy."

2 As taught in the first chapter of this book, we must employ sound exegetical principles when interpreting Revelation. That includes due consideration of what the message meant to John's first-century audience.

3 Reese makes a strong biblical case for placing the Rapture/Resurrection at the time of Israel's conversion at the end of the Tribulation and inauguration of the Millennium (Zach. 12–14; Rom. 11:25–26). Reese, *The Approaching Advent of Christ*, 19. Cf. Ladd, *The Blessed Hope*, 62–94. For Douglas Moo's defense of the posttribulation position on Revelation 20:4–5, see Moo, "A Posttribulation Response [to Hultberg] in *Three Views on the Rapture* by Blaising, et al. (2010), 174–75. For a prewrath critique of Moo's position, see Hultberg, "A Case for Prewrath Rapture" in *Three Views on the Rapture* by Blaising, et al. (2010), 150–52. Posttribulationists point to Matthew 24:29–31 as additional support for their theory. We discussed that in chapter 10: "Matthew 24:32–44: Second Coming."

4 See chapter 6: "Midtribulation Position: Including Prewrath Interpretation."

5 "The chief interpretive problem is whether the consequences of the opening of the seven seals, the blowing of the seven trumpets, and the pouring out of the seven bowls represent imaginative descriptions of essentially the same eschatological events described in different ways (the recapitulation theory) or they should be understood as presenting the linear unfolding of an eschatological scenario culminating in the dénouement of the New Jerusalem." David E. Aune, *Revelation 1–5*, Word Biblical Commentary, vol. 52, David Hubbard and Glenn Barker, gen. eds. (Dallas, TX: Word Books, 1997) xcv.

6 J. Ramsey Michaels, *Interpreting the Book of Revelation* (Grand Rapids: Baker Books, 1992), 54.

7 For an example of this approach, see Craig S. Keener, *Revelation*, The New Application Commentary (Grand Rapids: Zondervan, 2000).

8 Craig S. Keener, *Revelation*, The NIV Application Commentary: From Biblical Text . . . to Contemporary Life, Terry Muck, gen. ed. (Grand Rapids: Zondervan) 34. Expressing a view similar to that of Keener, Ladd says, "It is noteworthy that both the seals and the trumpets bring us to the end." Ladd, *A Commentary on the Revelation of John*, 121.

9 Cf. Criswell, *Expository Sermons on Revelation*.

10 Michaels, *Interpreting the Book of Revelation*, 57.

11 Ibid

12 Bickle, *Book of Revelation Study Guide*, 6–7.

13 Bickle, *Studies in the Book of Revelation*, 25.

APPENDIX B: BIBLICAL IMMINENCE

Therefore keep watch, because you do not know on what day your Lord will come.

Matthew 23:42 NIV

✦ ✦ ✦ ✦ ✦

The biblical concept of imminence as it relates to the Rapture is more complex than I previously thought, and my understanding of the subject evolved significantly during this study. For those two reasons, I find it necessary to provide this summary of the matter as I currently see it.[1] Cognizant of the hermeneutical spiral discussed in the preface, I remain open to further learning on this matter. Certainly, imminence is an important aspect of the Lord's return.

It is a mistake to begin with a preconceived idea of imminence and impose it on the scriptural revelation. Instead, we must begin with an inductive study of all the biblical texts about the timing of the Rapture and let a biblical concept of imminence emerge. I began with an over-simplified concept of imminence as an "at any moment" Rapture. But that does not convey the full revelation in the New Testament.

The emphasis in Scripture is for Christian to stay prepared for the Lord's coming because "you do not know on what day your Lord will come" (Matt. 24:42 NIV). History has taught us the folly of thinking we know! The many failed predictions have not only been an embarrassment for the church but have also resulted in wrecking individual lives. We do not know! It is both prideful and presumptuous to think we do. Jesus reinforced this truth when he said, "But about that day or hour no one knows, not even the angels in heaven, nor the Son, but only the Father" (Mark 13:32 NIV). Passages such as these support an "at any moment" Rapture.

However, there is another side of this issue that cannot be ignored. The Bible teaches Christians to be alert to the signs of Christ's coming as well. If "at any moment" were the complete revelation, Jesus's and the apostles' delineation of signs that alert us to the nearing of his return would be of little value. In Mark 13 Jesus gave the parable of the fig tree, then said, "Even so, when you see these things happening, you know that it is near, right at the door" (v. 29). Paul wrote in 1 Thessalonians 5:1-4, "But concerning the times and the seasons, *brethren, you* have no need that I should write to *you*. For *you* yourselves know perfectly that the day of the Lord so comes as a thief in the night. For when *they* say, 'Peace and safety!' then sudden destruction comes upon *them*, as labor pains upon a pregnant woman. And *they* shall not escape. But *you, brethren*, are not in darkness, so that this Day should overtake *you* as a thief" (emphasis added). Clearly, Paul is making a distinction between the way his coming will take the world off guard, but not take vigilant Christians by surprise. Therefore, the "at any moment" concept must be tempered by exhortations to know "the times and season."

Noah's flood took the world by surprise even though the preparation of the ark was a sign warning them in advance. The wicked could not discern the times. Yet, Noah was not taken off guard by the event, even though he could not predict precisely when the Father would release the floodgates. His assignment was to obediently make the preparation as instructed by God. Our preparations are found, not in building arks or bunkers, but in nurturing our intimacy with the Lord and doing what he tells us to do on a daily basis.

What we see in the New Testament is truth held in the tension of suddenness on the one hand and sign indicators on the other hand. This tension can be uncomfortable to our modern rationalism. It challenges us in much the same way the truths of freewill and predestination do. If we emphasize one side of the revelation to the neglect of the other, the result is an unbalanced understanding of the subject. The ongoing debate concerning imminence is often fueled by arguing one side of the revelation and discounting the other side. I prefer to let the scriptures stand as revealed even when my understanding is incomplete (1 Cor. 13:9).

It is a mistake to let a preconceived idea of imminence dictate one's whole eschatology. Instead, we should embrace both sides of revelation on the subject. That yields a balanced position based on Scripture. I believe in the freewill of man and God's sovereign planning/fulfillment of man's redemption. In my finite mind, I cannot fully explain how God accomplishes that. And I do not believe anyone else can either (Deut. 29:29). Certainly, a finite human being trying to rule the universe would have to opt for one to the exclusion of the other. But it is not beyond the ability of an infinite God. I believe in an impending sudden Rapture, and no one knows when it will happen. But I also believe Christ and the apostles gave us signs to observe that alert us that his coming is near. I accept the tension of those two truths.[2]

Revelation on this subject is given, not so we can neatly place events on an end-time chart, but so we would stay spiritually alert and always prepared for our Lord's return. The real question is: Are you abiding in Christ in such a way that whenever he returns, you are ready to receive him?

Endnotes: Appendix B

1 The reader can use the subject index, "imminence," to review previous discussions.

2 Pretribulationists insist that their concept of "at any moment" imminence disqualifies the possibility of the other models (Pentecost, *Things to Come*, 204). If we only had those scriptures that support the revelation as "at any moment," then their position must be accepted. But the other passages leave the "at any moment" concept of imminence modified in a way that eliminates it as a final litmus test. On the other hand, posttribulationists who remove the unexpectedness and suddenness of Christ's coming in favor of watching signs go too far (Gundry, *The Church and the Tribulation*, 43). George Ladd and Douglas Moo take a better, less extreme position. They argue for a posttribulation position, but acknowledge the *uncertainty* found in the New Testament tension of truth. See Ladd, *A Theology of the New Testament*, 203; Moo, "A Case for the Posttribulation Rapture" in *Three Views on the Rapture* by Blaising, et al. (2010,), 235–39.

APPENDIX C: DISCUSSION QUESTIONS BY CHAPTER

As iron sharpens iron, so one person sharpens another.

Proverbs 27:17 RSV

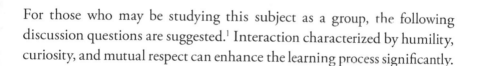

For those who may be studying this subject as a group, the following discussion questions are suggested.[1] Interaction characterized by humility, curiosity, and mutual respect can enhance the learning process significantly.

Preface

1. What question is the focus of this study? Why is the subject so narrowly defined?
2. What signs do you see that indicate we are living in the end times?
3. What previous teaching have you had on this subject? Which of the three models (pre-, mid-, or posttribulation) was emphasized in the instruction?
4. In your own words, explain the difference between the pretribulation, midtribulation, and posttribulation positions concerning the timing of the Rapture.
5. What assumptions does the author make concerning the Rapture and Second Coming that all three camps agree on?

6. What is a hermeneutical spiral, and how does it relate to our current study?

7. What questions would you like to ask before we proceed?

Chapter 1: Interpretation Method for Understanding End-Time Prophecy

1. What are the two main methods of interpreting Scripture, and why is one preferred above the other?

2. Why is establishing the interpretation method to be used so important as a foundation for this study?

3. What are some of the problems inherent in the allegorical method?

4. What are some of the challenges in using the literal (grammatical-historical) method?

5. What is "the law of double-reference" encountered in biblical prophecy?

6. What is the difference between premillennialism and amillennialism? Historically, who was instrumental in popularizing amillennialism?

7. What comments or questions would you like to process before we proceed to the next chapter?

Chapter 2: Daniel's Seventieth Week: The Tribulation Period

1. What are the two purposes of the Tribulation period discussed in this chapter?

2. What other purpose would posttribulationists add?

3. What passage in Scripture tells us the Tribulation period will last seven years? What other passages defining the last half (3½ years) of that period tend to reinforce this interpretation?

4. When did the clock begin on Daniel's 70 weeks (490 years) as described in Daniel 9:25

5. In Daniel 9:26:

   What event does "Messiah shall be cut off" (v. 26) refer to?

   Who are "the people of the prince"?

   What event does the phrase "Shall destroy the city and the sanctuary" refer to (Matt. 24:2)?

6. In Daniel 9:27:

   Who is "he" that will confirm a covenant with Israel (and other nations) for seven years?

   What is the abomination (commonly called the abomination of desolation) in this verse, and when will it happen in relation to the seven years?

   How do we know that the defilement of the temple by Antiochus IV in about 167 BC was only a foreshadowing of the ultimate fulfillment?

7. What indications do we have that there is a gap of time (church age) between Daniel 9:26 and 9:27?

   Why did God add this gap of time between Daniel's 69th week and the 70th week in God's program for Israel?

   Why did God not specifically define this gap in the Daniel 9:26-27 passage?

8. What comments or questions would you like to process before we proceed to the next chapter?

Chapter 3: Partial Rapture Theory: A Variant of Pretribulationism

1. What are the four basic methods of interpreting the book of Revelation? Why is the futurist interpretation preferred over the other three?

2. What is the partial Rapture theory? How does it differ from the traditional pretribulation position?

3. What do you consider as strengths in the partial Rapture theory?

4. In the author's story about a church that held the partial Rapture theory, Dr. Tow said that any error in the doctrine itself was not as serious a problem as something else? What was the more serious problem in that story? How does it serve as a warning for us?

5. What do you consider to be the most significant weakness in the partial Rapture theory?
6. Why does Dr. Tow not accept the parable of the wheat and tares and the parable of the ten virgins as support for a partial Rapture position? Do you agree with him? If so, why; if not, why not?
7. Overall, do you think the partial Rapture theory is supportable as the explanation of the Rapture? Why or why not?
8. What comments or questions would you like to process before we proceed to the next chapter?

Chapter 4: Pretribulation Position: Strengths

1. What are some biblical truths that you feel are essential to orthodox faith and, therefore, not negotiable, or subject to compromise?
2. Which strength of the pretribulation model do you consider the strongest argument for that position? Why do you consider it particularly important?
3. Why does the word "saints" in Revelation 13:7 not prove that the church is on earth during the Tribulation period?
4. In what way might the heavenly scene in Revelation 4 and subsequent heavenly scenes tend to support the pretribulation position? Who do you think the 24 elders in Revelation 4 represent?
5. Recalling the two purposes of the Tribulation period discussed in chapter 2, why do pretribulationists contend their position aligns with those purposes better than the other two models? Do you agree? Why or why not?
6. How do pretribulationists define imminence, and why do they feel imminence supports their position more than the other two positions?
7. What comments or questions would you like to process before we proceed to the next chapter?

Chapter 5: Pretribulation Position: Weaknesses

1. Which weakness of the pretribulation position do you consider the most significant and why?
2. How do posttribulationists use 1 Thessalonians 1:3–10 to defend their position against the other two positions?
3. Why does 2 Thessalonians 2:1–12 pose a difficulty for the pretribulation position? How do pretribulationists seek to defend their position in this passage? Do you feel their defense is sustainable?
4. What makes 2 Thessalonians 2:1–12 a difficult passage to interpret? What interpretation of the restrainer in verses 6–7 do various scholars propose? Why is it difficult to identify who or what the restrainer is? Why is this important to the pretribulation argument?
5. Do you feel the relatively recent articulation of the pretribulation model is a significant argument against it? Why or why not?
6. Why do midtribulationists and posttribulationists accuse pretribulationists of escapism? Do you feel the accusation is justified? Why or why not?
7. What are the three Greek words used in the New Testament in reference to *both* the Rapture and the Second Coming? What does the fact that each term is used indiscriminately for the Rapture and the Second Coming imply?
8. What comments or questions would you like to process before we proceed to the next chapter?

Chapter 6: Midtribulation Position: Including Prewrath Interpretation

1. Both the midtribulation and the prewrath models place the Rapture after the abomination at the middle of the seven-year Tribulation period. How would you briefly distinguish between the two models?
2. What do you consider to be the greatest weakness in these two models?

3. What do you consider to be the greatest strength in these two models?
4. What is the problem with identifying the timing of the Rapture using one's interpretation of pictures and symbols in the book of Revelation?
5. In your opinion what is the strongest challenge against identifying Revelation 7:9 as the raptured church?
6. How does 2 Thessalonians 2:1-4 support the midtribulation and prewrath positions?
7. What are your thoughts about how God will present Christ with a bride that is holy without spot or wrinkle?
8. What questions remain in your mind about the midtribulation and prewrath positions?

Chapter 7: Posttribulation Position

1. What do you consider to be the strongest argument for the posttribulation position, and why?
2. Why is the New Testament writers' use of the three Greek words *parousia, apokalupsis,* and *epiphaneia* when referring to both the Rapture and Second Coming an important argument for posttribulationism? How weighty is this argument in your mind?
3. In your evaluation of 2 Thessalonians 1 and 2, do you think the pretribulation rebuttal to the posttribulation interpretation is strong or weak? Why?
4. Do you think the posttribulation and midtribulation positions prepare Christians to stand firm under hardship and persecution more than the pretribulation position? What are the consequences for pretribulationists if one of the other theories is correct? What are the consequences for midtribulationists and posttribulationists if pretribulationism is correct? Is this a valid argument against pretribulationism? Why or why not?
5. What do you consider the greatest weakness in the posttribulation position? Explain your answer.

6. Do you think posttribulationists provide an adequate answer for how the Millennium is populated with people still living in mortal bodies? Why or why not?

7. Compare the pretribulation versus the posttribulation positions on imminence. Which position explains the whole New Testament revelation on this subject better? Explain your answer.

8. Compare the pretribulation and posttribulation explanation of 1 Thessalonians 5:9. Which position offers the most convincing interpretation of that promise? Explain your answer.

9. What comments or questions would you like to process before we examine the Olivet Discourse?

Chapter 8: Matthew 24:1–14: Conditions During Church age

1. Why is it important to carefully examine the Olivet Discourse when attempting to answer the question: Will Christians go through the Tribulation period?

2. What do you consider the greatest challenge in accurately interpreting the Olivet Discourse? Explain your answer.

3. Why is it important to determine who the disciples represent (the nation of Israel, the church, or both) before interpreting the details of the discourse? To whom do you think the discourse is directed? Who did Matthew have in mind as his reading audience? Explain your answers.

4. How does the fact that Jesus himself did not know the day of his return (Matt. 24:36) complicate interpreting the discourse? What errors have some scholars made when incorporating this reality in their interpretations of the discourse? How does this inform our understanding of biblical imminence?

5. How does Matthew 23 contextually inform Jesus's message in Matthew 24 and 25? How does Matthew 23 inform our understanding of Jesus's target audience in the Olivet Discourse? What does Jesus predict in Matthew 24:2?

6. How does Matthew 24:6, 14 inform us that the conditions described in verses 4-14 will exist during the church age? How does the metaphor of birth pains that Jesus introduced in verse

8 inform us that the intensity of these conditions will increase as the end is approached?

7. Explain the parallel of Matthew 24:4-14 with Revelation 6? How are they the same? How do they differ?

8. What comments or questions would you like to process before we proceed to the next chapter?

Chapter 9: Matthew 24:15–30: The Great Tribulation

1. How does Jesus's statement in Matthew 24:15 relate to Daniel 9:27 that we studied in chapter 2? According to Daniel 9:27, when does the abomination of desolation occur in relationship to the seven-year Tribulation period?

2. What is redaction criticism, and how does it relate to our study of the Olivet Discourse?

3. How does an examination of the differences between Luke 21:20–24 and Matthew 24:15–29 reveal the distinct theological objectives of each author concerning the abomination of desolation? What is the significance of Luke's statement in 21:24 compared to Matthew statement in 24:21, 29? How do those verses establish different timeframes for Luke 21:20–24 versus Matthew 24:15–29? What event is Luke focused on in those verses, and what event is Matthew focused on?

4. What is the magnitude of tribulation in 70 AD recorded by Josephus compared to the scope of suffering during World War II and prophesied in Revelation 6:8? Why is this relevant to how we interpret Matthew 24:15–22 considering Jesus's statement in Matthew 24:21?

5. How do some preterists try to avoid the obvious implications of erroneously identifying Matthew 24:15–22 with the destruction of the temple (70 AD) when they interpret events described in Matthew 24:29–30 and Luke 21:25–27?

6. Why must Matthew 24:29–30 be taken literally? What scriptural basis do we have for a literal interpretation? What are the doctrinal dangers associated with allegorizing/spiritualizing Matthew 24:30?

7. Why does Jesus give so much warning about deception in Matthew 24? What are the implications of this for our day and time?
8. What comments or questions would you like to process before we proceed to the next chapter?

Chapter 10: Matthew 24:31–44: The Second Coming

1. Why is Matthew 24:31 particularly relevant to answering our question: Will Christians go through the Tribulation period? How do the interpretations of this verse differ between pretribulationists and posttribulationists? Which camp do you tend to agree with on this verse and why?
2. What is the main point (exhortation) made in the parable of the fig tree (Matthew 24: 32–33)? How does this inform our understanding of imminence?
3. What are the major interpretations of "generation" in Matthew 24:34, and how does this impact our understanding of the Olivet Discourse? What is the strength of the preterist argument? What is the strength of the futurist argument? Which interpretation do you think is right, and why?
4. Explain the debate between pretribulationists and posttribulationists on whether the one *taken* is taken in salvation or taken in judgment in verses 40–41. Which camp has the strongest argument in your opinion and why?
5. What is the primary point/exhortation in Jesus's story recorded in Matthew 24:42–44? What application can you make to our own lives?
6. What does Titus 2:11–14 teach about how to wait for our Lord's return?
7. What comments or questions would you like to process before we proceed to the next chapter?

Chapter 11: Matthew 24:45–25:30: Watching for the Return

1. What is the main point of Jesus's Olivet Discourse? How does this correspond with Paul's exhortation in 1 Thessalonians 5:2–9?

2. What is your understanding of what it means to "keep watch" (*grēgoreō*)?

3. Describe the mistake made by the wicked servant in Matthew 24:45–52? What were the consequences of his decision? What lessons do you draw from this parable?

4. What was the difference between the wise versus foolish virgins in Matthew 25:1–13? What was the consequence of their error as recorded in verse 12? What lesson can be learned about partial preparation from this parable? What other lessons do you draw from the story?

5. Contrast the mistake made by the servant in Matthew 25:25–27 with the mistake made by the servant in Matthew 24:49. What does the combination of these mistakes say about our own preparations for Christ's return? What lessons do you find in the parable of the talents?

6. There is debate about whether these stories contrast dedicated believers versus carnal believers or contrast true professors of faith versus unsaved professors. What does the severity of judgment in 24:51; 25:12; 25:30 suggest? How does this impact the use of these parables to support a midtribulation position?

7. What comments or questions would you like to process before we proceed to the next chapter?

Chapter 12: Matthew 25:31–46: Judgment of the Sheep and Goats

1. Explain the dispensational pretribulationist interpretation of this passage. Why is this interpretation problematic for posttribulationism?

2. How does the eternal nature of the judgments pronounced in 25:46 tend to discredit the pretribulation interpretation?

3. Explain the interpretation offered in this book and essentially supported by Moo and Keener. Compare this interpretation with the pretribulationist interpretation and explain why you would choose one over the other.

4. How does the interpretation offered by Tow, Moo, and Keener further the posttribulation argument about populating the Millennium with mortal people? What is your understanding of how the Millennium will be populated with mortals?

5. Do you think this is a judgment of nations as a group or individuals who make up the nations? Explain the reason for your answer.

6. Who do you think are Christ's "brethren" in 25:40? Explain the reason for your answer. How does this decision affect the way you interpret the passage?

7. In what way does the parable of the wicked servant, the parable of the ten virgins, and the parable of the talents illustrate the practical point of Jesus's teaching in Matthew 24:1–44? In what way does Matthew 25:1–46 drive home the seriousness of heeding the message of this sermon?

8. What comments or questions would you like to process before we proceed to the conclusion of this book?

Conclusion and Appendices

1. Why did Dr. Tow not begin with the book of Revelation as his foundation for answering the question: Will Christians go through the Tribulation period? Do you agree with this approach? Why or why not?

2. Once a foundation is laid for establishing the timing of the Rapture using more direct statements on the subject in the Olivet Discourse and the epistles, how does the book of Revelation enrich our understanding of end-time events?

3. Explain your understanding of imminence at this point. Do you feel the Bible teaches exclusively an "at any moment" concept? Do you dismiss the "at any moment" concept since we are given signs alerting us to Christ's coming? Do you feel there is a tension of

truth on the subject in the New Testament that warns us to stay ready for an "at any moment" Rapture but also exhorts us to watch the signs indicating his return is drawing near? Explain why you have arrived at your conclusion.

4. What part of this study was most helpful to you? What part remains unclear or confusing?

5. Recognizing we will all continue to be learners in the school of Christ, which position do you lean toward at this point? What strengths in that position have persuaded you the most? What weaknesses in that position cause you some continued reservation?

6. Do you feel humility, teachability, and respect toward those who differ with you on this issue is important to maintain? Do you feel breaking fellowship with other Christians over differences about this is appropriate? Why or why not?

7. How has this study motivated you to stay spiritually alert and prepared for Christ's coming? How might you use what you have learned to encourage others to do the same?

Endnotes: Appendix C

1   These questions are appropriate for college or seminary level and may be too challenging for groups less committed to the learning process. For those groups, more general questions may be more effective in drawing out discussion. Of course, this list of questions is not exhaustive, but the ability to answer these questions is a strong indication the reader understands the material.

SELECTED BIBLIOGRAPHY

Allison, Jr., Dale C. *Matthew: A Shorter Commentary.* New York: T & T Clark International, 2004.

Anderson, Robert. *The Coming Prince.* London: Hodder & Stoughton, 1909.

Archer, Jr., Gleason L. (gen. ed.), Paul D. Feinberg, Douglas J. Moo, and Richard R. Reiter. *The Rapture: Pre-, Mid-, Post-Tribulational?* Grand Rapids: Zondervan, 1984.

—. *Three Views on the Rapture: Pre-, Mid-, or Post-Tribulational?* Grand Rapides: Zondervan, 1996. Originally published as *The Rapture: Pre-, Mid-, Post-Tribulational.*

Arnold, Clinton. "Academic Forum, Segment I: Initial Remarks." *The Glorious Return of Our King.* Center for Biblical End-Time Studies, International House of Prayer. Kansas City, MO, November 7, 2019.

Aune, David E. *Revelaion 1–5.* David Hubbard and Glenn Barker, eds. Word Biblical Commmentary, vol. 52A. Dallas, TX: Word Books, 1997.

Barker, Kenneth L., ed. *The NIV Study Bible, 1985.* Grand Rapids: Zondervan, 1995.

Beare, Francis Wright. *The Gospel According to Matthew.* San Francisco, CA: Harper & Row, 1981.

Beechick, Allen. *The Pretribulation Rapture.* Denver, CO: Accent Books, 1980.

Bickle, Mike. *Book of Revelation Study Guide.* Kansas City, MO: Forerunner Books, 2009.

—. *Studies in the Book of Revelation.* Kansas City, MO: Forerunner Books, 2014.

Black, David Alan, and David S. Dockery. *New Testament Criticism &*
Interpretation. Grand Rapids, Zondervan, 1991.

Blaising, Craig, Alan Hultberg (gen. ed.), and Douglas J. Moo. *Three*
Views on the Rapture: Pretribulation, Prewrath, or Posttribulation.
Grand Rapids: Zondervan, 2010. Previously published with different
contributors in 1984 and 1996.

Bock, Darrell L. *Luke.* Baker Exegetical Commentary on the New
Testament, Moises Silva, ed., 2 vols. Grand Rapids: Baker Books,
2004.

Boice, James Montgomery. *The Gospel of Matthew, An Expositional*
Commentary: Vol. 2, The Triumph of the King Matthew 18–28. Grand
Rapids: Baker Books, 2001.

Bonhoeffer, Dietrich. *The Cost of Discipleship.* New York: Macmillan,
1960. Translated from the German *Nachfolge* first published 1937 by
Chr Daiser Verlag Möchen by R. H. Fuller, with some revision by
Irmgard Booth.

Brown, Michael L., and Craig S. Keener. *Not Afraid of the Antichrist: Why*
We Don't Believe in a Pre-Tribulation Rapture. Minneapolis, MN:
Chosen, 2019.

Bruner, Fredrick Dale. *Matthew: A Commentary.* rev. 1990. The Churchbook
Matthew 13–28, vol. 2. Grand Rapids: Eerdmans, 2004.

Carson, D. A. *Matthew, Mark, Luke.* The Expositor's Bible Commentary,
vol. 8, F. E. Gabelein and J. D. Douglas, eds. Grand Rapids:
Zondervan, 1984.

Chafer, Lewis Sperry. *Systematic Theology.* 1947–1948, 7 vols. Dallas, TX:
Dallas Seminary Press, 1974.

Cranfield, C. E. D. *The Gospel According to Mark.* rev. and enl. ed., 1959.
Cambridge Greek Testament Commentary, C. F. D. Moule, ed.
Cambridge: Cambridge Univeristy Press, 1972.

Criswell, W. A. *Expository Sermons on Revelation: Five Volumes Complete*
and Unabridged in One, 1962. Grand Rapids: Zondervan, 1978.

—. *Expository Sermons on the Book of Daniel.* 4 vols. Grand Rapids:
Zondervan, 1972.

Danker, Fredrick William, ed. *A Greek-English Lexicon of the New*
Testament and Other Early Christian Literature. 3rd ed. Based on Walter
Bauer's *Griechish-deutsches Wörterbuch zu den Schriften des Neuen*

Testaments und der frühchristlichen Literatur, sixth edition, Kurt Aland and Barbara Aland, with Viktor Reichmann, eds. and on previous English editions by W. F. Arndt, F. Chicago: University of Chicago Press, 2000.

Edersheim, Alfred. *The Life and Times of Jesus the Messiah,* Part II, 1971. Grand Rapids: Eerdmans, 1984.

English, E. Schuyler. *Re–Thinking the Rapture.* Travers Rest, SC: Southern Bible, 1954.

Farrar, W. *The Gospel According to St. Luke in Greek: with Maps, Notes and Introduction.* Cambridge: Cambridge University Press, 1910.

Fee, Gordon D. *The First and Second Letters to the Thessalonians.* The New International Commentary on the New Testament, Bruce Stonehouse, Gordon Fee, and Joel Green, eds. Grand Rapids: Eerdmans, 2009.

—. *The First Epistle to the Corinthians.* The New International Commentary of the New Testament, Bruce Stone and Gordon Fee, eds. Grand Rapids: Eerdmans, 1987.

Fee, Gordon D., and Douglas Stuart. *How to Read the Bible for All Its Worth: A Guide to Understanding the Bible.* Grand Rapids: Zondervan, 1982.

France, R. T. *Matthew.* Tyndale New Testament Commentaries. Grand Rapids: Eerdmans, 1985.

Freeman, James M. *Manners and Customs of the Bible.* Plainfield, NJ: Logos International, 1972.

Friberg, Timothy, Barbara Friberg, and Neva F. Miller. *Analytical Greek Lexicon to the New Testament.* Baker Greek New Testament Library. Grand Rapids: Baker Books, 2000. Accessed in electronic data base: Bibleworks, version 6.0, 2003.

Gibbs, Jeffrey A. *Jerusalem and Parousia: Jesus' Eschatological Discourse in Matthew's Gospel.* Staint Louis, MO: Concordia Academic Press, 2000.

Giblin, Charles H. *The Threat of Faith: An Exegetical and Theological Re–examination of 2 Thessalonians 2.* Rome: Pontifical Biblical Institute, 1967.

Govett, R. *The Saints' Rapture to the Presence of the Lord Jesus.* Miami Springs, FL: Conley & Schoettle Publishing, 1984. Originally published in London during the mid-1800s.

Graham, Billy. *The Reason for My Hope: Salvation.* Nashville, TN: Thomas Nelson, 2013.

Green, Gene L. *The Letters to the Thessalonians,* The Pillar New Testament Commentary, D. A. Carson, ed. Grand Rapids: Eerdmans, 2002.

Green, Joel B., *The Gospel of Luke,* The New International Commentary on the New Testament, N. B. Stonehouse, F. F. Bruce, and Gordon D. Fee, eds. Grand Rapids: Eerdmans, 1997.

Gundry, Robert H. *First the Antichrist: A Book for Lay Christians Approaching the Third Millennium and Inquiring Whether Jesus Will Come to Take the Church out of the World before the Tribulation.* Grand Rapids: Baker Books, 1997.

—. *Matthew: A Commentary on His Literary and Theological Art.* Grand Rapids: Eerdmans, 1982.

—. *The Church and the Tribulation.* Grand Rapids: Zondervan, 1973.

Guthrie, Donald. *New Testament Introduction.* rev. ed., 1961. Downers Grove, IL: InterVarsity Press, 1990.

Hagner, Donald A. *Matthew 14–28.* Word Biblical Commentary, Vol. 33B, D. A. Hubbard and G. W. Barker, eds. Dallas, TX: Word Books, 1995.

Harrison, Norman B. *The End: Re-Thinking the Revelation.* Minneapolis, MN: The Harrison Service, 1941.

Hayford, Jack W., ed. *The New Spirit Filled Life Bible.* Nashville, TN: Thomas Nelson, 2002.

Hendriksen, William. *Exposition of the Gospel According to Matthew.* Grand Rapids: Baker Book House, 1973.

Holmes, Michael W. *1 & 2 Thessalonians.* The NIV Application Commentary, Terry Muck, ed. Grand Rapids: Zondervan, 1988.

Ironside, H. A. *Lectures on the Epistle to the Colossians.* Neptune, NJ: Loizeaux Brothers, 1929.

Josephus, Flavius. *Josephus: Complete Works.* Trans. by William Whiston. Grand Rapids: Kregel, 1981, Originally published about 75– 93 AD.

Kaiser, Walter C. Jr., P. H. Davids, F. F. Bruce, and M. T. Brauch. *Hard Sayings of the Bible.* Downers Grove, IL: InterVarsity Press, 1996.

Kaiser, Walter C., and Moises Silva. *An Introduction to Biblical Hermeneutics: The Search for Meaning.* Grand Rapids: Zondervan, 1994.

Keener, Craig S. *A Commentary on the Gospel of Matthew.* Grand Rapids: Eerdmans, 1999.

—. *Revelation.* The New International Commentary. Grand Rapids: Zondervan, 2000.

—. *The IVP Bible Background Commentary: New Testament.* Downers Grove, IL: InterVarsity Press, 1993.

Kistemaker, Simon J. *Exposition of the Book of Revelation. New Testament Commentary.* Grand Rapids: Baker Books, 2001.

Kittel, G., and G. Friedrich, eds. *Theological Dictionary of the New Testament,* translated by G. W. Bromiley. 10 vols. Grand Rapids: Eerdmans, 1964-1979.

Klein, William, Craig Blomberg, and Robert Hubbard, Jr. *Introduction to Biblical Interpretation.* Grand Rapids: Thomas Nelson, 1993.

Knight, Walter B., ed. *Knight's Master Book of New Illustrations.* 1956. Grand Rapids: Eerdmans, 1979.

Ladd, George Eldon. *A Commentary on the Revelation of John.* Grand Rapids: Eerdmans, 1972.

—. *A Theology of the New Testament.* rev. ed., 1974. Grand Rapids: Eerdmans, 1993.

—. *The Blessed Hope.* Grand Rapids: Eerdmans, 1956.

Lewis, C. S. *Mere Christianity.* London: C. S. Lewis Pre. Ltd., 1952.

Lindell, H. G. and Robert Scott. *Lindell-Scott Greek-English Lexicon.* Oxford: Oxford University Press, 1843. Accessed in Electronic Database: Bibleworks. v. 6.0. 2003.

Loyd-Jones, Martyn. *Life in Christ: Studies in 1 John.* Wheaton, IL: Crossway, 2002.

MacArthur, John. *Matthew 24–28.* The MacArthur New Testament Commentary. Chicago: The Moody Bible Institute, 1989.

Marshall, I. Howard. *The Gospel of Luke: A Commentary on the Greek Text.* The New International Greek Testament Commentary. Grand Rapids: Eerdmans, 1989. Originally published by Paternoster Press in 1978.

McQuilkin, Robertson. *Understanding and Applying the Bible,* rev. ed., 1983. Chicago: Moody Press, 1992.

Michaels, J. Ramsey. *Interpreting the Book of Revelation.* Grand Rapids: Baker Books, 1992.

Moo, Douglas J. *The Epistle to the Romans,* The New International Commentary on the New Testament, N. Stonehouse, F. F. Bruce, and Gordon Fee, eds. Grand Rapids: Eerdmans, 1996.

Moore, A. L. *The Parousia in the New Testament.* Leiden, Netherlands: E. J. Brill, 1966.

Morgan, G. Campbell. *The Gospel According to Luke.* 1931. Grand Rapids: Fleming H. Revell, 1992.

Morris, Leon. *New Testament Theology.* Grand Rapids: Zondervan, 1986.

—. *The First and Second Epistles to the Thessalonians. 1959.* The New International Commentary on the New Testament, F. F. Bruce,. ed. Grand Rapids: Eerdmans, 1979.

—. *The Gospel According to Matthew.* Grand Rapids: Eerdmans, 1992.

—. *The Gospel According to St. Luke.* 1974. The Tyndale New Testament Commentaries, R. V. G. Tasker, ed. Grand Rapids: Eerdmans, 1980.

—. *The Revelation of St. John.* The Tyndale New Testament Commentaries, R. V. G. Tasker, ed. Grand Rapids: Eerdmans, 1981.

Mounce, Robert H. *Matthew.* 1985. New International Biblical Commentary, W. W. Gasque. ed. Peabody, MA: Henderson, 1991.

Newman, Barclay M., Jr. "A Concise Greek-English Dictionary of the New Testament." In *The Greek New Testament,* Barbara Aland, Kurt Aland, Johannes Karavidopoulos, Carlo M. Martini, and Bruce M. Metzger, eds. United Bible Societies, 1983.

Nigro, H. L. *Before God's Wrath: The Bible's Answer to the Timing of the Rapture,* rev. ed. Lancaster, PA: Strong Tower Publishing, 2002.

Nolland, John. *The Gospel of Matthew: A Commentary on the Greek Text.* The New International Greek Testament Commentary, . H. Marshall and D. A. Hagner, eds. Grand Rapids: Eerdmans, 2005.

Osborne, Grant R. *Revelation.* Baker Exegetical Commentary on the New Testament, Moises Silva, ed. Grand Rapids: Baker Academic, 2002.

Payne, J. Barton. *The Imminent Appearing of Christ.* Grand Rapids: Eerdmans, 1962.

Pentecost, J. Dwight. *Things to Come: A Study in Biblical Eschatology,* 1958. Grand Rapids: Zondervan, 1973.

Peters, George N. H. *The Theocratic Kingdom.* Vol. 2. Grand Rapids: Kregel, 1952.

Reese, Alexander. *The Approaching Advent of Christ.* London: Marshall, Morgan and Scott, 1937. Repr., Grand Rapids: Grand Rapids International, 1975.

Robertson, Archibald T. *Word Pictures in the New Testament,* 6 vol. Originally published by Harpers, & Brothers, New York in 1930. Accessed in electronic data base: Biblesoft. 2010.

Rogers, Cleon L. Jr., and Cleon L. Rogers III. *The New Linguistic and Exegetical Key to the Greek New Testament.* Grand Rapids: Zondervan, 1998.

Rosenthal, Marvin. *The Pre-Wrath Rapture of the Church.* Nashville, TN: Thomas Nelson, 1990.

Rydelnik, Michael, and Michael Vanlaningham. The Moody Bible Commentary. Chicago: Moody Publishers, 2014.

Ryrie, Charles C. *What You Should Know about the Rapture.* Chicago: Kregel, 1952.

Sauer, Erich. *The Triumph of the Crucified.* Grand Rapids: Eerdmans, 1951.

Scofield, C. I., ed. *The New Scofield Reference Bible.* 1909. London: Oxford University Press, 1967.

Showers, Renald E. *The Pre-wrath Rapture View: An Examination and Critique.* Grand Rapids: Kregel, 2001.

Sliker, David. *Biblical Foundations of Eschatology.* Kansas City, MO: Forerunner Books, 2006.

—. *End-Times Simplified: Preparing Your Heart for the Coming Storm.* Kansas City, MO: Forerunner Books, 2005.

—. *The Nations Rage: Prayer, Promise and Power in an Anti-Christian Age.* Minneapolis, MN: Chosen Books, 2020.

Smith, William. *Smith's Bible Dictionary.* Peabody,, MA: Hendrickson, 1990. Originally published in London in 1863. Accessed in electronic data base: Biblesoft 2010.

Spurgeon, Charles H. *A Treasury of Spurgeon on the Life and Work of Our Lord.* 6 vols. Grand Rapids: Baker Book House, 1979.

Strong, James. *New Exhaustive Strong's Numbers and Concordance with Expanded Greek-Hebrew Dictionary.* Nashville: Thomas Nelson, 2010. Originally published: *The Exhausive Concordance of the Bible,* Cincinnatit: Jennings & Graham. 1890. Accessed in electronic data base: Biblsoft, 2010.

Stronstad, Roger. *The Charismatic Theology of St. Luke.* Peabody, MA: Hendrickson, 1984.

Tasker, R. V. G. *The Gospel According to St. Matthew.* Tyndale Bible Commentaries. Grand Rapids: Eerdmens, 1961.

Thayer, Joseph. *Thayer's Greek Lexicon.* Orignally published by Harper & Brothers, 1896. Accessed in electronic data base: Biblesoft 2010.

Thomas, David. *The Gospel of Matthew: A Homiletical Commentary.* Grand Rapids: Kregel, 1979.

Tow, Richard W. *Authentic Christianity: Studies in 1 John.* Bloomington, IN: WestBow Press, 2019.

Van Kampen, Robert. *The Rapture Question Answered: Plain and Simple,* 1997. Grand Rapids: Fleming H. Revell, 2002.

—. *The Sign.* Wheaton, IL: Crossway, 1992.

Wallace, Daniel B. *Greek Grammar Beyond the Basics: An Exegetical Syntax of the New Testament with Scripture, Subject, and Greek Word Indexes.* Grand Rapids: Zondervan, 1996.

Walvoord, John F. *The Blessed Hope and the Tribulation: A Historical and Biblical Study of Posttribulationism.* Grand Rapids: Zonderban, 1976.

—. *The Rapture Question,* rev. ed., 1957. Grand Rapids: Zondervan, 1979.

Walvoord, John F., and Roy B. Zuck. *The Bible Knowledge Commentary: An Exposition of the Scriptures by Dallas Seminary Faculty,* New Testament edition. Wheaton, IL: Victor Books, 1983.

Wiersbe, Warren W. *Be Ready.* Wheaton, IL: Victor Books, 1979.

Wilkins, Michael J. *Matthew,* The NIV Application Commentary, Terry Muck, ed. Grand Rapids: Zondervan, 2004.

Witherington III, Ben. *Matthew,* Smyth & Helwys Bible Commentary, M. K. Elroy, ed. Macon, GA: Smyth & Helwys Publishers, 2006.

Woods, Andy. *The Falling Away: Spiritual Departure or Physical Departure.* Taos, NM: Dispensational Publishing, 2018.

Yeager, Randolph O. *Renaissance New Testament,* vol. 3. Bowling Green, KY: Renaissance Press, 1978.

Zodhiates, Spiros. *The Complete Word Study Dictionary: New Testament.* 1992. Iowa Falls, IA: World Bible Publishers, Inc., 1994.

ALSO BY THE AUTHOR

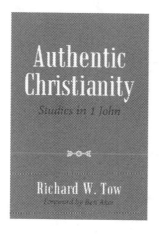

Ironically, as we improve methods and techniques, we are reaching fewer people with the gospel. There are deeper issues that are not being adequately addressed. Sadly, some are suggesting that we redesign Christianity to suit the tastes of our culture. This is producing an alarming departure from scriptural truth. In Authentic Christianity, Dr. Tow challenges the deceptions inherent in that movement and calls the church back to New Testament Christianity in doctrine and lifestyle. He does this by providing a theologically sound exposition of 1 John with relevant, practical application. The Christianity Jesus died for works if we will fully commit to it!

PURCHASE AT WESTBOWPRESS.COM/ BOOKSTORE OR AMAZON.COM

SCRIPTURE INDEX

SUBJECT INDEX

Printed in the United States
by Baker & Taylor Publisher Services